Entangled Heritages

Relying on the concept of a shared history, this book argues that we can speak of a shared heritage that is common in terms of the basic grammar of heritage and articulated histories, but divided alongside the basic difference between colonizers and colonized. This problematic is also evident in contemporary uses of the past. The last decades were crucial to the emergence of new debates: subcultures, new identities, hidden voices, and multicultural discourse as a kind of new hegemonic platform also involving concepts of heritage and/or memory. Thereby we can observe a proliferation of heritage agents, especially beyond the scope of the nation-state. This volume gets beyond a container-vision of heritage that seeks to construct a diachronic continuity in a given territory. Instead, authors point out the relational character of heritage focusing on transnational and translocal flows and interchanges of ideas, concepts, and practices, as well as on the creation of contact zones where the meaning of heritage is negotiated and contested. Exploring the relevance of the politics of heritage and the uses of memory in the consolidation of these nation-states, as well as in the current disputes over resistances, hidden memories, undermined pasts, or the politics of nostalgia, this book seeks to seize the local/global dimensions around heritage.

Olaf Kaltmeier is Full Professor for Ibero-American History and Director of the Center for InterAmerican Studies at Bielefeld University, Germany.

Mario Rufer is Full Professor-researcher at Universidad Autónoma Metropolitana-Xochimilco, in Mexico City.

InterAmerican Research: Contact, Communication, Conflict
Series Editors: Olaf Kaltmeier, Josef Raab, Wilfried Raussert, Sebastian Thies

The Americas are shaped by a multitude of dynamics which have extensive, conflictive and at times contradictory consequences for society, culture, politics and the environment. These processes are embedded within a history of interdependence and mutual observation between North and South which originates in the conquest and simultaneous 'invention' of America by European colonial powers.

The series will challenge the ways we think about the Americas, in particular, and the concept of area studies, in general. Put simply, the series perceives the Americas as transversally related, chronotopically entangled and multiply interconnected. In its critical positioning at the crossroads of area studies and cultural studies the series aims to push further the postcolonial, postnational, and cross-border turns in recent studies of the Americas toward a model of horizontal dialogue between cultures, areas, and disciplines.

The series pursues the goal to 'think the Americas different' and to explore these phenomena from transregional as well as interdisciplinary perspectives.

Forthcoming title

Mobile and Entangled America(s)
Maryemma Graham, Wilfried Raussert

Entangled Heritages
Postcolonial perspectives on the uses of the past in Latin America

Edited by

Olaf Kaltmeier
(Center for InterAmerican Studies, Bielefeld University)

and

Mario Rufer
(Universidad Autónoma Metropolitana, Xochimilco)

LONDON AND NEW YORK

First published 2017 by Routledge

2 Park Square, Milton Park, Abingdon, Oxfordshire OX14 4RN
52 Vanderbilt Avenue, New York, NY 10017

Routledge is an imprint of the Taylor & Francis Group, an informa business

First issued in paperback 2019

Copyright © 2017 selection and editorial material, Olaf Kaltmeier and Mario Rufer; individual chapters, the contributors

The right of the editor to be identified as the author of the editorial material, and of the authors for their individual chapters, has been asserted in accordance with sections 77 and 78 of the Copyright, Designs and Patents Act 1988.

All rights reserved. No part of this book may be reprinted or reproduced or utilised in any form or by any electronic, mechanical, or other means, now known or hereafter invented, including photocopying and recording, or in any information storage or retrieval system, without permission in writing from the publishers.

Notice:
Product or corporate names may be trademarks or registered trademarks, and are used only for identification and explanation without intent to infringe.

British Library Cataloguing-in-Publication Data
A catalogue record for this book is available from the British Library

Library of Congress Cataloging-in-Publication Data
Names: Kaltmeier, Olaf, 1970– editor, author. | Rufer, Mario, editor, author.
Title: Entangled heritages: postcolonial perspectives on the uses of the past in Latin America / edited by Olaf Kaltmeier and Mario Rufer.
Description: New York, NY : Routledge, 2016. | Includes bibliographical references.
Identifiers: LCCN 2016002253| ISBN 9781472475435 (hardback) |
ISBN 9781315579849 (ebook)
Subjects: LCSH: Latin America – Civilization – 21st century. |
Latin America – Historiography.
Classification: LCC F1408.3 .E577 2016 | DDC 980.04 – dc23
LC record available at https://lccn.loc.gov/2016002253

ISBN: 978-1-4724-7543-5 (hbk)
ISBN: 978-0-367-28144-1 (pbk)

Typeset in Times New Roman
by Florence Production Ltd, Stoodleigh, Devon, UK

Contents

List of figures vii
Notes on contributors ix
Acknowledgments xi

Introduction: the uses of heritage and the postcolonial condition in Latin America 1
Olaf Kaltmeier and Mario Rufer

1 On the advantage and disadvantage of heritage for Latin America: heritage politics and nostalgia between coloniality and indigeneity 13
 Olaf Kaltmeier

2 ¡Mexicanos al grito de guerra! How the *himno nacional* became part of Mexico's heritage 37
 Sarah Corona Berkin

3 Making heritage – the materialization of the state and the expediency of music: the case of the *cuarteto característico* in Córdoba, Argentina 47
 Gustavo Blázquez

4 Is Spanish our language? Alfonso Reyes and the policies of language in postrevolutionary Mexico 69
 María del Carmen de la Peza

5 Cultural management and neoliberal governmentality: the participation of Perú in the Exhibition *Inca—Kings of the Andes* 87
 Gisela Cánepa

6 Commemorate, consecrate, demolish: thoughts about the Mexican Museum of Anthropology and its history 109
 Frida Gorbach

7 Going back to the past or coming back from the past? Governmental policies and uses of the past in a Ranquel community in San Luis, Argentina 123
María Celina Chocobare

8 Unearthing *patrimonio*: treasure and collectivity in San Miguel Coatlinchán 137
Sandra Rozental

9 Processes of heritagization of indigenous cultural manifestations: lines of debate, analytic axes, and methodological approaches 153
Carolina Crespo

10 The ambivalence of tradition: heritage, time, and violence in postcolonial contexts 175
Mario Rufer

Index 197

Figures

10.1 Museo Nacional de Antropología 184
10.2 Museo Nacional de Antropología 186

Notes on contributors

Gustavo Blázquez is Researcher at the National Council of Scientific and Technical Research (CONICET), Argentina, and Professor at the Universidad Nacional de Córdoba (UNC).

Gisela Cánepa Koch is Professor for Social Anthropology at the Department of Social Sciences at the Catholic University of Peru.

María Celina Chocobare is a PhD student in Social Anthropology at Universidad Nacional de Cordoba, Argentina.

Sarah Corona Berkin is Professor for Communication Studies at Universidad de Guadalajara, México.

Carolina Crespo is Researcher at the National Council of Scientific and Technical Research (CONICET), Argentina, and Professor at Universidad de Buenos Aires (UBA).

Ma. del Carmen de la Peza is Distinguished Professor at Universidad Autónoma Metropolitana-Xochimilco, in Mexico.

Frida Gorbach is Senior Professor-Researcher at Universidad Autónoma Metropolitana-Xochimilco, in Mexico City.

Olaf Kaltmeier is Full Professor for Ibero-American History and Director of the Center for InterAmerican Studies at Bielefeld University, Germany.

Sandra Rozental is Assistant Professor at Universidad Autónoma Metropolitana-Cuajimalpa, in México City.

Mario Rufer is Full Professor-Researcher at Universidad Autónoma Metropolitana-Xochimilco, in Mexico City.

Acknowledgments

We are especially grateful to CONACyT in Mexico for funding the project 'Memorias subalternas y tensiones de la nación en el sur global.' Their support made possible our seminar in Chapala, México, where we started to think about this book. Laura Nava, Luz María Quirarte, Erika Ramírez, Álvaro Méndez, and Tony Ramírez provided all the administrative support in the whole process. Maai Ortiz and Alberto Navarrete were efficient assistants and sharp intellectual partners. The BMBF-founded Research Network for Latin America 'Ethnicity, Citizenship, and Belonging' facilitated a visiting scholarship of Mario Rufer at Bielefeld University.

We are especially grateful to Lucía Cirianni and Mario de Leo Winkler who did a great job in the revision of the texts and the translation from Spanish into English. Pablo Campos supported the editing process. We also would like to express our gratitude to Kirstin Howgate and Brenda Sharp from Ashgate Publishing for their confidence in this publication project.

Introduction

The uses of heritage and the postcolonial condition in Latin America

Olaf Kaltmeier and Mario Rufer

In the last decades, we have witnessed a strong expansion and diffusion of cultural heritage. From the most distant town to international forums, we observe the growing use of heritage rhetoric and practices. Subsequently, the proliferation of studies on heritage in Latin America has achieved, in the last few years, a notorious level of development and sophistication. The analyses go from an exploration of the senses pushed by the instituted actions (agents in statehood or supra-state interventions regulated by transnational mechanisms), to less programmatic social actions geared to claim denied, silenced, or hidden senses of origin and provenance, and even studies of layout, management, and promotion of heritage and its links to cultural consumption. This book, gathering the main contributions of the aforementioned branches, follows, however, a divergent question. The question that we editors formulated at the beginning was: Is there a specificity in the formulas of how the politics and narratives on heritage and heritizing are conceived, exploited, administrated, signified, and appropriated in Latin America, part of the *global south*?

A first warning that might seem obvious should be mentioned: that question rose from the basic premise of not assuming that heritage *exists* previously to the skein of politics and poetics that constitute it, the way Carolina Crespo notes in this work. We do not think, as editors, that there is a historical *a priori* regarding something that *must be* considered, registered, or legitimized as 'heritage.' What interested us from the beginning was to deconstruct and analyze a triple process from *global south* contexts: first, how does the notion of heritage became a central input with strong political connotations in actions with instituting goals (from the state or supra-state) as well as in actions 'from the bases' or peripheral to institutional wishes (rural communities, indigenous communities, sectors identified with certain sociopolitical causes). Second, we were interested in working on the ways and processes through which the notion of heritage was objectified and turned from a political gesture to an unquestionable object (Appadurai 1981; Arantes 1984; Castañeda 1996; Ferry 2005; Florescano 1993; Rozental 2014; Vaca and García 2012): as if heritage 'exists' (and in every case it should be known what to do with it). The discussion turned on the terms of the establishment of rules, norms, and guidelines that could specify the regulation of the witness-objects (material objects or, in the last decades, also 'intangible'). Third, we explore how notions and uses of heritage are transformed and act as transformers of the current cultural regimes in Latin America, especially in neoliberal and post-neoliberal contexts (Comaroff and Comaroff 1993; Herwitz 2012). The nucleus of the discussion consists in ambiguous dynamics of the commodification of heritage as an object or as a reference in the marketing surrounding places—from the city to the nation.

Heritage, memory, postcoloniality

In the two movements mentioned previously, we saw a base discussion dangerously diluted. The editors of this volume sustain that we pertain in societies that were gestated, administered, and politically regulated in modern-colonial power regimes: societies historically traversed by the 'coloniality of power' (Quijano 2000). In this sense, we believe it is necessary to 'perceive a historic continuity between the conquest, the colonial order of the world and the postcolonial republic formation that extends until the present' (Segato 2007b, 158; see also Turner 2000, 15–18). Of course we are not talking of continuities in the terms that classical structuralism perceived them or as a certain serial historiography conceived them, but instead as immutable series that weigh as historical sentences above the social subjects that live them. We speak, instead, of recognizing the silenced mimetic continuities, parodied under the apparent chiasm of the 'national subject,' protected by the disciplines under which shadows they were built upon, assumed, and practiced as 'new political orders,' metamorphosed in the apparent historic singularity of the national being present as autochthony, tradition, heritage (Rufer 2012).

Following Segato, we understand that:

> all states—colonial or national, the difference is irrelevant here—are *otherness-like, otherness-phobic and otherness-producer at the same time*. It allows the deployment of its others to enthrone itself, and any political process must be understood through those vertical processes of gestation of the whole ensemble and the cornering of identities.
>
> (Segato 2007, 138, original emphasis)

If it happens in that manner, then what is the relationship of the narratives of heritage/heritizing and contemporary gestures of 'community management'? What link exists between the administration of allowed identities inside 'neoliberal multiculturalism' and the overwhelming necessity of heritizing everything? And fundamentally, which political operations—and which senses of direction—are encased (several times hidden) in the apparent drive to make everything heritage?

Hence, the aim of the book is to explore the relevance of the politics of heritage and the uses of memory in the consolidation of these nation-states, as well as in the current disputes over resistances, hidden memories, undermined pasts, or the politics of nostalgia; the book also seeks to seize the local/global dimensions around heritage—with the intervention of UNESCO and other agents (see Kaltmeier, this volume; Castañeda 2009). At the same time, the relationship between collective memory (as a process created over the base of superimposed discursive devices) and heritage is marked by the difference with which the past is considered from the modern idea of rupture (Vaca 2012). The notion of heritage is inextricably linked to the modern will of indexical ordering of the past and showing it as 'legacy' through precise and institutionalized actions (generally, at least until World War II, as actions of any kind of state formation) (Hansen and Stepputat 2001; Pérez Monfort 2011).

It is relevant to mention that several of the authors participating in this book started their research exploring the field of politics of memory and the 'uses' of the past in the present. We explored how the 'administration of the past' (Rufer 2008) turned into one of the key gestures of the postcolonial nation. The different 'productions of history' (Cohen 1994) in textbooks, new museums, intervention and reposition of monuments, group, sectorial, or community actions to interpose hegemonic narrations of the past, have put the semic-discursive production on the past/memory/history triad on fertile moving terrain.

Was the new heritage boom linked with this performative gesture of the politics of memory in postcolonial contexts? That question is indirectly sustained in the texts of Kaltmeier, Rufer, and Crespo in this volume. Kaltmeier starts from a distinction that permeates this book as an epistemic gesture: 'While in Western European countries, heritage has been transformed into a depoliticized lifestyle factor, heritage in postcolonial contexts has become a battleground on the interpretation of history and its projection into the future' (see Kaltmeier, this volume). From this point of view, Kaltmeier will insist on the need to link the relevance of the politics of heritizing with the concept of indigeneity and coloniality in Latin America. To answer the initial question, the author unravels the role that is met by the forms of gestation and signifying heritage in postcolonial contexts, marked by the presence (demographical, political and public) of indigenous populations. Here, it is therefore worked in a double tension of conjuncture. On the one hand, one that marks colonial difference: starting with the quinzcentennial of the incorrectly called 'Discovery' of America, the discussion over heritage-acquired specific dimensions in terms of complaints, claims, and projections for the future of indigenous communities that repositioned their presence, memory, and legacy in the long Latino-American temporality. On the other hand, coloniality is also present in the gesture that tries—with precise policies—to domesticate this semi-political gesture in the new policies of identity of the multicultural nation-state (in its neoliberal and national-popular versions, depending on the case).

Carolina Crespo (in this volume) progresses in that direction by directly dissecting the poetics of the limits of 'the permitted otherness' in the present policies of heritage, fundamentally from indigenous populations. It is a clear analytical bet that also permeates all the works in this book; Crespo notes that she conceives the vision of heritage as process and political practice, pondering less what it is from a normative analysis, than that which different social sectors are making out of it and the relations and implications that this generates. This requires being thought of more as a space for consensus, as a field of forces that involves tension in certain relations, subjectivities, emotional attachments, types of knowledge and visions of the social world and of the space inside the procedures of construction and dispute for hegemony.

The question over political tension between heritage and memory is also developed in the text by Rufer. The author presents how the notion of heritage, in certain cases, is used to absorb 'the political' of memory: sometimes memory can work like an enunciative strategy—of communal, sectorial, etc. (De Certeau 1980); as disruptive narratives with those trying to administer the past and transform it into a locked archive of the revisionist perspective. But the notion of heritage sometimes works in a functional manner to liberal multiculturalism, fundamentally acting as a 'poisoned gift': with the promise of being the reflection of the identity that is 'now recognized' and pondered upon, that identity stays, nevertheless, enclosed over itself in the non-profanation logic of heritage: it must be guarded, extremely cared for, subtracted to experience. For the author, this is a reediting of the colonial will over the administration of the past and the present. Nevertheless, it presents its own fissures: from its precise analysis, Crespo, Rufer, and Kaltmeier explain how communities resignify and return the 'heritizing' gesture with the uneasy will of the action of memory (Pollack 2006). Therefore, with the concept that pertains to the hegemonic guidelines, they build a supplement of meaning (Bhabha 2002): crossing out the conservative gesture of institutional politics of heritage, imprinting a gamut of political senses over incompleteness, loss, hierarchy, and grievance.

Heritage and nation-state

From the nineteenth century onward, the uses of cultural heritage supported the modern nation-state building processes in the Americas, as well as their identity politics as homogenous territories. Nevertheless, in Latin American postcolonial societies, heritage can be conceived of a Western gift related to coloniality that regulates the narration of histories. In this sense especially, the narration and conception of indigeneity and coloniality pose a problem to heritage politics in the Americas.

The colonial rupture makes it impossible to construct a historical continuity from a remote past to the contemporary nation. Relying on the concept of 'shared history,' we argue that we can speak of a shared heritage that is common in terms of the basic grammar of heritage and articulated histories, but divided alongside the basic difference between colonizers and colonized. This problem is also evident in contemporary uses of the past. The last decades were crucial to the emergence of new debates: subcultures, new identities, hidden voices, and multicultural discourse as a kind of new hegemonic platform also involving concepts such as heritage and/or memory. Thereby we can observe a proliferation of heritage agents, especially beyond the scope of the nation-state (Escalante Gonzalbo 2011).

One main concern of this volume is to get beyond a container-vision of heritage that seeks to construct a diachronic continuity in a given territory. Instead, we want to point out the relational character of heritage focusing on transnational and translocal flows and interchanges of ideas, concepts, and practices, as well as on the creation of contact zones (Pratt 1998) where the meaning of heritage is negotiated and contested (López Caballero 2011).

In order to understand the entangled and relational character of heritage, we have to rethink our concepts. Several theoretical displacements seem necessary: we no longer think of culture as a system but also as a resource; we no longer deal only with historiographies, but also with 'uses of the past'; we no longer work only with identities but also with 'processes of identification.' Heritage is also analyzed from its processes of construction in relation to the aforementioned variables (culture, identity, the past).

It is also evident that the relationship between heritage and nation-states must be able to show the *performative dimension of the state*. What concrete form does a policy of identities acquire when otherness that is controlled and limited by actions of statehood becomes an oppositional cultural good within the forces that play for the equilibrium of power. Celina Chocobare analyzes this side working on the uses of the past and the Ranquel 'identity' in San Luis, Argentina. Looking for a repositioning that would evidence the identity specificity (and exceptionality) of the region, the government of San Luis in Argentina proposes actions of specific recognition of the Ranquel indigenous community, and to achieve it deploys a series of particular uses of the past through local legislative resources and cultural management. The paradoxes of these uses of indigenous heritage highlight the ambiguity between politics of identification and the administration of difference. Gustavo Blázquez also shows how the notion of culture becomes a specific tool for the government and administration. The author discusses how a resource so seemingly innocuous such as popular music (the Argentinian *cuarteto cordobés* in this case) acquires a crucial dimension: its process of heritizing, analyzed from an ethnographic sensibility, unveiling the form in which the state reinvents itself day-by-day, extending its sovereignty over that which it defines as traditional, popular, and culturally 'proper.'

On a different note, Frida Gorbach explores the way certain fundamental pieces of the hegemonic and monumental construction of national identity such as the National Museum of Anthropology of Mexico still continue reediting the fortress of the anthropology/heritage/nation-state triad. Starting with the exhibition of the relationship between dramaturgy and the power of ceremony that celebrated the 50 years of the National Museum, the author underpins a careful text on the diverse narratives (from classical authors up to contemporary works of art). These narratives discuss how, even in times of the recognition of otherness and exhibition of diversities, the nation-state reinvents the rubric of heritizing and the documentary/monumental gesture of disciplinary power and the exhibition complex.

Beyond 'the stone' as a key material testimony of the relation triad already explained, we question what happens with the most rooted and naturalized exponents of the national symbolic universe: do anthems, rosettes, flags, and their uses still have something to tell us? How can we reframe the question by its political dimension in diffuse texts of loss of allure of the homogeneous nation, and yet, of horrible reissues of nationalist pulsations, even in their versions of a 'pluricultural nation'? On the other hand, we were aware of the lack of attention over one of the most recently referred elements such as heritage (in the logic of 'rescue' and 'no profanation') but less analyzed in their processes of negotiation: language. How can we critically analyze the undeniable defense of indigenous languages in Latin America, but in a context of discontinuity with key historical references that make that defense a decontextualized cause in the concrete social scene of 'linguistic dispossession' that many communities live today?

On the first point, Judith Butler and Gayatri Spivak marked the political character of singing and performing publicly the national anthems in diasporic and migration contexts in the book *Who Sings the Nation State* (2009). In this volume, Sarah Corona Berkin takes this question to the study of graphic representations of the Mexican national anthem in different states. The author shows how the national anthem was disseminated in a process that unified heritizing with mandatory pedagogy in the plot of national postrevolutionary conformation in that country. The crucial part of Corona Berkin's argument is that the preoccupations of the postcolonial nation-state to retain the authority of representations over the Mexican identity are perceived by those who are *enabled* to sing/perform the anthem in the images of the unique and free textbook edited by the *Secretaría de Educación Pública* (SEP; Ministry of Education): children, women, indigenous people, mestizos, and whites form a mosaic of identity/otherness that can only be understood in inter-positional terms, with a politically precise, contextual, and temporal sense of direction.

The second aspect, related to language, is examined by María del Carmen de la Peza—also in Mexico. Starting from a triple analysis: theoretical (on community, heritage, and language), historical (on the contextual dimension of pilferage and linguistic exclusion), and intellectual (on the specific oeuvre of Alfonso Reyes), the author highlights the paradox of heritizing the languages in Mexico. On the one hand, she explains how the 'right' of language was conceived as intangible heritage based on recent politics of UNESCO. However, the process of colonial-national *'castellanización'* (the compulsory immersion into Spanish language) meant the 'prohibition' of accessing one's own language, its *deauthorizing*. In that moment, the interdiction of the possibility of speaking is inaugurated as an implicit beginning of the (post)colonial policy of language. That policy was never justly reverted because access to Castilian was always marked by the original foreclosure of dispossession violence of the mother tongue. That way, the author states: 'Even though the Mexican State has privileged Spanish as the national language for the effects of public and political interaction, most Mexicans are functional illiterates and do not live Spanish as their own language' (see De la Peza, this volume). A pluricultural state that acknowledges the value of linguistic diversity with the rhetoric of intangible heritage does not take responsibility for those primary processes, and overall, it continues administering which subjects,

Introduction: the uses of heritage   7

when, in which way, over which things and in what language, and who can actually speak (and who will continue to be unable to do so).

Seen from the perspective of everyday reproduction of statehood, the policies of heritage escort the processes of identification and otherness, even when they are 'poetics of recognition' over those who have been silenced in the long history of the modern nation. In ways of classifying, naming, and producing heritage by legitimizing the existence of precise heirs (indigenous peoples, afro communities, subnational collectivities), an aporetic reproduction is produced: in the action through which they are recognized, those 'other interns' are also moved into a differentiated and otherness producing partiality; and they form part of the nation-state that in the processes recognizes and grants, continues to exercise the power of the legislative perspective, administrating subjectivities/subjections, and extending its sovereignty (Briones 2005). This point created the ethic of suspicion by which this book addresses the problem of heritage linked to diversity, difference, and differentiation as historical, contextual, and political complex phenomena.

Heritage, difference, and signification

We have highlighted that in the face of institutional wishes, there are diverse and contextual processes of tension and response. The classical notions of heritage linked to a transferable property by basic rules of lineage and heritage that form a 'legacy' (Vaca 2012) are intertwined in processes of hegemonization of the national state (Florescano 1993) and also with dense forms in local and community spheres that signify and process the sedimentations of postcolonial capitalism (Ferry 2005; García Canclini 1993). Definitely, as expressed by Sandra Rozental in this volume, communities have learned and processed that heritage is something that has the form of a 'potential expropriation': something that can be extracted, taken, disappeared (as a relic/monument that 'belongs' to the whole nation—and therefore disappears from the community environment and the links it strengthened —or as a good-merchandise that is privatized and turned into cumulative wealth). How is heritage sectorized, how does it affect regulations and community links, how does it interweave with the logic of resources, consumptions, or fetishism, and how they signify precise categories in those processes? Rozental uses her text to work those textured questions, through the Mexican community of Coatlinchán, and from the communal circulation of stories of 'buried treasures.' The author links the historical meaning of 'treasures' in the production of history, with the affective stories of violence, exploitation, and dispossession lived and conjured up by the community.

At the same time, the practices of definition, classification, visibility, and recognition normally pay little attention to the processes of silencing and to the place of those processes of construction of heritage narratives. On the one hand, there are a series of managers and authorities of ordering, taxonomy, and selection of narratives destined to become part of exhibited cultural heritage (either in terms of objects, accounts, or 'culture'). On those managers and authorities (and on the codified construction of their authority and legitimacy), little has been researched. At the same time, violent and traumatic processes that are at the base of the modern conformation of communities (and in the distribution and negotiation of their identities in the *glocal* concert) usually are aborted in heritage narratives. Carolina Crespo and Mario Rufer devote themselves to analyze these processes of silencing with epistemological potential.

Crespo draws attention to how events of displacement, pilferage, and plundering make certain accounts gradually excluded from the narratives on local memories—even from communal circulation. Without doubt, in the construction of the notion of heritage by indigenous communities, these processes of silencing are key elements to understanding what is at play in the construction of an 'archive' as a regime of the enunciable in systems of heritizing.

Rufer, through the exploration of Mexican community museums, analyzes the way in which they are perceived (and negotiated) in the limits of present-day heritage narratives; the author specifically analyzes how the modalities of cultural management of diversity tries to delimit the intensity, topic, and direction of community discussions on belonging, local history, heritage, memory, and violence; at the same time, he returns to the specific gesture of how this institutional intent is circumvented, in how it is adapted and questioned in a specific way through narratives created in communities that process and return the 'poisoned gift' of the state with an iconoclastic force that strains the hegemonic direction.

Heritage, transnationalism, and neoliberalism

In the nineteenth and the first half of the twentieth centuries, the nation-state can be conceived of, in Bourdieu's terms, as a 'reserve bank of consecration' that allocated and administrated symbolic capital. This especially included the recognition and the mise-en-scène of heritage. In the last third of the twentieth century, this model of state formation has been transformed through neoliberal waves of globalization. In regard to the conceptualization and administration of heritage, we can identify three main dynamics in this cultural–political context.

The first dynamic concerns the ongoing commodification and the penetration of the market in nearly all aspects of social life. This includes the field of cultural production where authors such as George Yudice and Toby Miller have identified an 'expediency of culture' and the growing impact of cultural industry, which in postcolonial societies especially includes the marketing of cultural heritages. Cultural studies scholars and cultural sociologists have argued for the existence of an ongoing de-differentiation between economy and culture in late capitalist societies. In a similar vein, Daniel Mato (2007) points out that the classical definition of cultural industries, introduced by Theodor W. Adorno and Max Horkheimer, is now being substituted by dynamics in which all industries make use of culture and of heritage. In this sense, not only is the cultural commodified, but also other commodities and objects underlie logics of cultural marketing that often finds expression in heritage branding. The search for an authentic and unique heritage in postcolonial societies in Latin America is often related to colonialism, indigeneity, and Afro-Americanity (see Kaltmeier and Cánepa in this volume) Cultural studies scholar Graham Huggan (2001) speaks in this context about the emergence of a veritable 'postcolonial alterity industry,' where the construction of exotic alterity serves as a means to enter the market.

The growing commodification of all social relations also implies the reshaping of the relationship between state and market. As Foucault advises, this should not be reduced to a simple equation of 'more market' means 'less state.' Instead we deal with new forms of governmentality that also include the emergence of new forms of cultural politics, including the redefinition of heritage. This finds its expression in the contemporary trends of 'city marketing' and 'nation branding.' Gisela Cánepa problematizes with her case study on the museum exhibition *Inca—Kings of the Andes* 'on an emerging cultural regime, paying specially attention to the way it is operating in Peru since the neoliberal reforms implemented by Alberto Fujimori in the early 1990s and in the postwar context' (in this volume).

In a similar vein, Gustavo Blázquez analyzes (in this volume) how the invention of the musical format of the *cuarteto* in Córdoba as cultural heritage is related to the 'transformation of culture into expediency and the legitimization of the figure of 'cultural manager' as a technician specialized in designing and administrating cultural policies.'

At his point, the debate of cultural homogenization in globalization process resurges, as some authors argue that a globalized and normed heritage produces 'landscapes of consumption tending to consume their own contexts,' not least because of the 'homogenizing effect on places and cultures' of tourism (Sack 1992, 158–159), while on the other hand authenticity and local particularity is needed to make the heritage game work.

A second dynamic is the growing interconnectedness of horizons of interaction in regard to heritage. After World War II, we can observe the emergence of a real transnational heritage field with a broad array of institutionalized actors and new experts. Especially the concept of world heritage, and its subsequent amplification from monuments, to areas, to landscapes, to immaterial heritage, has not only been a normalizing instance but also a catalyzer and transformer of heritage. Thereby, supranational institutions like UNESCO are increasingly becoming embattled arenas for heritage politics, that not only attend the petitions of nation-states but that develop their own heritage agendas, thereby creating spaces of intervention for sub-national actors. In this sense, local communities are also increasingly involved in the heritage field, as it is highlighted by Herwitz (2012, 5): 'This common language (of heritage, the authors) makes identity a globally comprehensible, consumable item and provides local populations with a relevant profile. Having (suddenly) a *heritage* makes you (potentially) an international player.'

Beyond the homogenization tendency through market logic, the question arises: to what extent does the internationalization of heritage regimes with its rules of certification and codification as well as its cultural grammar also lead to a homogenization of heritage. On the other hand, it can be argued that the inclusion of new actors in the heritage field constantly challenges established rules of the game and leads to a permanent transformation of heritage and its uses (see Kaltmeier, this volume).

Although there exists a strong link between the proliferation of heritage and the neoliberal market regime, heritage can function also as an obstacle toward commodification. Post-neoliberal Latin American governments in Ecuador and Venezuela are involved in neo-nationalist heritage discourses that are related to the foundational narratives of the nineteenth century with reference to heroes of the national pantheon such as Simón Bolívar or Eloy Alfaro. In doing so, such heritage politics may repeat the silencing of indigenous and Afro-American presences that characterized postcolonial heritage politics since the nineteenth century. However, in Bolivia, the Evo Morales government is engaged in the re-foundation of the nation through a deep process of decolonization and reinvention of indigenous heritage that may lead to a significant rupture in the established patterns of Latin American postcolonial heritage politics.

This collection of essays is the outcome of an intensive interdisciplinary and intercultural interchange of ideas. The authors united here have worked together since 2012 on the idea of 'Entangled Heritages in Latin America.' We have discussed their approaches and concepts in panels organized at the Biannual Conference of the International Association of Inter-American Studies 2012 in Guadalajara, Mexico, and 2014 in Lima, Peru, as well at the 2013 conference of the *Consejo Europeo de Investigaciones Sociales de América Latina* (CEISAL) in Porto, Portugal. In 2013, we deepened the interchange of ideas through an exchange with the BMBF-Research Network for Latin America 'Citizenship, Ethnicity, and Belonging' and in a three-day workshop on the banks of the Lake Chapala in Guadalajara. We hope that the reader will be able to see and enjoys this intense exchange while reading the essays presented in *Entangled heritages. Postcolonial perspectives on the uses of the past in Latin America*.

References

Appadurai, Arjun. 1981. 'The past as a scarce resource.' *Man*, 16 (2): 201–19.
Arantes, Augusto. 1984. *Produzindo o passado: estratégias de construção do patrimônio cultural*. São Paulo: Editorial Brasiliense.
Bhabha, Homi. 2002. *El lugar de la cultura*. Buenos Aires: Manantial
Briones, Claudia. 2005. 'Formaciones de alteridad, contextos globales, procesos nacionales y provinciales.' In *Cartografías argentinas. Políticas indigenistas y formaciones provinciales de alteridad*, ed. Claudia Briones. Buenos Aires: Antropofagia.
Castañeda, Quetzil E. 1996. *In the museum of maya culture. Touring Chichen Itza*. Minneapolis: University of Minnesota Press
Castañeda, Quetzil E. 2009. 'Notes on the Work of Heritage in the Age of Archaeological Reproduction'. *Ethnographies and Archaeologies: Iterations of the Past*. Florida: University Press of Florida, 109–19.
Cohen, David W. 1994. *The combing of history*. Chicago: University of Chicago.
Comaroff, Jean, and John Comaroff. 1993. 'Introduction.' In *Modernity and its malcontents. Ritual and power in postcolonial Africa*, ed. Jean Comaroff, and John Comaroff. Chicago: University of Chicago.

De Certeau, Michel. 1996. *La invención de lo cotidiano. 1 Artes de hacer*. México. Universidad Iberoamericana. [1980].
De la Peña, Guillermo. 2011. 'La antropología, el indigenismo y la diversificación del patrimonio cultural de México.' In *La antropología y el patrimonio cultural de México*, ed. Guillermo De la Peña. Mexico City: CONACULTA.
Escalante Gonzalbo, Pablo. 2011. 'Introducción.' In *La idea de nuestro patrimonio cultural*, Vol. 2, ed. Pablo Escalante Gonzalbo. Mexico City: CONACULTA.
Ferry, Elizabeth Emma. 2005. *Not ours alone: Patrimony, value, and collectivity in contemporary Mexico*. New York: Columbia University.
Florescano, Enrique. 1993. 'El patrimonio cultural y la política de la cultura.' In *El patrimonio cultural de México*, ed. Enrique Florescano. Mexico City: CONACULTA – Fondo de Cultura Económica.
García Canclini, Néstor. 1993. 'Los usos del patrimonio cultural.' In *El patrimonio cultural de México*, ed. Enrique Florescano. Mexico City: CONACULTA – Fondo de Cultura Económica.
Guerrero, Andrés. 2003. 'On imagining/writing postcolonial histories. Points and counterpoints.' In *After Spanish rule. Postcolonial predicaments of the Americas*, ed. Mark Thurner, and Andrés Guerrero. Durham: Duke University.
Herwitz, Daniel. 2012. *Heritage, culture and politics in the postcolony*. New York: Columbia University.
Huggan, Graham. 2001. *The postcolonial exotic: Marketing the margins*. London: Routledge.
López Caballero, Paula. 2008. 'Which heritage for which heirs? The pre-Columbian past and the colonial legacy in the national history of Mexico.' *Social Anthropology*, 16 (3): 329–45.
Mato, Daniel. 2007. 'Todas las industrias son culturales: crítica de la idea de 'industrias Culturales' y nuevas posibilidades de investigación.' *Nueva época*, 8: 131–53.
Pérez Monfort, Ricardo. 2011. 'Nacionalismo y representación en el México posrevolucionario (1920–1940). La construcción de estereotipos nacionales.' In *La idea de nuestro patrimonio cultural*, ed. Pablo Escalante Gonzalbo, Vol. 2. Mexico City: CONACULTA.
Pollak, Michael. 2006. *Memoria, olvido, silencio. La producción social de identidades frente a situaciones límite*. La Plata: Ediciones al margen.
Pratt, Mary Louise. 2007. *Imperial eyes. Travel writing and transculturation*. London: Routledge [1992].
Quijano, Aníbal. 2000. 'Colonialidad del poder, eurocentrismo y América Latina.' In *La colonialidad del poder. Eurocentrismo y ciencias sociales. Perspectivas latinoamericanas*, ed. Eduardo Lander. Buenos Aires: CLACSO.
Rozental, Sandra. 2014. 'Stone Replicas: The Iteration and Itinerancy of Mexican Patrimonio.' *The Journal of Latin American and Caribbean Anthropology*, 19 (2): 331–56.
Rufer, Mario. 2010. *La nación en escenas. Usos del pasado y políticas de la memoria en contextos poscoloniales*. Mexico City: El Colegio de México.
Rufer, Mario. 2012. 'Introducción: nación, diferencia, poscolonialismo.' In *Nación y Diferencia*, ed. Mario Rufer. Mexico City: ITACA-CONACyT.
Sack, Robert D. 1992. *Place, modernity and the consumer's world*. Baltimore: Johns Hopkins University.
Segato, Rita. 2007a. 'El color de la cárcel en América Latina. Apuntes sobre la colonialidad de la justicia en un continente en desconstrucción.' *Nueva Sociedad*, 208 (March-April): 142–61.

Segato, Rita. 2007b. 'Raza es signo.' In *La nación y sus otros*. Buenos Aires: Prometeo.
Vaca, Agustín, and Estrellita García. 2012. 'Notas en torno de los fundamentos teóricos del patrimonio cultural.' In *Procesos del patrimonio cultural*, ed. Agustín Vaca, and Estrellita García. Mexico City: El Colegio de Jalisco.
Yudice, George. 2003. *The expediency of culture*. Durham: Duke University.

1 On the advantage and disadvantage of heritage for Latin America
Heritage politics and nostalgia between coloniality and indigeneity

Olaf Kaltmeier

Heritage is booming all over the world. Within the last years, we have witnessed an amazing qualitative and quantitative expansion of heritage policies. Not only have international heritage organizations like the famous UNESCO World Heritage Center expanded their scope dramatically, but the cultural industry also seems to be booming with a 'heritage lifestyle' marked by nostalgia, vintage, and a 'retro' look. Performance and narration of heritage are related to a globally established form, although its appropriation depends on local patterns. This is especially the case in Latin America, where the general heritage boom—which is also set according to a growing cultural industry—is intrinsically entangled with questions of coloniality and indigeneity.

While in Western European countries, heritage has often been transformed into a depoliticized lifestyle factor, in postcolonial contexts heritage has also become a battleground for the interpretation of history and its projection into the future. According to David Herwitz, this is the main reason why decolonizing societies enter the heritage game and make their own heritage, although heritage itself is a Western device.

> To do so is a rehabilitating move, a way of self-assigning a future by taking over the ideology which allows them to ascribe origin and destiny to the past, accretion and transmissibility to their 'values.' And a central part of the postcolonial dialectic is re-conceptualizing the precolonial past as a heritage, finding a way to claim that past as the origin of one's future.
> (Herwitz 2012, 21)

This use of heritage has its pitfalls, since heritage is a discourse and a practice that is not rooted in indigenous policies of the past but introduced by the colonizers, which implies certain logics of representation, categorization, and exhibition. While heritage is based on these logics of representation, categorization, and exhibition, usually made by experts, it is articulated with the affective and emotional side of nostalgic feelings that, in the Americas, are related to the antagonist patterns of coloniality and indigeneity. Thereby, nostalgia is not a simple sighing for yesterday; instead, it serves as a means to confront a conflictive present and an uncertain future (Kaltmeier 2015b).

The decolonial engagement with heritage and nostalgia is particularly relevant for those Latin American countries that have a considerable indigenous population and where attempts are made at imagining the nation in relation to a precolonial heritage. The indigenous uprising in Ecuador in 1990 and the hemispheric indigenous protest movement of 1992 around the 500th anniversary of the European conquest of the Americas marked a turning point in the field of indigeneity and initiated a new politicization of the indigenous question in Latin America. This new visibility of the indigenous, the introduction of ethnic symbols and semantics into public spaces, and the reinvention of ethnic identities shape the political culture of the Latin American countries since the 1990s, and query the principles of vision and division of a social world based on coloniality. A fundamental aspect of these movements was their struggle for cultural-political recognition, including the matter of heritage.

Although Latin America's policies have been multilayered and special emphasis has been placed by the public on the memory of South American military dictatorships, coloniality and indigeneity can be seen as fundamental temporal layers of the Americas. Following a discussion on the fundamental contemporary dynamics of heritage, this article focuses on its entanglements first with coloniality, and, second, with indigeneity. These two fundamental aspects of the colonial situation are re-actualized in many and different ways in the field of heritage. In this context, this article analyzes paradigmatic constellations spanning from Mexico to Chile where different actors—from social movements to cultural entrepreneurs, state agencies and NGOs—try to make use of heritage, and where they reinterpret history through heritage in several ways. In doing so, we explore to what extent is it possible to articulate difference or even resistance within the established idiom of heritage.

The power of heritage

Probably, every human society engages in practices of memory in order to build identity and belonging. However, the notion of heritage that alludes to practices and discourses made by scientific experts emerged around the second half of the nineteenth century in the context of nation-building. The nation's attempt at a diachronic and harmonious narrative is at odds with the dynamics of industrial revolution, internal migration, and massive processes of urbanization disrupting the processes of identity formation. In Europe, the emergence of the discourse of heritage was linked to romanticism and to ideas such as 'arcadia,' 'origin,' and 'authenticity.' Therefore, the discourse of heritage is offered as a way to heal the flaws of modernity. It promises continuity and stability, continuing an invented origin that was lost in the processes of modernization (Herwitz 2012, 18; Smith 2006, 17). Especially in postcolonial conditions, however, the use of heritage for nation-building is somehow ambiguous. Due to the colonial situation, the past is not only a positive reference with which to narrate a story of progress; rather, it is marked by trauma and colonial shame.

In Latin America, the idea of heritage emerged as homologous and interchangeable with European notions, but unlike them, it was marked by the colonial situation. Thus, the indigenous as well as the colonial are seen as a resource in different junctures, but also as a hindrance and an obstacle for the construction of identities. Since the 1860s, colonial architecture and urbanism were seen by Latin American elites mostly as an obstacle to modern urban development as established by the Paris model. By the liberal republics, the Hispanic heritage was seen as an obstacle for modernization and civilization, while conservative sectors relied on hispanism to forge the nation. For the *criollo* elites, the treatment of indigenous peoples within national history was equally a problem. Without the indigenous origin, it became difficult to form a national narrative as deep as that shown by European discourses. Therefore, indigenous peoples were—in many countries—petrified and exhibited as an artifact of the past, while contemporary indigenous populations were forced into assimilation processes.

From the national perspective, the image of heritage rises as a mosaic, fragmented according to national borders. This national segmental rationale is increasingly intertwined with a transnational field of heritage. Especially after World War II and through international and supranational organizations such as UNESCO, the Organization for World Heritage Cities, the International Council on Monuments and Sites (ICOMOS), the International Centre for the Study and Preservation of Cultural Property (ICCROM), and regional associations such as the Latin American and Caribbean Organization of Historic Centers, a transnational field of heritage emerged where architects, archeologists, urbanists, sociologists, economists, ecologists, and other experts participate in an interdisciplinary manner and from their own specific discourses.

Heritage is thus established, after World War II, as a technocratic discourse produced by experts. With its universalizing scope construed in terms of 'world heritage,' the strong nineteenth-century link between heritage and nation is loosened and heritage becomes depoliticized. If, drawing on Pierre Bourdieu, we had to define de *nomos* of the heritage field, we could claim that it is the decision on which tangible or intangible goods are to be preserved and which are not. It is in this sense that Jesús Martín-Barbero (2010a, 5) points out:

> The craft of memory [as that of heritage, O.K] is therefore that of not mere accumulation but that of sieving, which is to say selection and redressing. Values are also included here, since memory also exercises its craft on them by re-valuing as well as de-valuing.

Making this decision is not in the least a democratic exercise; it depends on the control over economic, social, and cultural capital (García Canclini 1999). It is based on a fairly simplistic attitude before the contradictions and complexities of history, which led Eduardo Kingman and Ana María Goetschel (2005), drawing on their experience in Quito's historic city center, to understand it in Foucauldian terms as a disciplinary device that trivializes memory. Heritage is in this sense intrinsically linked to power. Laurajane Smith coined the concept 'authorized heritage discourse,' which 'focuses attention on aesthetically pleasing material objects, sites, places, and/or landscapes that current generations 'must' care for, protect and reserve' (2006, 29) in order to create identity. The decision to preserve is informed by the geopolitics of mainstream knowledge, which is currently related to the historical emergence of the West throughout the long sixteenth century and its Eurocentric production of knowledge. On the level of discourse, it can be conceived as an iteration of national Western discourse on a global scale, thus universalizing the European forms and concepts of heritage. In spite of its global character, it is ultimately nation-states that are responsible for proposing and managing world heritage sites.

Recently, however, there are several tendencies in the proliferation of heritage. Within UNESCO definitions, the concept of heritage has been increasingly widened. It was first centered on monuments; by the mid-seventies, it came to include urban settings, which, as it happened with the historic center of Quito on 1978, can be declared to be world heritage, as it was also the case for cultural landscapes after 1992. It is especially with the emergence of intangible heritage, which was adopted by UNESCO in 2003, that a proliferation of heritage was directed also to local and regional communities and was no longer limited to state agencies. Nearly every single community, municipality, or region is identifying its specific heritage. Thus, heritage came to be considered as a *fait social total*. As a social fact in Durkheimian terms, heritage consists of representations and actions, and thus exerts a coercive power over the individual. Thereby it encompasses legal, economic, religious, aesthetic, morphological, and other aspects of social life (Mauss 2009). Within the context of contemporary identity policies in the Americas, George Yudice (2003) has argued that there is a performative imperative to reveal identity. In the same way, we can identify a heritage imperative of showing historically bound identity and belonging.

Although we agree with the aforementioned critique of heritage as a Eurocentric realm of power, we also think there are ways of counter-conduct or even resistance. In regard to his discussion on governance, Foucault stated: 'Where there is power, there is resistance.' In his lecture from March 1, 1978, at the Collège de France, Foucault discussed the possibility of resistance against the new pastoral power. He discussed both passive and active forms of resistance. But his main interest was directed towards those practices of counter-conduct emerging within the new power regime. In concert with this Foucauldian approach, we are also mainly interested in the practices of counter-conduct within the field of heritage that have the productive function of challenging orthodox forms and creating new knowledge.

This is particularly the case in postcolonial contexts where heritage is simultaneously adopted and altered. In this context, Herwitz proposes the following understanding of the use of heritage: 'Heritage practice was a 'gift' in the double edged sense of offering and poison' (2012, 8). On the one hand, it enables postcolonial nations in a mixture of mimicry and assimilation to construe themselves as nations and insert themselves within global history. On the other hand, it defines a discursive frame to express these demands and its forms of representation, such as museums, history books, archaeological sites, and so on.

Beyond the analysis of heritage as discourse, I want to emphasize its material dimension, which is especially expressed by the category of tangible heritage. Here, the way coloniality has shaped the heritage landscape is rendered evident. As Bertolt Brecht (1964, 261) wrote: 'Always the victor writes the history of the vanquished. He who beats distorts the faces of the beaten. The weaker departs from this world and the lies remains.' Similarly, Eric Wolf (1982) has argued that many colonized peoples have been subjected to the state of 'peoples without history.' If this is so for historiographical discourse, it is even more relevant for the case of appropriated and transformed space as it is shown by monuments, cities, and cultural landscapes. The exclusion of the subaltern from the material text of space is even deeper there than in written and told history. Access to capital is of paramount importance for the construction of material goods that are considered by experts in the field of heritage. Besides, lack of capital limits the selection of construction materials, so artifacts made by the subaltern usually have less durability. The monuments remain and the barracks of the workers disappear.

To perform such an appropriation and transformation of the environment, economic, cultural, and social capital are needed. In pervasive colonial contexts, this capital is mostly generated through appropriation and exploitation of a social class constructed in racial terms by a white *mestizo* elite. It is therefore worth emphasizing along with Walter Benjamin, that 'there is no document of culture that is not at the same time a document of barbarism' (1974, 253). These considerations are still absent from the discourse of heritage agencies that praise many monuments in the Americas for their colonial character.

Nostalgia and heritage nowadays

After World War II and the subsequent wave of decolonization, we can observe a depoliticization of heritage that was followed in the 1990s by an increasing dynamic of commodification of heritage in the postmodern condition. The end of the bipolar world brought about by the fall of the Soviet Union inspired neo-Hegelian philosopher Francis Fukuyama to declare the 'end of history' at an age of global capitalism. This dynamic goes along with a remarkable return of nostalgic attitudes and feelings. Linda Hutcheon (1998) even argues that nostalgia is the main cultural force in the 1990s: 'Perhaps nostalgia is given surplus meaning and value at certain moments—millennial moments, like our own. Nostalgia, the media tell us, has become an obsession of both mass culture and high art.'

We are witnessing a certain crisis of the future that relates to the end of great narratives of development and progress. However, this does not mean history has come to an end. On the contrary, the omnipresence of cultural heritage projects, policies of memory, nostalgia, 'retro' and vintage fashion trends, as well as historical shows indicate not the end of history but rather an oversaturation of history in contemporary life.

While the heritage policies adopted during the nineteenth century and early twentieth century were informed by the nation-building project, in our postmodern and—even at a global scale—neoliberal times, we notice a use of heritage that has an economic aim. With the neologism 'histourism' (Römhild 1992), merging 'history' and 'tourism,' and the wordplay 'pasttime of past time' (Hutcheon 1988), scholars have highlighted the leisure aspect in the commodification of heritage, which is echoed in 'retro' fashion trends promoted by cultural industries. Cultural heritage does not escape the capitalist economy, which is characterized by an ever closer entanglement of the economic and the cultural. Thus, heritage is saliently presented as a commodity that can be consumed according to the laws of capitalism. In their critique of the economization of ethnicity, John and Jean Comaroff (2009, 10) point out:

> Heritage is culture named and projected into the past, and simultaneously, the past congealed into culture . . . It is identity in tractable, alienable form, identity whose found objects and objectifications may be consumed by others and, therefore be delivered to the market.

This is also the case for many Latin American countries where ethnic and heritage tourism with its specific gift markets is booming (DeHart 2010).

But in postcolonial situations, it is not only a proliferation and commodification of heritage that can be observed; a striking re-politicization of heritage that can also be related to feelings of postcolonial nostalgia is equally relevant. Postcolonial scholars have pointed out the importance of nostalgic moments in the political-cultural claims of the colonized (Hutcheon 1998; Simonse 1982). Especially in postcolonial studies, a discussion on melancholy emerged, inspired by Freud's essay on *Mourning and Melancholy*, which addresses the melancholic clinging to the precolonial past. Homi Bhabha departs from the existence of a hybrid third space where the precolonial experience cannot be recovered. This revolt is only possible in these fragmented third spaces.

> All these bits and pieces in which my history is fragmented, my culture piecemeal, my identification fantasmatic and displaced; these splittings of wounds of my body are also a form of revolt. And they speak a terrible truth. In their ellipses and silences they dismantle your authority.
> (Bhabha 1992, 66)

Acknowledging the importance of nostalgia for resistance, José Rabasa's (2008) criticism is set against the backdrop of a critical lecture of Aztec codices that interpret the Spanish conquest from Bhabha's conception, because here revolt can only be articulated in terms of yet another version of Western discourse. Arguing against this vision, Rabasa criticizes the underlying idea of projecting Western mental categories—as described by Freud—on indigenous populations, and points out the possibility of queer and gay narratives as well as sudden shifts from moaning to mania. It seems that Rabasa hints at an indigenous locus of enunciation beyond the mourning for lost and domesticated third spaces. In regard to indigenous nostalgia and heritage policies, we would like to argue from a position placed between Bhabha and Rabasa, as we will try to show that indigenous actors are located and how they have located themselves in the logic and language of heritage, while there is always a surplus of meaning that challenges the established discourses.

This re-politicization concerns the content—the selected objects—as well as the procedure of selection: who has the right to select, and following which criteria? Within the frame of heritage proliferation, it has been the indigenous peoples who have probably queried heritage the most. Beyond heritage practices that are differentiated by Laurajane Smith, on the one hand, through ways of handling and managing heritage, and, on the other hand, through practices of cultural consumption of heritage, we intend to critically analyze the concepts of temporality imbedded in heritage discourses and practices. The following questions arise: What is the importance of nostalgia and heritage in the recent wave of globalization? And, what kind of history is being targeted by heritage policies?

These questions are highly relevant for Latin American countries, since the region is densely entangled with Western Europe and North America. International and transnational heritage organizations intervene in the region, tourists and 'cosmopolitical' elites visit the region and transport their imaginaries, cultural industry disseminates, and cultural-economic heritage flows. Despite this tendency towards a homogenization of heritage discourses and practices, it is of paramount importance to take into account the particular heritage logics inherent to Latin American countries. Although there are endless varieties of local and regional heritages in Latin America, it seems possible to identify in the contemporary struggle on heritage one fundamental contradiction that is related to a key historical experience: coloniality.

The coloniality of heritage policies

In the Latin American context, we are witnesses to a real struggle over heritage and interpretations of history. After the neoliberal wave of social, political, and economic transformations of Latin American societies, we notice a massive process of deconstruction of modernity. In the face of economic crisis, we confirm a polarization of the social structure that led to the pulverizing of the working class and a profound crisis of the middle classes. The social imaginary of progress and development, as framed by Western standards, was hereby dissolved. In the current debate on modernity's heritage, the latter is often discussed under the concept of 'ruins' (Stoler 2013). An emblematic aspect may be the 'self-musealization' of the Latin American capital of modernity—the city that was shaped in the form of an airplane, Brasilia. After only 27 years since its construction, the capital of Brazil has the reputation of being the only city in the world built during the twentieth century to have been granted (on 1987) the rank of Historical and Cultural Heritage of Humanity by UNESCO.

Nevertheless, most of the heritage debate in Latin America revolves around a deeper temporal layer: coloniality. Coloniality is understood not as a historical or aesthetic (in terms of colonial art or architecture) age, but as a long duration temporal layer that is reinterpreted, re-semanticized, and reused under different contexts and whose repercussions continue until today (Quijano 2000). A key element of coloniality is the establishing of a system of domination based on ethnic divisions. In the case of Latin America, the invention of the indigenous as an identity category must be mentioned. Two faces of the colonial situation are currently reemerging within the heritage field. On the one hand, we see monuments and urban settings being given new importance. On the other hand, it is no longer only the prehistoric monuments but also indigenous practices and customs that are being targeted by heritage.

Thus, speaking about coloniality does not mean referring to a historical structure of empire. As Stoler argues, 'It is rather to understand how those histories, despite having been so concertedly effaced, yield new damages and renewed disparities.' In this sense, she proposes a conceptual shift from ruin to ruination: 'Our focus is less on the noun ruin than on 'ruination' as an active, ongoing process that allocates imperial debris differentially and ruin as a violent verb that unites apparently disparate moments, places, and objects' (2013, 7). Using terms such as 'rot,' 'debris,' and 'ruination,' the rhetoric Stoler proposes is very strong and hints at forgotten aspects of the history of empires and their aftermaths, but in this contribution we are more interested in the other side of heritage policies: preservation, recuperation, and splendid exposure. Nevertheless, I think that Stolers's observations are first helpful to take into account the dynamic, renewed, and re-appropriated aspects of the social life of historical artifacts, and second, to underline with Frantz Fanon the destructive tangible and intangible, often sociopsychological aspects of coloniality.

Most of the Latin American sites that have been granted cultural heritage status by UNESCO are located in urban areas and constitute colonial monuments or settings. This close link between heritage and coloniality is neither new nor is it arbitrary. With the example of Quito, Ernesto Capello (2011, 61–84) has proved how the idea of material preservation of the colonial past is linked to nineteenth-century hispanism, which has been renewed in several conjunctures. In the 1920s, hispanophile intellectuals like Cristobál de Gangotena y Jijón and José Gabriel Navarro articulated the idea of preservation with the ideological defense of white supremacy and the defense of the civilizational efforts of Hispanic colonialization. In 1934, in the context of the 400th anniversary of the Spanish foundation of Quito, the imagination of Quito as the most Castilian city in the Americas was greatly influential. From that point on, there is a clear line of continuity toward twentieth-century heritage practices, as they explain local dynamics in order to understand why Quito was the first urban setting to be granted world heritage status by UNESCO. However, facing indigenous mobilizations and criticisms generated by the debate on the 500th anniversary of the colonization of the Americas, it is surprising to see that international organizations such as ICOMOS or UNESCO continue to repeat an acritical discourse on the colonial. In its 1991 report,

UNESCO argued with respect to the declaration of Lima as a world heritage site: 'the historic cores of the town recall Lima at the peak of its development in the Spanish kingdom of Peru,' while ICOMOS revealed in its 1991 report that 'the historic center of Lima bears excellent witness to the architecture and urban development of a Spanish colonial town of great political, economic and cultural importance in Latin America.' The Eurocentric nature of these claims is evident, since, in them, Lima is seen as a colonial extension of Europe, a fact that justifies its status as world heritage. The contributions made by the indigenous population and African slaves remain invisible. Also, the documents do not reach a problematization of the colonial process. Through the discourse's style of we can observe these institutions' attitude, which are considered to be absolute authorities in the definition of which artifact possesses the value required to be preserved. It is an inventory of coloniality that, furthermore, elevates the latter to the status of world heritage. The geopolitical perspective that is particular to the European colonizer becomes universal in these discourses, and is even awarded with the status of cultural heritage of humanity. With this transfer of coloniality into the cultural sphere, the transcendence of its inherent violence is trimmed off.

From a semiotic perspective, we could argue that, in this way, the meanings, or the signified of the signifier 'coloniality,' are erased; that is to say—colonial violence, exploitation, ethnocide, mistreatment, and racism are eliminated. In heritage policies pointing toward an international audience, it is essential to erase the notions of violence associated with coloniality to be able to overcome 'colonial shame.' Only through the elimination of violence and overcoming of colonial shame can coloniality become a key moment for city marketing and the attraction of cosmopolitan tourists. Therefore, our contention is that appropriation of coloniality and its usage as a resource for restructuring urban spaces is only possible if the concept is de-historicized. I understand this operation of de-historicizing the historical concepts for economic usages referring to the strategies of the marketing of the *retro* in terms of retro-coloniality (Kaltmeier 2011, 99–104). This is about a paradoxical way of emptying meanings and using signifiers. We thus can understand retro-coloniality as a collective symbol covering and connecting fields of practices such as heritage, tourism, and quotidian culture.

In Lima, heritage policies for recovering the historic center have found, along with its 'colonial inventory,' a fertile ground among Lima's upper middle class. (Cánepa 2013; Kaltmeier 2015a). The high level of acceptance and success of heritage policies based on coloniality can be explained by the upper middle class's attitude of colonial nostalgia. Faced with increasing miscegenation, Lima's upper middle class's loss of identity and in a context of massive migration and diminishment of spaces for the middle class, the concept of 'colonial arcadia' emerged in their collective imagination during the seventies. According to José Guillermo Nugent, the colonial arcadia is not a representation of the city but an imaginary that expresses 'the world as it should be' (1992, 45). On the basis of these nostalgic narratives, urban history is reinvented in colonial terms.

In other Latin American countries, we notice similar identity dynamics among the upper middle class. In Argentina, the use of an aristocratic-colonial imaginary of rural life, which is understood by Maristela Svampa as a cultural mimesis in the fashion of the homesteading elite's lifestyle, functions as a mechanism of social distinction (Svampa 2008). Likewise, the Ecuadorian upper middle class recurs to the colonial vis-à-vis its identity crisis, introduced with the economic crisis and the emergence of the indigenous movement in the 1990s.

It is also important to underline the commercial dimension of retro-colonial heritage policies, since, in order to attract tourists, it is relevant to erase the dimension of colonial violence. The consumption of coloniality in 'histourism' has to be a nostalgic and aesthetic enjoyment. This is how the musealized historic center becomes a crucial element for cultural industries, especially for tourism. This is how it is promoted by the Master Plan of Lima's Center of December 21, 1998: 'the historic center as a touristic and cultural space at an international level, fostered by public and private investment.' It is remarkable that the historical foundation of this imagining of a colonial urban landscape is highly questionable. Apart from some outstanding sacral buildings, the majority of the buildings is of republican origin. Therefore, I prefer to speak of a retro-colonization of the urban imaginary, alluding to the economic interests involved in selling the past, and the postmodern Zeitgeist.

This retro-colonialization of urban imaginaries is not limited to an idealistic and aesthetic debate about epistemological violence; instead, it is related also to material violence. Peruvian intellectual Gonzalo Portocarrero (2009) pointed out in his interpretation of José Maria Arguedas's 'Los Ríos Profundos' that space is not simply a stage for human action, but that it—in this case the cathedral of Cusco—provokes behaviors and emotions. The flogging of indigenous supporters of the indigenous president of Bolivia, Evo Morales, following colonial punitive rituals in the central plaza of Sucre, the so-called colonial 'white city,' is an extreme example that brings to light the performative dimension of this re-colonization (Ströbele-Gregor 2011). However, in the process of producing an image of the city for city branding, we can also observe massive identity-related conflicts with the local—most often popular or indigenous—urban lower classes. This is expressed by the displacement or resettlement of 'dangerous classes' (Foucault), a process that can take place by force, as in the case of Lima (Dias Velarde 2001), through negotiations, as it happened in Quito (Hanley and Ruthenberg 2005), or in the context of catastrophes, as in post-Katrina New Orleans (Jakob and Schorb 2008). We can also observe an intensification of disciplinary practices and spatial control by police patrols and camera surveillance. Most importantly, there is also a process of gentrification and displacement of the immobile by means of rising land rents and speculation. In the public debate, coloniality and its commodification as an attractive redevelopment strategy are so hegemonic that there is virtually no space for critical interventions that raise the question of the colonial trauma and its perpetuation by cultural heritage in programs of urban renewal.

In order to describe the processes of appropriation of urban cultural areas, the feudal alluding concept of gentrification has been consciously chosen by urbanists. The term derives from 'gentry,' an English historical social class located between low and middle nobility. The word 'gentrification' describes processes of urban transformation in which the original population of a deteriorated and pauperized area is progressively displaced by a wealthier upper middle class one. In Europe, artists, bohemians, and alternative sectors are considered to be *first-stage gentrifiers*; after their intervention in deteriorated historical areas, attractiveness of these sectors rises and gains more attention, which is reflected by rent prices. This dynamic facilitates speculation and it generally derives in the expulsion of the subaltern sectors. In contrast to the processes of gentrification in Europe and the United States, the main *first-stage-gentrifier* in Latin American colonial city centers is not the bohemian but the state, or the municipal government, in cooperation with the main actors in the field of heritage.

These dynamics also change the public character of Latin American urban spaces, where the *plaza* (Rosenthal 2000) has often fulfilled the function of a *sui generis* public space. However, we see that modernization through heritage destroys the social relations that are crucial to urbanity construction. With Jürgen Habermas, we can speak of a forceful process of 're-feudalization of the public' through the pressure of commercial and political interests (Habermas 1962) that are, in many contemporary Latin American cases, cities articulated by a modernization through heritage. According to historian Eduardo Kingman's (2004, 28) analysis:

> Campaigns are developed for the control of the [historic] center and for the generation of a heritage culture (understood as the equivalent of civic culture); plans of social sustainability and cultural reactivation are designed, and actions are taken against sectors that are considered dangerous such as sex workers, beggars, street vendors, parking attendants, charlatans, and popular artists.

The people allowed in this landscape are mainly upper middle class and tourists who participate in the short circuit of consumption. It is a fast urban life of brief pleasure while the social dimensions of informal exchange and encounter—so characteristic of public space—are in danger of distinction.

Nevertheless, one could argue that heritage may also be used to stop processes of capitalist urban renewal. In fact, the construction of the Waldschlößchen Bridge in Dresden, which crosses the Elbe Valley that is recognized by UNESCO as world heritage, initiated a polemic between 'traditionalists' and 'modernizers.' In 2006, UNESCO included the Elbe Valley in the list of 'endangered world heritage' only to permanently cross it off the list three years later. Its absence in the canon of world heritage is still visible, although it could be said—in a reference to Derrida— that it was crossed, but not erased.

However, I have some doubts about whether this antagonism between 'modernization' and 'tradition' is really paradigmatic for the relation between heritage and urban renovation in the current context. If we look at Latin America, we see a series of projects of urban development that are intrinsically intertwined with heritage interventions at historic centers. Projects such as the construction of a highway running above and under the Rímac River in Lima, the cable railway connecting La Paz and El Alto, or the subway project at Quito with a station planned for the

San Francisco square come to mind. All these projects are—at least partly—justified with the rhetoric of heritage. Only small groups of urban dwellers and local intellectuals confront these dynamics of urban renewal in the name of heritage defense.

The indigeneity of heritage

Indigeneity results from violent colonial encounters and constitutes the other side of coloniality. Rather than thinking of it as a fixed identity, it can be conceived as an ongoing process and a relational category, which includes both self-identification and identifications by others such as colonizers, settlers, the church, the state, and—with a high amount of symbolic capital—scholars. Thereby, indigeneity is intrinsically related to history, since concepts such as 'indigenous,' 'native,' 'aboriginal,' and 'first nations' 'all refer etymologically to priority in time and place' (Pratt 2007, 398). The relational construction itself is embedded in struggles around recognition and redistribution. In a nutshell, to put it in the words of Andrew Canessa, 'indigeneity is about history and power' (2012, 207), or—in this context—heritage and power. In this sense, the use of indigeneity for the construction of heritage is not limited to indigenous actors.

The use of pre-Hispanic monuments for the construction of national heritage was a key element of Latin American postcolonial societies, especially in countries where the Inca, Mayan, and Aztec civilizations once existed. Undoubtedly, indigenism was the most influential discourse of the twentieth century, as it poses the inclusion of the indigenous in the nation-building process. In this sense, it is not surprising that Peru, one of the hotspots of classical indigenism, uses the indigenous to frame its new national corporate identity as 'Marca Perú' (Cánepa 2013). In a similar vein, Guillaume Boccara and Patricia Ayala (2012, 211) offer proof that Chile's National Monuments Council

> has been developing multiple strategies and work lines oriented towards the display and installation of a discourse through which Chile is construed and imagined as a multicultural nation, using monuments, archaeological sites, and local customs (tangible and intangible heritage). Some of these strategies are the use and visibility of archaeology, the change and widening of the notion of heritage, institutional uncentering, and designation of Advisors Councils, the World Heritage Project, the formation of the Indigenous Heritage Area, and the celebration of Heritage Day. In this context, the Council has come to constitute an institution for the control of differences, redefinition of the relationship of indigenous peoples with their past, nationalization of their memory, and commodification of their culture as well as a central and hegemonic agency of the struggles for the control of heritage, some of which have been contested by indigenous groupings that make heritage claims and query archaeology.

Likewise, Nadja Lobensteiner (2010) reveals how the exhibition 'Mapuche: Chile's seeds' displayed at the Capital Museum of Beijing in 2008 served as a promotion of Chile's cultural heritage in China while, simultaneously in Chile, the Mapuche movement and its struggles for recognition were facing extreme repression.

Despite the state's important role in heritage politics, as opposed to nineteenth-century heritage politics, the scenario has changed. Nation-states are no longer the unquestioned protagonists of heritage. With the emergence of a powerful political movement, indigenous peoples also managed to establish themselves in the heritage field. On the one hand, they are actors who take advantage of the proliferation of heritage by placing themselves in the debates as landmarks for the recognition of intangible heritage. Likewise, the idea of the origin, inherent to heritage discourse, allows the political and legal argument used by indigenous peoples to defend their territorial rights—they were here before the colonizers.

On the other hand, they question existing heritage policies for their ethnocentric nature. In this sense, Walter Mignolo (2005, 1) indicates that

> we must remember that at the same time that Europe accumulated money through the extraction of gold and silver in the sixteenth century, and through the exploitation of the Caribbean plantations and the massive slave trade of the seventeenth century, Europe also accumulated meaning and the reproduction of the coloniality of knowledge.

Beyond the debate on stolen artifacts that are exhibited in museums, another debate emerges, that of the control of the past. This implies control over artifacts and relics expropriated from indigenous communities through acts of violence. Furthermore, it poses the question of who is entitled to control which history. This question has the potential to effectively challenge the legitimacy of scientific discourse on heritage and the authority of the experts in the field.

First, I want to explore how indigenous movements and communities make tactical use of heritage by addressing their demands in the discursive frame of heritage. They use heritage in this way for the defense of their territory, as in the case of the struggle against mega projects. Faced with the construction of the Ralco dam in the Bío River in Chile, the Mapuche-Pehuenche communities identified heritage sites in order to stop the project (Kaltmeier 2004). One of these sites was an indigenous cemetery that provoked a legal-administrative debate among the Indigenous National Commission (CONADI) and the National Monuments Council. The interpretation made by the latter is, as explained by Paola González Carvajal (2008, 153),

> that the Council, in order to define a criterion that allows the distinction between historical indigenous cemeteries and archaeological cemeteries in the absence of a legal concept for 'historical indigenous cemetery' and in the context of evaluating the environmental impact of the Ralco Hydroelectric Plant Project, recurred to the definitions established in the version from March 1997 of the 'Draft Law for the Protection and Enhancement of the Nation's Monumental Heritage.'

A key aspect of the discussion was whether or not an indigenous archaeological cemetery can have any use in the present or not. The tendency to petrify the indigenous heritage is evident. Although in the Ralco case, the National Monuments Council has declared its irresponsibility, the debate on the issue of the dam continued within the heritage field, which—along with the argument of the place's natural heritage—was argued upon great moral power and ability to mobilize dissent.

A more recent tactical use of heritage was made by the National Ecuadorian Indigenous Organization (CONAIE). Against the efforts of President Correa's administration, which tried to displace CONAIE from their traditional location in Quito, they decided in December 2014, as expressed by their president Jorge Herrera, 'to declare the CONAIE central office as heritage of the indigenous peoples and nations.'[1] Thus, tactical positioning within the idioms of heritage and its legal framework allowed indigenous people to fight against projects of development that affect deeply and even destroy their livelihoods.

Second, beyond this tactical use of heritage for the defense of their communities and territories, they have also formulated heritage demands that oppose those of hegemonic heritage projects. Here, we have the case of the struggle over indigenous artifacts that are exhibited in museums. In 2007, the Atacamean communities at the north of Chile were successful in their demand that the mommies of their ancestors that were exhibited in the San Pedro de Atacama Museum were withdrawn from there and returned to them. The museum had been built by a Jesuit missioner, Father Gustavo Le Paige, who had been sent to the Atacama Desert in the 1950s. During his stay there and until his death, he collected 5,000 pre-Hispanic mommies (Ayán 2014). One of the female mommies displayed in the museum was even given the nickname 'Miss Chile.' In this way, it came to be the embodiment of a search for the origins of the Chilean nation, an act that was considered a sacrilege by the indigenous communities.

But indigenous peoples do not only demand the restitution of artifacts to their communities; they also question the orthodox rationale in exhibitions, which found its repercussion in the established world of museums. In 2007, the Bolivian government of the indigenous president Evo Morales placed the demand for decolonization on top of the official agenda; it demanded the repatriation of the Niño Korin collection displayed at the Museum of World Culture in Gothenburg, Sweden. This collection consists basically of a Bolivian medicine man's grave that was purchased in 1973 by Henry Wassén, who was the director of the Ethnographic Museum at that time. This demand for repatriation by the Bolivian government was later extended to all Bolivian objects in museum collections, about 17,000 in total. This demand for repatriation and decolonization inspired Adriana Muñoz from the Museum of World Culture to organize a self-reflexive project on the collection and the problem of exhibition funded by the Swedish Arts Council. With the participation of Beatriz Loza and the Kallawaya Walter Quispe, the power of labeling artifacts was brought into question. Of particular importance was the fact that the Kallawaya, an itinerant ethnic group of healers from the Bolivian highlands, have gained specific symbolic capital through their inclusion in the

UNESCO list of intangible heritage in 2006 (Muñoz 2009). This decolonial perspective was reinforced by the inclusion of Walter Mignolo, from Duke University, in the process. The project led to the report 'The Power of Labelling' (Muñoz 2009), a documentary film, and an exhibition. The issue of repatriation is still unresolved and is being debated by the Swedish Ministry of Foreign Affairs and the Bolivian government.

This example demonstrates the extent to which the inclusion of heterodox actors—such as indigenous people, or in particular Kallawaya—can change the mode of operation in the heritage field and produce alternative meanings. These changes are reinforced by the self-reflexive power held by cultural production as well as the imperative to produce something new, akin to the latest academic fashions such as postcolonialism.

Third, with regard to this last experience, we can argue that the appropriation of cultural heritage by indigenous peoples is not limited to the appropriation of artifacts or to the defense of traditional rights and territories. Instead, there are several cases that make evidence of the fact that the historiographical concepts and the Western rationale on matters of heritage itself is put into question. This can lead not only to a redefinition of practical logics and discourses in the field of heritage but to the elaboration of heritage policies beyond established forms.

In the Andean region, we have to mention here the Katarista movement in Bolivia. It was formed in the early 1970s by young urban Aymaras whose parents had migrated from the rural areas to El Alto, La Paz. In the center of the cultural politics of the Katarista was the appropriation of the (symbolic) figure of Tupac Katari (Julián Apaza), who together with Tupac Amaru II in Peru was the main leader of the indigenous revolution of the 1780s. With the *Manifiesto de Tiwanaku* of 1973, the movement gained national and international attention—notwithstanding the dictatorship of Hugo Banzer. It was a cornerstone in a new dynamic of decolonization and it put autonomy in the center of the political organization process. This includes the definition of a national heritage of their own as opposed to that of the *mestizo* Bolivian nation:

> True development is based on culture. People attach great value to their culture. The systematic attempt to destroy the Qhechwa and Aymara cultures is the source of the nation's frustrations. Politicians from the dominant minorities have attempted to create a type of development based solely on a servile imitation of the development of other countries, while our cultural heritage is totally different.

Here, the articulation of a different cultural heritage—basically understood in terms of the whole ensemble of artifacts, practices, and ideas of the Qhechwa and Aymara—serves as an antipode to Western forms of national modernization. Although, the forms of expression—monuments for Tupac Katari, manifesto, and national discourse—are based on a modern grammar of heritage.

Also, particular places and artifacts are used to projecting their own visions of heritage against the normalizing imaginations of national development.

Anthropologist Rafael Castillo has demonstrated that Iximché, the ancient city of the Kaqchiquele people, was built as a 'place of memory' of importance to Guatemala's history.

> Iximché, as it is presented to us nowadays, bears many historical events on its old buildings that go as far back in time as the sixteenth century Kaqchiquele rebellion, and are as current to our eyes as those claims made by certain peoples on their rights to their culture and their territory, and also as those claims that recur to monumentality in their search for national meaning through rituals of memory.
>
> (Castillo n.d.)

The latter was revealed in 2007, when the 'Declaration of Iximché' was formulated within the Third Continental Summit of Indigenous Peoples and Nationalities, where the struggle of indigenous peoples for the recognition of their culture, autonomy, and self-determination is evoked in the context of the decolonization of knowledge. Whereas Iximché was included in the nation-building process in the early twentieth century by *mestizo* intellectuals, it was not until the end of the twentieth century that intellectuals and indigenous organizations—in the context of the peace-building process after the civil war—reclaimed the Mayan heritage for an alternative narrative of the nation. A crucial element is the construction of a Pan-Mayan identity whose values are seen as the cure for a society stricken by civil war and genocidal practices. This has repercussions for tangible heritage: 'Due to the symbolic importance of pre-Hispanic times, material remains of that period have been attached with new meanings as well. For example, public ceremonies involving different communities are held in archaeological parks to demonstrate Mayan unity' (Frühsorge 2008). Thus, what emerges is real heritage tourism from the indigenous communities toward archaeological sites.

We can observe a similar process of appropriation of world heritage by indigenous movements in Bolivia. Here, the appropriation of cultural heritage and its redefinition according to a decolonization of society and a new foundation of the nation reaches its peak at the ceremonies of inauguration of Evo Morales as president of Bolivia in 2006 and 2010, held at Tiwanaku. Tiwanaku was recognized by UNESCO in 2000 as world cultural heritage, for being the cultural and spiritual center of the Tiwanakota civilization. While UNESCO acknowledges the archaeological character of the site, the Aymara nation takes it as a reference for the construction of their identity. Therefore, Tiwanaku—Bolivia's most important archaeological site—became the exemplary place to express the 'new national foundation' project. President Morales was invested with the title of Apu Mallku of the Multinational State after a ceremony where the *amautas* (wise men) performed purification rituals and covered him with a robe. On top of the robe, he wore a gold pectoral armor representing the union of the ruler with his ancestors, and on his head was placed a *chuku* or four-pointed hat representing the union of all of Bolivia's regions. Previously, through other rituals, the *amautas* had consecrated the pyramid and the Kalasasaya temple. At the end of the ritual, an old woman from Tiwanaku accompanied Evo Morales to the Kalasasaya temple, at whose main door he received two batons of command from a girl and a boy who had been born in the area. As has been argued by anthropologist Nancy Postero (2007), this celebration is not only about an indigenous victory on the political field, it has deep cultural meaning. It was perceived by many Bolivians as a ritual of change that also interrupted the flux of time. It marks the beginning of another historical age, which in the Andean world is understood in terms of *pachakuti*, a word that contains opposed connotations of catastrophe and renovation. This conception of temporality is well known in the Andean world. According to Javier Sanjinés's reasoning: 'Over the past two and a half centuries, the constant indigenous insurgencies in the Andean region have been marked by a very particular consciousness of awaiting the catastrophic overturning of the colonizer's historical time' (2013, 47). This holds implications to how heritage is understood, since it is not seen as past in the sense of a linear progress but as temporal co-presence in terms of a persistence of the past in the now.

And in this past, remembering a cultural heritage of their own is the base to confront the future. Yet, also among and within the different indigenous peoples, there are quite diverse and often contradictory ideas about the outreach of *pachakuti*. The indigenous-modernist perspective is probably best expressed by Evo Morales in his third inaugural speech at Tiwanaku, on January 21, 2015.

> Brothers and sisters, when we speak of recovering and strengthening our cultural heritage, our identity as a multinational state, many people think we are planning to return to the past. No, we are not planning to return to a romanticized past, but [undertaking] a scientific recuperation of the best of our past to combine it with modernity [. . .] a modernity that allows us to make industries without danger to Mother Earth, with a modernity that allows us to develop with Pachamama.

Nevertheless, the modernization perspective inherent in the economic program of the Morales administration also creates heritage conflicts. The construction of a highway from Brazil to the Pacific Coast passing through the protected area and native land of the Isiboro Secure National Park and Indigenous Territory (Parque Nacional y Territorio Indígena Isiboro-Secure or Territorio Indígena y Parque Nacional Isiboro Secure, TIPNIS) generated conflicts about heritage. The local indigenous population defended their cultural heritage and autonomy in alliances with environmental NGOs and activists who defended the natural heritage of the region. In order to give the conflict an even greater importance in the field of heritage, Bolivian activists demanded that TIPNIS be declared World Cultural and Natural Heritage by UNESCO (Luksic 2012).

Outlook

By the end of the nineteenth century, German philosopher Friedrich Nietzsche warned about a present that is oversaturated with past. Since too much history can become an obstacle for the social definition of an expectations horizon. Or, in the words of Nietzsche, 'the danger of destruction from being swamped by what is foreign and past, from 'history'.' With the emergence of heritage as *fait social total* in the postmodern world, the danger perceived by Nietzsche is within reach. To be more precise, heritage is about antiquarian history that belongs 'to the man who preserves and honors, to the person who with faith and love looks back in the direction from which he has come.' In a similar way, renowned urbanist and architect Rem Koolhaas (2012) alerted that

> ... there is [...] a prolific global desire to preserve all other genre of architecture. In 1972, a UN convention on the protection of cultural and natural heritage set out the criteria of heritage selection which we still abide to today. Nearly 12 percent of the planet is currently marked as 'preserved,' continuing to cordon off greater areas as 'off-limits' at an alarming fast rate.

While we share the diagnosis of a proliferation of heritage, we disagree with the assumption that heritage is mainly concerned with the past. Instead, it seems that heritage serves as a fruitful field to struggle about possible futures. In this sense—as we have shown in this article—discussing the usefulness and the inconveniences of history for life without distinguishing between different social groups turns out to be very complicated. Therefore, we have to adjust the matter and wonder who is finding which heritage boom useful. Thereby we maintain our focus on the antagonism of coloniality versus indigeneity without addressing the complex heritage politics of Bolivarianism.

Indigeneity has been—and probably still is—the greatest challenge for the heritage field in Latin America. Many indigenous movements have undertaken a 'tiger's jump to the past' in order to recover its heritage in struggle. They rewrite history. While doing this, they recur to given historiographical and heritage related formats, but they amplify and widen the contents of the archive, thus challenging the 'authorized heritage discourse.'

Indigenous peoples have become new players of the heritage game that are characterized by their high degree of authenticity and, since the 1990s, they are protected by multicultural policies of recognition and anti-discriminatory codes of conduct. These aspects were converted into symbolical capital, recognized in the heritage field. Indeed, it is nowadays impossible to think about declarations on indigenous items without the participation of indigenous people. This inclusion of indigenous people as experts leads, on the other hand, to a devaluation of the symbolic capital held by experts in the field of heritage and a partial democratization of the heritage field. Indigenous peoples have used this inclusion in the heritage field to transform the existing logics of operation, to narrate other histories, and to use heritage in conflicts regarding the political or economic fields.

Nevertheless, this inclusion also has its pitfalls. There is the danger of exoticization and folklorization of the indigenous, because the search for uniqueness, authenticity, aesthetics, and the spectacular—inherent to heritage – hardly takes into account daily life indigeneity and cultural creolization.

On the advantage and disadvantage of heritage 31

Furthermore, these outstanding objects, sites, or practices, ennobled by heritage, can become easily prominent features of marketing strategies. The political and economic expediency of heritage is obvious and it may lead to absurd projects of discovering indigenous heritage, which is totally disconnected from the experiences of the local population (see Rufer's paper in this volume).

The heritage boom and its economic success have also impacted local social structures. The indigenous experts may be transformed into true heritage brokers, who use their new symbolic capital not only in the heritage field but also in politics and economics in order to improve their social position.

But indigenous heritage has been, over the last two decades, not only important for indigenous peoples. The indigenization of heritage in Latin American countries was of particular importance in the Andean world. Nancy Postero notes that Evo Morales's first ceremony is not only addressed to the indigenous population; every year, the Andean New Year is celebrated at the Gate of the Sun in Tiwanaku where middle-class *mestizos* participate in search for alternatives to the technical life of the cities as well as new spiritual experiences (Postero 2007, 16).

Nevertheless, for the established white *mestizo* elites, the use of heritage has been more complicated. Not all relied on neo-indigenist identity constructions. Middle classes and upper middle classes, especially comprised of white *mestizo* people, were confronted with a threefold identity crisis in many Latin American countries until the end of the 1990s. First, they were affected by the end of the great narratives of modernity, since the expectations horizon they had longed for throughout the decades vanished. Second, especially middle classes were affected by the economic crisis that started in the 1980s, so they faced a process of differentiation, particularly downward. Third, indigenous mobilizations have achieved deep redefinitions of Latin American nations toward a multicultural and multinational approach, so the white *mestizo* man lost his position as a model for the citizen, defined in political and cultural terms. This also brought into question the reference to Europe as the origin and future of cultural heritage. Looking at the monumentality of the colonial heritage allows them to carry out a monumental reading of history and provides them with security to face the future. Moreover, this is so because the colonial no longer has negative connotations, since it has been recognized worldwide by organizations with a high level of credibility, as in the case of UNESCO.

Likewise, the reference to colonial heritage creates stability in the world. This is particularly important in the face of the dynamics of the recent globalization wave, characterized by 'liquefaction' (Bauman 2000) of social relations, and by 'contingency' and social 'disembedding' (Altvater and Mahnkopf 1999). Faced with these tendencies, it offers 'stability, security, and embeddedness.' In this way, the heritage boom can be related to attempts to provide collective and individual identities with meaning before modern dissolution of certainties and lifestyles that have been rendered habitual. This moment of construction is differentiated by its self-reflexive character of other historical narratives that attempt to 'naturalize' themselves.

Nevertheless, by the 2000s and 2010s, it seemed that in many Latin American countries, the reference to colonial heritage had lost its significance. In Rafael

32 *Olaf Kaltmeier*

Correa's Ecuador, the 'citizen's revolution' is a form of neo-developmentalism that revitalizes the great narrative of progress. In neoliberal Peru and Chile, the middle and upper middle classes also rely on cosmopolitical and postmodern lifestyles. In all cases, we also detect a renewed nationalism that is distributed by superficial country-branding marketing campaigns such as 'All you need is Ecuador' and 'Marca Perú.' In order to present unique selling products, they offer and advertise different kinds of 'heritage products.'

While Nietzsche calls for a deep knowledge of the past, currently the past is often an unknown terrain for most people. Heritage is emptied of its contents— especially in the case of the colonial, which is precisely required to be emptied of meaning in order to get rid of the connotations of violence and racism. The experience of heritage is limited to an aesthetic experience and a lifestyle, both closely linked to processes of cultural consumption.

Heritage actors are not innocent in this operation, as they have disconnected the artifacts from history. A highly problematic aspect of that conception of heritage is that the decision to preserve it or not is anchored to an object or site. The object of heritage becomes a fetish, since it is assumed that there are certain qualities inherent to the object at stake. Thereby, heritage undertakes the operation of separating this object from its context, which makes it impossible to understand its meaning. Jesús Martín-Barbero (2010b, 5–6) underlines this aspect:

> The past thus stops being a part of memory, and it becomes an ingredient of the pastiche, that operation that allows us to mix facts, sensibilities and styles, and texts from any time, without the slightest articulation with the contexts and undercurrent movements of that time.

But embeddedness matters. Reconnecting history to heritage would mean to take into account social, political, and cultural contestation that is also inherent to the material objects, as there is no artifact of culture that is not at the same time an artifact of barbarism. This negative dialectic is particularly important for the Americas, shaped by coloniality. It is the insurgent heritage articulated by subaltern actors, such as indigenous peoples, that has brought into question the technocratic understanding of heritage. In this sense, heritage has to be reconnected in a self-reflexive manner to our own procedures to produce heritage. If we want to de-fetishize heritage, we have to take a close look at the production of heritage.

Note

1   See http://ecuadorinforma2013.blogspot.de/2014/12/conaie-resolvio-declarar-patrimonio-de.html

References

Altvater, Elmar, and Birgit Mahnkopf. 1999. *Grenzen der Globalisierung. Ökonomie, Ökologie und Politik in der Weltgesellschaft*. Münster: Westfälisches Dampfboot.

Ayala, Patricia, and Guillaume Boccara. 2012. 'Patrimonializar al indígena. Imagi-nación del multiculturalismo neoliberal en Chile.' *Cahiers des Amériques latines*, 67: 207–28.

Ayán Vila, Xurxo M. 2014. 'El Patrimonio de los vencidos: arqueología en comunidades subalternas.' *Tejuelo*, 19: 109–42. http://iesgtballester.juntaextremadura.net/web/profesores/tejuelo/vinculos/articulos/r19/07.pdf

Bauman, Zygmunt. 2000. *Liquid Modernity*. Cambridge: Polity.

Benjamin, Walter. 1974. *Über den Begriff der Geschichte*, In: *Illuminationen. Ausgewählte Schriften*. Vol. 1 Frankfurt/Main: Suhrkamp.

Bertolt, Brecht. 1964. 'Die Verurteilung des Lukullus.' *Gesammelte Werke. Stücke*, Vol. 7. Berlin: Suhrkamp.

Bhabha, Homi. 1992. 'Postcolonial Authority and Postmodern Guilt.' In *Cultural Studies*, eds., Lawrence Grossberg, Cary Nelson, and Paula Treichler, 56–68. New York: Routledge.

Cánepa, Gisela. 2013. 'Nation-Branding. The Re-foundation of Community, Citizenship and the State in the Context of Neoliberalism in Peru.' *Medien Journal—Zeitschrift für Kommunikationswissenschaft*, 37 (3): 2—18.

Canessa, Andrew. 2012. 'New Indigenous Citizenship in Bolivia. Challenging the Liberal Model of the State and its Subjects.' *Latin American and Caribbean Ethnic Studies*, 7 (2): 201–22.

Carrión, Fernando, and Manuel Dammert. 2011. 'Quito`s Historic Center: Heritage of Humanity or of the Market?' In *Selling EthniCity. Urban Cultural Politics in the Americas*, ed. Olaf Kaltmeier, 171–88. Farnham: Ashgate.

Castells, Manuel. 1996. *The Rise of Network Society*. Oxford and Malden, Mass.: Blackwell.

Castillo, Rafael. n.d. 'Iximché, un lugar de memorias en Guatemala.' www.hcentroamerica.fcs.ucr.ac.cr/Contenidos/hca/cong/mesas/x_congreso/cultura/memorias-guatemala.pdf

DeHart, Monica. 2010. *Ethnic Entrepreneurs. Identity and Development Politics in Latin America*. Stanford: Stanford University.

Dias Velarde, Patricia. 2001. 'El espacio urbano en la recuperación del Centro Histórico de Lima.' In *Centros Históricos de América Latina y el Caribe*, ed. Fernando Carrión, 347–63. Quito: FLACSO.

Frühsorg, Lars. 2008. 'Excavating Utopia? Indigenous Youths and Archaeological Heritage in Guatemala.' www.academia.edu/211620/Excavating_Utopia_Indigenous_Youths_and_Archaeological_Heritage_in_Guatemala

García Canclini, Néstor. 1999. 'Los usos sociales del patrimonio cultural.' In *Patrimonio Etnológico. Nuevas Perspectivas de Estudio*, ed., Encarnación Aguilar Criado, 16–33. Granada: Consejería de Cultura – Junta de Andalucía.

González Carvajal, Paola. 2004. 'Proteccción jurídica del patrimonio cultural: Logros y ecrucijadas del patrimonio antropoarqueológico chileno.' *Chungará*, 36: 509–22.

González Carvajal, Paola. 2008. 'Atamiento jurídico de los restos óseos indígenas en Chile.' In *Bioética en investigación en Ciencias sociales*, ed., Elizabeth Lira Kornfeld, 141–60. Santiago: CONICYT.

Habermas, Jürgen. 1990. *Strukturwandel der Öffentlichkeit: Untersuchungen zu einer Kategorie der bürgerlichen Gesellschaft*. Frankfurt a.M.: Suhrkamp.

Hanley, Lisa, and Meg Ruthenberg. 2005. 'Los impactos sociales de la renovación urbana: el caso de Quito, Ecuador.' In *Regeneración y revitalización urbana en la Américas: hacia un Estado estable*, eds., Fernando Carrión and Lisa Hanley, 209–40. Quito: FLACSO.

Herwitz, Daniel. 2012. *Heritage, Culture, and Politics in the Postcolony*. New York: Columbia University.

Hutcheon, Lisa. 1988. *A Poetics of Postmodernism. History, Theory, Fiction*. New York: Routledge.
Hutcheon, Lisa. 1998. 'Irony, Nostalgia, and the Postmodern.' www.library.utoronto.ca/utel/criticism/hutchinp.html#N54
Jakob, Christian, and Friedrich Schorb. 2008. *Soziale Säuberung*. Münster: Unrast.
Kaltmeier, Olaf. 2011. 'Urban Landscapes of Mall-ticulturality: (Retro-)Coloniality, Consumption, and Identity Politics: The Case of the San Luis Shopping Center in Quito.' In *Selling EthniCity. Urban Cultural Politics in the Americas*, ed., Olaf Kaltmeier, 95–116. Farnham: Ashgate.
Kaltmeier, Olaf. 2015a. 'Colonialidad, nostalgia y patrimonio: conflictos sobre espacio, historia e identidad en el centro histórico de Lima.' In *Cruzando fronteras en las Américas: Las dinámicas de cambio en la política, la cultura y los medios. Vol. 2. Fronteras discursivas: Migración, Resistencia, Patrimonio*, eds., Sofía Mendoza Bohne, Yolanda Minerva Campos García, and Olaf Kaltmeier, 99–116. Guadalajara: Universidad de Guadalajara.
Kaltmeier, Olaf. 2015b. 'En búsqueda de la ciudad perdida. Género, erotismo y nostalgia en el paisaje urbano de Quito.' In *De Patrias y Matrias: Gender and Nation in the Americas*, eds., Sebastian Thies, Gutiérrez de Velasco, Luz Elena, and Gabriele Pisarz Ramírez. Trier: WVT.
Kingman, Eduardo. 2004. 'Patrimonio, políticas de la memoria e institucionalización de la cultura.' *ICONOS: Revista de Ciencias Sociales*, 20: 26–34.
Kingman, Eduardo, and Ana María Goetschel. 2005. 'El patrimonio como dispositivo desciplinario y la banalización de la memoria: una lectura desde los Andes.' In *Regeneración y revitalización urbana en las Américas: hacia un Estado estable*, eds., Fernando Carrión and Lisa Hanley, 97–110. Quito: FLACSO.
Koolhaas, Rem. 2012. www.designboom.com/architecture/rem-koolhaas-oma-cronocaos-preservation-tour-part-three/
Lobensteiner, Nadja. 2010. 'La exposición 'Mapuche: Semillas de Chile' como 'embajada cultural': Aspectos de un discurso político-cultural chileno.' *Forum for Inter-American Research*, 3 (1). www.interamerica.de.
Luksic, Alvaro. 2012. 'Plantean que el Tipnis sea declarado Patrimonio Natural de la Humanidad.' *El País Online*, July 15, 2012. www.elpaisonline.com/index.php/2013-01-15-14-16-26/local/item/17692-plantean-que-el-tipnis-sea-declarado-patrimonio-natural-de-la-humanidad.
Martín-Barbero, Jesús. 2010a. *La reinvención patrimonial de América Latina*. Murcia: Sphera Pública (Special Issue).
Martín-Barbero, Jesús. 2010b. 'El futura que habita la memoria.' https://esjatologico.files.wordpress.com/2010/09/el-futuro-que-habita-la-memoria2.pdf
Mauss, Marcel. 2009. *Ensayo sobre el don: forma y función del intercambio en las sociedades arcaicas*. Madrid: Katz Barpal.
Mignolo, Walter. 2000. *Local Histories/global Designs*. Princeton: Princeton University.
Nietzsche, Friedrich. 1996. *Vom Nutzen und Nachtheil der Historie für das Leben*. München: DTV.
Nugent, José Guillermo. 1992. *El laberinto de la choledad*. Lima: Fundación Ebert.
Portocarrero, Gonzalo. 2009. 'La resistencia como fundamento de la libertad.' Speech at the symposium 'Multiculturalism and Beyond.' ZiF-Bielefeld University, July 23, 2009. http://gonzaloportocarrero.blogsome.com/2009/08/31/la-resistencia-como-fundamento-de-la-libertad/#more-275>
Postero, Nancy. 2007. 'Andean Utopias in Evo Morales's Bolivia.' *Latin American and Caribbean Ethnic Studies*, 2 (1): 1–28.

Pratt, Mary-Louise. 2007. 'Indigeneity today.' In *Indigenous Experience Today*, eds., Marisol de la Cadena and Orin Starn, 397–404. New York: Berg.
Quijano, Aníbal. 2000. 'Colonialidad del Poder, Eurocentrismo y América Latina.' In *Colonialidad del Saber, Eurocentrismo y Ciencias Sociales*, ed., Edgardo Lander. CLACSO-UNESCO.
Rabasa, José. 2008. 'Thinking Europe in Indian Categories, or, "Tell Me the Story of How I Conquered You."' In *Coloniality at Large: Latin America and the Postcolonial Debate*, eds., Mabel Moraña, Enrique Dussel, and Carlos Jáuregui, 43-76. Durham: Duke University.
Römhild, Römhild. 1992. 'Zur Kritik der Idyllisierung.' In *Reisen und Alltag: Beiträge zur kulturwissenschaftlichen Tourismusforschung*, eds., Dieter Kramer and Ronald Lutz, 121–30. Frankfurt a.M.: Universität Frankfurt.
Rosenthal, Anton. 2000. 'Spectacle, Fear, and Protest: A Guide to the History of Urban Public Space in Latin America.' *Social Science History*, 24 (1): 33–73.
Sanjinés, Javier. 2013. *Embers of the Past. Essay in Times of Decolonization*. Durham: Duke University.
Simonse, Simon. 1982. 'African Literature between Nostalgia and Utopia: African Novels since 1953 in the Light of the Modes-of-Production Approach.' *Research in African Literatures*, 13 (4): 451–87.
Smith, Laurajane. 2006. *Uses of Heritage*. London: Routledge.
Stoler, Ann Laura. 2013. '"The Rot Remains"; From Ruins to Ruination.' In *Imperial Debris. On Ruins and Ruination*, ed., Ann Laura Stoler, 1–38. Durham: Duke University.
Ströbele-Gregor, Juliana. 2011. 'Black Day in the White City. Racism and Violence in Sucre.' In *Selling EthniCity. Urban Cultural Politics in the Americas*, ed., Olaf Kaltmeier, 71–90. Farnham: Ashgate.
Svampa, Maristella. 2008. 'Kontinuitäten und Brüche in den herrschenden Sektoren.' In *Sozialstrukturen in Lateinamerika: Ein Überblick*, eds., Dieter Boris, Therese Gerstenlauer, Alke Jenss, Kristy Schank, and John Schulten, 45–71. Wiesbaden: VS-Verlag.
Wolf, Eric R. 1982. *Europe and the People Without History*. Berkeley and Los Angeles: University of California.
Yudice, George. 2003. *The Expediency of Culture*. Durham: Duke University.

2 ¡*Mexicanos al grito de guerra!*[1]

How the *himno nacional* became part of Mexico's heritage

Sarah Corona Berkin

In the words of Edgar Morin, the nation appears at once

> anthropomorphic, theomorphic and cosmomorphic, because it expresses itself in human terms, resents offenses, has a sense of honor and a will to power and glory; theomorphic by virtue of the cult and religion of which it is the object; and cosmomorphic for bearing within itself all its territory, cities, countryside, mountains, and oceans.
>
> (Morin, in Giménez 1993)

Common metaphors concerning the *Himno Nacional Mexicana*, the Mexican national anthem from here on abbreviated HNM, include 'the voice of Mexico calling to us' and reminding us that the *Patria* is *our home*, in words that give order to the national cosmos and without which 'the universe's multiple voices would confuse us in despair and anguish' (Serra Rojas 1954).

For Guillermo Bonfil Batalla, patrimony or heritage is precisely that collective emotional and cultural resource that allows one—and many—to feel and inhabit the nation. It is the repository of cultural elements—some tangible, others intangible—that a given society considers its own, and which it draws upon in confronting problems (any kind of problem, from great crises to apparently trivial everyday matters); in formulating and attempting to achieve its aspirations and plans; in imagining, enjoying and expressing itself' (Bonfil Batalla 1993, 21).

In this paper, I examine how the HNM became heritage, its process during different historical periods, and the ways schools affected its teaching and diffusion. I address the national anthem from the vantage point of heritage, considered by Florescano to be 'one of the solidest elements of social identification.' I observe with Vaca (2012) that, different from the concept of collective memory, heritage is a result of modernity. With weakening of a memory originally linked to times of the Church, its rituals, and religious events, there was consequent weakening of the past as a means of guiding social behavior. Still, memory does not completely disappear as a guide for new behavior, but remains in its civil form, which we call heritage. It doesn't seek to eliminate 'nor abolish the past, nor discard history, but rather to filter through reason and rational critique, all that pertains to humans, individually and socially' (Vaca 2012, 12). The concept of heritage is thus a tradition anchored in processes of rationality, secularization, and nineteenth-century nationalisms. Next, I'll describe the history of the appearance of HNM, its consolidation as an official anthem, and the educational process that has brought it heritage status.

The history of the *himno nacional*: marching toward heritage status

The Mexican national anthem appeared later than those of other Latin American countries that had also achieved independence during the nineteenth century, and whose anthems originated in the process of forming their national states: Venezuela's dates from 1810; Argentina, 1813; Ecuador, 1830; Uruguay, 1833; and Paraguay, 1846. In Mexico, it was only after consolidating independence, and then not until 1853—during one of Antonio López de Santa Anna's dictatorial periods and amid the chaos of losing national territory—that a contest was launched to generate a national anthem. This had been tried several times before, beginning in 1821, with no success at defining either popular taste or that of the authorities. Santa Anna applied himself to the task hoping that patriotic sentiment would deflect attention from imminent civil war.

But this was also the moment in which the nation was finally taking shape; after losing a war to the United States, the northern frontier was for the first time precisely understood, and Mexico was more consciously naming that territory which it had to defend, and thus sing about as a nation.

In 1854, Santa Anna announced a contest in which the musicians and poets of the era might compete. Francisco González Bocanegra, a romantic poet from the state of San Luis Potosí, came out as the winner from among 26 contestants. Immediately afterward, the call for musical entries was answered, and chosen from among various proposals was that of Catalonian Jaime Nunó, who had previously taught military music in Cuba.

An honorary jury was assembled, which selected the 'best' poem and music for the anthem. However, Santa Anna was not pleased with González Bocanegra and Nunó's winning piece, as the lyrics failed to flatter him as he'd hoped. The fact that the President did not appear at the theater for the work's premiere, or that despite there being an official contest winner, the legislature's official daily record announced there would be three anthems performed so that 'among these three, patriotic enthusiasm may adopt the one it likes best to celebrate the Republic's triumphs' (Diario Oficial September 1854, cited in Romero 1961, 114), was equivalent to undermining the recognition bestowed by the jury. Santa Anna did not even issue the decree declaring the contest winners for music and lyrics, which would have lent them legal status.

From its premiere in 1854 until the end of the nineteenth century, González Bocanegra and Nunó's HNM went from being just one more (and not the best liked) of the anthems played during the era to flatter successive governments: Santa Anna's several regimes, plus those of Ignacio Comonfort, Miguel Miramón, and Benito Juárez. The winning 1854 HNM passed relatively unnoticed for almost

50 years, for lack of acceptance by governments (and by those leaders who felt it paid them insufficient homage).

Nor did the resulting national disorganization upon Santa Anna's departure in 1855 create conditions for the HNM to be widely played. The national independence holidays on September 15 and 16, 1855, were suspended, although days later they were reinstated, alluding to the importance of patriotism:

> Mexico is again free, and shall use its rights to show the world that it knows to value the efforts and sacrifices of its nation's founders. And what better testimony could there be than a dignified and patriotic celebration of the anniversary of our independence?
>
> (El Siglo XIX, September 14, 1885, 4)

The HNM was not played during these festivities.

When Francisco González Bocanegra died in 1861, the press barely mentioned his death: when it did, it was for the loss of a young poet, never mentioning his authorship of the HNM. This anthem hadn't attained the legitimacy necessary for representing the nation, nor was its author recognized for his creation. Still, a local literary note in San Luis Potosí exalts Bocanegra for having been born in that region and for having written

> the forceful martial stanzas of that brave song which has so often led us to victory and will ever touch our souls, enveloping them in war-like ardor, inspiring the holy love of our homeland, personified for González Bocanegra by San Luis Potosí.
>
> (El Correo de San Luis, November 1888)

This notice demonstrates the battle for hegemony between the regions and the center of the republic.

González Bocanegra gained decisive national recognition as author of the HNM from the twentieth century. It wasn't until 1901 that Sánchez Marmolejo mentioned him as the 'author of our National Anthem' in the compendium entitled *Letras Patrias* (Romero 1961, 148). The first allusion to the work of the national anthem's author is in 1944 when Julio Jiménez Rueda included González Bocanegra for the first time in his anthology of *Letras mexicanas en el siglo XIX*. This long indifference to the author speaks of the slow process of drawing the HNM into the country's heritage.

Historian Romero explains how the Mexican Philharmonic Society, 'the most prestigious educational institution, with highest cultural ranking in Mexico, gathered the most distinguished intellectuals into its bosom, as well as those wielding greatest influence within the government' (1961, 137), in the program for its 1867 concert dedicated to Juárez, said:

> Mexico has no march that is truly and exclusively national, as neither that of Hertz nor Nunó's anthem fits the bill. It fell upon the Philharmonic Society

to fill this vacuum, and it thus charged Dr. Aniceto Ortega with composing such a march . . .

(Romero 1961, 137)

. . . to be played on said occasion. The Bocanegra–Nunó anthem was not officially used in civic ceremonies from Plan de Ayutla in 1854 until the fall of the Second Empire. This anthem arose from the conservatives, and liberals would not support it. In 1869, Ignacio M. Altamirano praised Aniceto Ortega's anthem, which aimed to replace that of Bocanegra–Nunó:

> The 'Zaragoza March' is Mexico's *Marseillaise* and from now on it will always be our call to arms. Ortega's inspiration is the daughter of victory and not of suffering; thus his harmonies never translate into laments nor complaints, but burst forth in shouts of joy, accented by triumph and enthusiasm. The *Marcha Zaragoza* shows not a people vacillating childishly in the face of battle, but one that walks erect and proud, triumphing upon the bloody battlefield and among the cadavers of the annihilated enemy.
>
> (Romero 1961, 139)

This march, as distinct from the earlier anthem, was more allied with the liberals—it being an homage to Zaragoza who defeated the French in the 1862 Battle of Puebla. This may also be the reason that, during the Empire of Maximilian, the HNM was played at official events and festivities that he and/or his wife attended.

In 1881, however, the HNM was still not national heritage. On March 13 of that year, the metropolitan newspaper *La Patria* (March 13, 1881, 3) published the following news item:

> What is known today as the National Anthem was the work of a Spanish 'philharmonist' named Jaime Nunó. It gained popularity and was vulgarized in times of the Empire, by orders of Maximilian. It thus cannot serve as the National Anthem, as neither its music nor its lyrics are as worthy as they should be, and they lack the requisite of nationality. To have our own anthem, we regard the following as necessary: 1st, that the government call for entries from poets and musicians throughout the Republic, for our Anthem's lyrics and melody. 2nd, that a qualified jury be named, to select and award the authors of the composition chosen as National Anthem. 3rd, to premiere this anthem next September 16th.

This item shows us that the HNM had not been consolidated as a legitimate and unquestionable referent for the nation. In 1882, various daily newspapers published a debate over the possibility of having a new *himno de paz*, that is, peace hymn or national anthem.

At the same time, there was a bad feeling among the population about the anthem's 'vulgarization':

¡Mexicanos al grito de guerra! 41

The abuse committed by playing the anthem just anywhere should be abolished. A ballerina raises her toes and her admirers ask that the anthem be played; a circus horse falls, or a bullfighter, and the anthem plays to distract the crowd; throw a parade for some sailors, or cats, and they'll be hailed by the anthem. Opening a pulquería, throwing a party for a comedian or light-opera star, this patriotic hymn is employed for everything, when it should only be heard on great solemn occasions, and for appearances by the nation's first magistrate.

(*El Telégrafo* November 3, 1881, 3)

With Benito Juárez's arrival as president, the González Bocanegra and Nunó anthem was seldom officially heard; both creators in fact feared for their lives, though perhaps not entirely with just cause. The first hid out, and the second left Mexico. But conservatives did not allow the HNM to wane. In a memorial celebration to Iturbide, following the attendant speeches and a churchly sermon, 'the Holy Mass continued, and upon raising the sacramental host, a magnificent orchestra played the national anthem, its notes filling the vaults of the lovely temple' (*El Amigo de la Verdad*, February 10, 1886).

It wasn't until 1872, with the death of Juárez and during the presidency of Sebastián Lerdo de Tejada, that official tension against the anthem began to loosen. We may also recall that it was Miguel Lerdo de Tejada, the president's brother, who as the highest official in Santa Anna's Ministry of Development, Colonization, Industry and Commerce, signed the famous 1853 call for national anthem entries.

In 1883, the police prohibited singing the anthem in non-official situations, and in 1891 the Ministry of War and the Navy referred to the prohibition: 'It is strictly forbidden for Military Bands to use the National Anthem beyond those cases specified by Law; the reception and leave-taking of the Flag, or honoring the Nation's Chief Magistrate' (Romero 1961, 190).

González Bocanegra had died of typhus very young, at 36, but in 1901 Jaime Nunó was found by chance in Buffalo, New York, during an important Pan-American Exposition, to which Mexico had sent a substantial number of representatives. His discovery and return to Mexico caused a great commotion, and that year the annual cry of independence was celebrated with the HNM, played by bands that Nunó himself conducted, and sung by a children's choir. The rally of popular emotion denotes how the HNM had been preserved in the collective memory. Military and school bands, which customarily played in town and city plazas, had the Bocanegra–Nunó anthem in their repertoires, and this probably allowed it to be remembered all those years. Another source of its heritage status was the school system. The book *El Amigo de los Niños Mexicanos*, with its 25 editions from 1890 onward, contained the anthem's lyrics.

During the festivities and warm homage paid to Nunó, a greeting was made in the Nahuatl language 'in the name of the indigenous race.' Nunó's visit was one of the most important moments for HNM's achievement of heritage status: it gave the anthem authenticity via its genuine creator and made indigenous people participants in the rebirth of the nation during the symbolic first year of the twentieth century. In that same context, during a session of the legislature on October 9, 1901, congressman Juan A. Mateos put forth an initiative to award Jaime Nunó a pension, with the following words:

> Once our compatriots at the Buffalo Exposition found the author of the National Anthem still alive, they offered him grand ovations, with good reason: this anthem, wrested from the hands of the tyrants, crossed the mountains of Ayutla and brought victory to the Reform and Constitutional movements. The hearts of our fathers and those of our sons have beaten to its rhythm.
> (Romero 1961, 176)

The HNM was made official, its origin under Santa Anna forgiven, and it was granted a history and a tradition.

As 1910 began, the debate between liberals and conservatives over the national anthem again heated up. For the former, Hidalgo was without a doubt the only father of Independence and Iturbide a secondary hero of doubtful patriotism; for the latter it was the opposite—Iturbide, author of the Plan de Ayutla, was the true Independence hero. Here were two ways of chronicling a nation, with that of the liberals winning out. Since 1910 was the first centenary of the independence, liberals looked on in dismay when Hidalgo wasn't mentioned in the nation's own song, but Iturbide was. The Centenary Commission proposed changing the awkward phrase 'Iturbide's the sacred flag' to 'the nation's sacred flag,' but conservative voices rose in protest against excluding Iturbide from the HNM. In a conciliatory gesture and to promote national integration, the Ministry of Public Education approved a version containing no proper names, to be used only in schools. It goes without saying that this later became the official national version of the HNM. From then on, no particular hero would be mentioned in its lyrics.

The year 1942 was decisive for the process of the HNM's patrimonial adoption. The *El Nacional* newspaper published the headline 'Yesterday Mexico stood unified before the nation's flag,' and a piece titled 'Country moved by profound patriotism' described the 'apotheotic spectacle of features unique in the annals of our civic life, where the notes of the National Anthem, ringing out from bands of musicians and thousands of throats, roused a supreme patriotic spirit in the multitudes' (*El Nacional*, February 25, 1942). On October 12, 1942, Día de la Raza, the remains of González Bocanegra and Jaime Nunó were exhumed with full honors and removed to the Rotunda of Illustrious Men. In his speech, poet Enrique González Martínez pronounced: 'No Mexican can hear or sing it without being profoundly moved. When far from his or her country its notes are heard, the music seems to work the miracle of filling the abyss of exile' (Peñalosa 1961, 168). In this way, the HNM was being sung to the land, to the *mestizo* race, and to national feeling.

In that same year of 1942, by decree of President Ávila Camacho, it was officially determined that performance of the HNM would include just four stanzas, interspersed with five renditions of the chorus.

Eric Hobsbawm observes that 'the invention of public ceremonies had the objective of transforming the republic's inheritance into a conjoint expression of

State pomp and power, and citizens' joy' (2012, 282). On September 15, 1954, with the motive of the HNM's centenary, conductor Luis Sandi Meneses led 13,000 children in a choral sing of the HNM at Constitution Plaza. This event, along with confirming the HNM without a doubt as official, served to establish guidelines for singing it. The HNM's music, originally conceived in E-flat major for military band instruments of the day and for trained singing voices, had to be converted to C Major to make it more suitable for untrained voices.

But it wasn't until 1984, with the government of Miguel de la Madrid, that this abbreviated form of the anthem became regulation. That year, with the publication of the Law for the National Seal, Flag and Anthem, the official words and music were defined with the purpose of assuring precision and uniformity in its singing, performance, publication, and recording. One of the main reasons for the new law was to replace the restrictive character of the 1967 legislation so that Mexicans would have access to their national symbols in daily life, while avoiding legal infractions. In this spirit, the prohibition against performing the national anthem at non-civic shows and social gatherings, and in all sorts of public establishments, was lifted, with the condition that it be interpreted in a respectful and solemn manner.

On December 8, 2005, article 39a was added to the Law for the National Seal, Flag and Anthem, announcing that indigenous people and communities could perform the national anthem, translated into their own languages. The National Institute of Indigenous Languages was selected to do the corresponding translations, which would be authorized by the Secretary of State and Ministry of Public Education.

Article 46 of this Law determined that the national anthem should be taught to children attending primary and secondary schools; it was modified in 2005 to also include preschools.

The national anthem: a matter for the schools

According to Bhabha (1990), the pedagogic condition of national symbols comes right down to their distinctive characteristics. The responsibility given to the Ministry of Education (SEP) for teaching the HNM allows us to understand the forms in which teaching accompanies the construction of Mexican social identity.

I have sought the presence of Mexican nationalism in the national educational process, which despite being homogenous and comprehensive as imparted by the SEP, shows tensions manifesting in textbooks, particularly when covering the HNM. National planning may be observed in the official pedagogic strategy for the anthem, which is illustrated with images of those considered Mexican. I analyze a collection of images accompanying the text[2] of the national anthem in its various versions, in textbooks dating from 1943 to 2012, with the objective of distinguishing those considered to be Mexicans who sing the HNM. Prior to the first date, I found only two references to the HNM in the body of textbooks, and these were unaccompanied by images. The governmental periods from Ávila Camacho (1940–1946) to Calderón (2006–2012) show what the process of HNM heritage status has meant to primary education books.

President Ávila Camacho, and his recently nominated presidential successor Miguel Alemán Valdés, moved to change the Mexican Revolutionary Party (PRM) into the Institutional Revolutionary Party (PRI), so it went from being a party of revolutionaries to an institution that again took up the colors of the nation's flag, and revived the national anthem.[3] In 1943, the anthem became official and an illustrated excerpt of its lyrics appeared, albeit hesitantly, in textbooks for first grade children.

The governments of Miguel Alemán (1946–1952) and Adolfo Ruiz Cortines (1952–1958) promoted the HNM with greater determination. During Miguel Alemán's presidency, a book on the HNM was produced, and profusely illustrated by Spanish refugee painter Bardasano. For his part, Ruíz Cortines had a brochure on the anthem published, its cover a nationalist engraving, and this stayed in print for over a decade.

With López Mateos (1958–1964) began another stage of illustrating the anthem. In the new universal depiction of the mother country on the covers of free textbooks (1959), López Mateos's approach complemented the ritual. The anthem was sung to a mother country that had to that point been *mestiza*—as opposed to Bardesano's classic-looking *Madre Patria*—and included the country's productive forces, as defined by the PRM. These included four sectors: workers, farmers, the military, and the public; now, the different organizations that were merging with the party were being added.

With Díaz Ordaz (1964–1970), a 1967 regularization of the anthem was accompanied by its history, in the form of a comic book. With expressive genre elements, it narrated the story of the authors, emphasizing their inspiration in creating the anthem. Free textbooks issued under reforms carried out during Echeverría's time in power (1970–1976) show less emphasis on Mexican nationalism and more on Latin American identity, with content addressing Latin American poetry and song, while excluding coverage of the HNM.

De la Madrid (1982–1988) legislated so that the anthem could be sung any place, at any time, beginning in 1984. This measure can be viewed in a free textbook photograph where a child prepares to listen to the anthem on a modern record player of that time. Salinas (1988–1994) and Zedillo (1988–2000) continued teaching the anthem. Mexico joined the globalization process, wagering that a quick and bold entrance on the world stage would accelerate its economic development. But on the other hand, after a decade of economic decline and growing social conflicts and demands, it needed to offer an image that would unite Mexicans around common symbols and stories.

At the end of the twentieth century, the PRI's seven decades in power came to an end. It had been a constant in the history of free textbooks and various citizenship models in Mexico. Beginning in 1959, through the 1972 and 1992 reforms, these programs were undertaken with the PRI occupying the presidency and in command of the government's principal institutions. Starting with the transformations we have reviewed as the HNM appeared in textbooks, differences can be observed between the visions for the nation each of these presidents furthered. Still, belonging to the same party represents a certain ideological and political unity, a certain common vision of history.

The most recent free textbook reform was that conducted with a party other than the PRI in power. For the 12 years from 2000 to 2012, Vicente Fox Quezada and Felipe Calderón, belonging to the conservative Partido Acción Nacional (National Action Party), occupied Mexico's presidency.

Books in this period broke with the nationalist discourse emanating from the Revolution, where the *patria* or homeland depended on Mexico's distinctive miscegenation (*mestizaje*) and the unity of its inhabitants. In place of a homogenous discourse, these books presented a fragmented, heterogeneous, and contradictory vision. All ideological proposals are valid, with no order nor dialogue; the civic pedagogic approach is a multiculturalist exploration, of differences on display. The fifth-year Civics text tells us: 'Instead of looking down on and rejecting people, get to know them. When you do, you'll wind up liking them because their different ways of being, thinking and living will make you glad.' The book in this case chooses a solution removed from any political path to solve the problem of different types coexisting. It's difficult to believe that affection and delight are plausible alternative methodologies for bringing twenty-first century Mexican nationals into agreement, or into a frictionless coexistence.

In this context, the anthem is treated as folklore, with the image of the flag in a handcrafted tin frame and mariachi figures made of straw. As an inclusive sample of all Mexicans, singing of the anthem in indigenous languages was made legal in 2005. Around the same time and contradictory to support for national diversity, a 2006 poster was published showing photographs of the Mexicans who sang the HNM: white European-featured adults, from a homogenous middle class. Indigenous people were not represented, nor those from the great national majorities. In this graphic, not only are Mexicans no longer *mestizos*, but there are no different social classes, nor occupations.

We find these recent textbooks embracing Mexican nationalism, while a national present that includes challenges and conflicts disappears. What do they offer instead? A version of a Mexico with room for all opinions, without need for discussion.

The HNM nevertheless remains a symbolic means of uniting the nation. In some years, official heritage-making has been more energetic than others: none prior to 1854, when there was not even a clear territory to call patria, but 1901 for example, when the Porfiriato dictatorship was consolidating the nation, and 1942, when Mexico was announcing itself a nation within a new order of nations. Today the state and the education system worry less about how to make the HNM work as heritage, but the process of its 'patrimonialization' lets us observe the historical ups and downs during the fight for nationhood.

Notes

1 Mexicans, heed the battle cry.
2 Free Textbooks or Libros de Texto Gratuitos (LTG) is the only official program in the West that distributes textbooks free of charge for teaching all children nationally. The

books are standardized, and obligatory for all Mexican children from first to sixth grades of primary school. In 2009, the program celebrated its 50th anniversary: up to that date it had published and distributed 5 billion free textbooks in Mexico. While the LTG program began in 1959, this article also considers earlier books, beginning in 1943 when the first illustrated allusion to the HNM appears in books directed at public education.
3   The Nation Revolutionary Party (PNR) was founded in 1928, restituted by the Mexican Revolutionary Party (PRM) in 1938, which changed its name to the Institutional Revolutionary Party (PRI) in 1946.

References

Abolición del. 'Himno Nacional.' March 13, 1881. *La Patria*, 3.
Bhabha, Homi. 1990. *Nation and Narration*. New York: Routledge.
Bonfil Batalla, Guillermo. 1993. 'Nuestro patrimonio cultural: un laberinto de significados,' In *El patrimonio cultural de México*, ed. Enrique Florescano. Mexico City: Conaculta.
Editorial. November, 1888. *El Correo de San Luis*.
García, Estrella, and Agustín Vaca. 2012. 'Notas en torno de los fundamentos teóricos del patrimonio cultural'. In *Procesos de patrimonio cultural*, eds. Estrella García and Agustín Vaca. Guadalajara: Colegio de Jalisco.
Giménez, G. 1993. 'Apuntes para una teoría de la identidad nacional.' *Revista sociológica*, 8 (21). Retrieved from www.revistasociologica.mx/pdf/2102.pdf
Hobsbawm, Eric. 2012. 'La fabricación en serie de tradiciones: Europa 1870–1914.' In *La invención de la tradición*, ed. Eric Hobsbawm, and Terence Ranger. Barcelona: Crítica.
Pacheco Moreno, Manuel. 1956. *El Himno Nacional*. Mexico City: Campeador.
Peñalosa, Joaquín Antonio. 1955. *Entraña poética del Himno Nacional*. Mexico City: Imprenta Universitaria.
¡Por Iturbide! February 10, 1886. *El Amigo de la Verdad*, 1.
Romero, Jesús. 1961. *La verdadera historia del Himno Nacional*. Mexico City: UNAM.
Serra Rojas, Andrés. 1954. 'Prólogo en Cid y Mulet.' In *México en un Himno*, Mexico City: Divulgación.
¡Viva la independencia nacional! September 14, 1885. *El Siglo XIX*, 4.

3 Making heritage – the materialization of the state and the expediency of music

The case of the *cuarteto característico* in Córdoba, Argentina

Gustavo Blázquez

> Let nothing be counted good, although, as always, it may seem really helpful, and nothing henceforth be considered honorable except what changes this world once for all: it needs it Like an answer to their prayers I came to the oppressors! Oh, goodness without results! Unnoticed attitude!
> —Bertolt Brecht, Saint Joan of the Stockyards

First steps

The first years of the twenty-first century saw me immersed in fieldwork focused on the so-called *cuarteto* dances of Córdoba, Argentina's second-largest city in demographic weight and economic gravitation. The goal of the ethnography was the analysis of the institution of 'compulsory heterosexuality' (Rich 1999) through ludic performances and choreographic practices associated with free time, amusement, and juvenile years. My interest lies in describing the politics and poetics of gender, class, and race, which organized these choreographies as well as the emerging subjectivities (Blázquez 2014).

Cuarteto balls were dancing reunions with live music by an orchestra exclusively formed by males, which mainly summoned together young people and adolescents from popular sectors of society. On a weekend, and only in the city of Córdoba, more than 20 balls were organized, which summoned up to 30,000 youths.

During the course of my research, I was obliged to comb out the social genesis of this local danceable musical genre called the *cuarteto característico*. I undertook the task from a critical analysis of a series of accounts, which formed an official(ized) narrative of the genre, which was repeated and repeated—always with differences—in books, magazines, webpages, songs, stories of life. I observed that the change of the meaning of the term cuarteto was 'naturalized' through this ensemble of narratives. Between 1940 and 1960, the word cuarteto referred to the number of players in the orchestras that interpreted joyful music, but never a type of music. The so-called 'cuartetos característicos' executed rhythms name as 'característicos,' like tarantellas, paso doble, *cumbias*, *paseítos*, marches, fox-trots, although they did it with a special accent created by Leonor Marzano, pianist of the first cuarteto característico titled 'Cuarteto Leo.'

In the years of ethnography, the people said they danced or listened to the cuarteto without those expressions appearing to have a lack of sense, different from other forms like dancing or listening to orchestra, trio, and quintet. The cuarteto orchestras were composed of 10 or more musicians; the rhythms, which weren't 'característicos,' had a strong influence of Caribbean music while adding winds and percussion. The cuarteto had turned into a musical genre, which was registered by the Diccionario de la Música Española e Hispanoamericana.

The performative force of that narration, empowered by wide dissemination and generalized acceptance of accounts, (re)constructed the historical continuity of the poetic form of the cuarteto, despite the important stylistic transformations. That story made the cuarteto, while endowing it with a history. Through that (hi)story, the cultural legitimacy of certain musicians, singers, and sonorities was (re)produced, while at the same time identifying those danceable rhythms with consumption by the popular sectors, first with the peasants and then with the urban workers (Blázquez 2008).

This article contemplates the analysis of one of the formalization moments of these heterogeneous ensembles of sonorities called cuarteto característico as 'popular Cordobese music,' which happened midyear in 2000. At that time, the House of Representatives of the Province of Córdoba declared its homage to the music of the cuarteto, which it referred to as 'the cultural emblem of the Province of Córdoba' (Decree 3626/00. June 7, 2000). From an analysis of that ceremony, it will be possible to observe how each observer built an account from which and in which it empowered its position while simultaneously building a general agreement that supported the 'cordobesity' of the cuarteto. This agreement, which lent meaning to the speeches of the congressmen, was (re)produced in the differential appropriation and in the significations attributed by diverse agents that participated in the performance. The different opinions, assessments, and appropriations of the homage show how any performance is made up of a confluence, not always peaceful, of perspectives and versions.[1]

More than a decade after these events, the Municipality of Córdoba declared the cuarteto a 'cultural heritage of the city' and began the mission for the official recognition of these sonorities in the list of intangible cultural heritage of humanity by UNESCO. Second, I consider that the new invention of the cuarteto, now as heritage, was produced within the context of the transformation of culture into expediency (Yudice 2002) and the legitimization of the figure of a 'cultural manager' as a technician specialized in designing and administrating cultural policies. By that time, I had already published a book with some findings from my research and hence was summoned as a specialist on the cuarteto by municipal authorities.

The set of actions implemented by the provincial and municipal state of Córdoba in relation to some sonorities of popular tone can be understood as part of the newly agreed value assigned to culture and new ways of managing it. In Argentina, like other places in the world, symbolic goods were transformed into important resources for social, economic, and political growth. The actions of the state extended in different spheres of social life, even in those considered intimate, while at the same time privatizing public spaces (Sabsay 2011). In this context, cultural policies will be analyzed as part of new government technologies where certain uses and symbolic goods are transformed into a resource. Power not only suppresses but also produces and makes it desirable to recognize itself in a specific cultural identity. The whole process of (trans)formation of popular sonorities into emblem and heritage in a specific territory has a certain glocal character, and its analysis will allow us to describe, in a micro scale, the mutation of the strategic position of culture with relation to state practices and changes in forms of governmentality (Foucault 1999). By analyzing the heritagization of the cuarteto, we can observe how the state was (re)produced in Córdoba. Some of the questions this article tries to answer include: Who created heritage and how? How was the state materialized in that process?

Culture as a form of government

With great performative force since the mid-nineteenth century, culture became a prominent instrument in the creation of national states while homogenizing the ensemble of legitimate knowledge, and simultaneously securing the conditions of differential access to that capital (Anderson 1993; Elias 1997; Hobsbawm and Ranger 1984). In this process, not exempted from brutality as forewarned by Walter Benjamin (1989), the state (re)presented itself as judge and guarantor of 'good taste' through its cultural institutions (museums, theatres, ballet groups, and symphonic orchestras), which exercised the guardianship over specific goods with some degree of democratic access. During the nineteenth and twentieth centuries, culture—understood as the ensemble of cultural goods and knowledge (especially artistic-literary)—was an instrument of civilization, nationalization, and construction of political hegemony on behalf of the state and national elites.

The idea of culture as a raw material to make state and govern populations and territories in a different way was added to the instrumental function in the last years. This new function bestowed on culture implied transformations of the definition of the term itself, which could no longer exclusively refer to pieces of the repertoire of 'high culture.' As part of this process, and mainly originating from the development of the Latin American Social Anthropology and British Cultural Studies, handicrafts and the collection of goods and practices associated with popular sectors were now collectively defined as culture. The term became plural and evolved to include 'cultures' and 'multiculturalism.'

State and supra-state organizations, like UNESCO, actively participated in helping stabilize the new definitions of cultures. For example, during the first National Argentinean Congress of Cultures, a grand event organized in 2006 by the Bureau of Culture of the Nation, the cultural areas of the provinces, and the Federal Council of Investment, it was established that 'cultures were the belle arts but also were, above all, the meaning we give to our methods of community living' (Conclusions of the First National Argentinean Congress of Cultures. Mar del Plata, August 27, 2006).

To make culture(s) resulted in a way to make state and the state became a place to fulfill culture(s), starting with specific government policies. Among these efforts, we can find the organization of events like the aforementioned Argentinian Congress of Cultures, which was repeated in the following years, and whose explicit goals were

> to build a space defined by the provinces, the municipalities and other social actors that intervene in the cultural makings of the country; to incorporate the definition of the role of culture within the national project, prioritizing the axes of social inclusion and the deepening of democracy; integrate the public cultural policies to the communal agents, as well as the government areas involved in social development—education, social communication, health, childhood, youth, tourism, etc.—as to favor the processes of decentralization, participation, articulation and strengthening of the State; and to broader the horizon of strategies and actions through incorporating the regional integration of Latin America.
> (Conclusions of the First National Argentinean Congress of Cultures. Mar del Plata, August 27, 2006)

It was no longer only a task of ideological indoctrination, manufacturing of consensus, or the fetishization of a determined group of goods as cultural heritage. Since the end of the Second World War and with increased strength since the 1980s in the USA, with different temporalities in Latin America, culture became a resource, a fuel, to make state and to stimulate development, growth, and strength.

As pointed out by Souza Lima and Macedo e Castro (2008), some common sense understands cultural policies as an action plan to guide decisions and actions, and, consequently, dedicated to the analysis of the conditions of emergency, mechanisms of operation, and probable impact on social and economic order of government programs. In these analyses, the actions of public policies are represented as the result of the capacity of a nation-state (liberal-democratic) to solve public problems. Those studies maintain a rational and instrumental vision of the state and try to understand their actions from the point of view of the efficiency of its practices. Therefore, public policies appear as the result of the identification of a 'social problem,' which will lead to the formulation of rational arguments that can explain them and from where collective solutions and plans of action arise. Their application, by technicians and specialists, and its final evaluation would complete an enchanted circle where the (in)capacity of action by the state to offer answers to social demands stands out.

Nonetheless, cultural policies could be understood as plans, actions, knowledge, and technologies of the government through which certain agents would—as part of a process that is socially flexible, contradictory, conflictive, changing, in perpetual movement—make the state. Even before a state, magically raised to the category of a manager of the social process capable of developing policies, we might find some practices and discourses that performatively make state when cited, again and again, as the rational and effective agent it proclaims to be.

A possible strategy to approach the state while seeking not to succumb to the brilliance of its own magic (Taussig 1997) is to penetrate its shortcuts and to ethnographically study how the 'mechanism works' (Foucault 1975) with the goal of dismantling and describing it in its specific workings. These approximations originate from the questioning of the programmatic definitions of government policies and abandon the somewhat paranoiac belief of the existence of a state. When transforming the S into a capital letter in a series of government practices of populations, formed by an ensemble of decisions and acts of will more or less systematic from certain social subjects on the use of instruments, rules, strategies, and objectives that regulate different social practices, it is possible to confront the constitutive force of the state, which is capable of creating itself and the realities it enounces. Policies that are pro-indigenous, educational, sanitary, for immigrants, for minors, for youths, among others, when seen from dark hallways and administrative intricacies, turn out to be heterogeneous annexes of administrative actions by state structures of everyday intervention in the social life of determined populations inside a specific territory (Cf. Castro 2009; Corrêa 2002; Lugones 2009; Pacheco de Oliveira 1988; Ramos 2002; Souza Lima 1995, 2002; Vianna 2002).

Before diving into these oblivious interventions in everyday life, I propose to find the state in the magnificent iridescence of its production, in the 'performances of state' or ceremonies organized by administrative nationalized bodies that produce the state as a defined agent of the social process (Blázquez 2012; Navallo 2007; Rufer 2010; Tamagnini, 2010). The performances of the state would be acts of the state; repeatedly executed, 'restored behaviors' (Schechner 2000), never original and always carried out for the second time, through which the state appoints itself and meets the citizens.

The first time

On June 7, 2000, the House of Representatives from the Province of Córdoba approved a declaration of 'homage to the cuarteto popular music from Córdoba, urging all composers, interpreters and promoters to continue its development and diffusion in all the national and international spheres as a cultural emblem from the Province of Córdoba' (Decree 3626/00). The next day, and in a hyperbolic form, the local newspaper announced the approval 'by unanimity of a project destined to declare cuarteto as a folklore genre from Córdoba' (*La Voz del Interior*, June 8, 2000. Section 2C, page 1), and established June 4 as the 'day of Cordobese popular music' (*La Voz del Interior* June 8, 2000. Section 2C, page 1). Through these acts, a group of practices centered on a type of danceable music were formalized, recognized as local, and made a symbol of the political-administrative unit.

According to the press, June 4 would become, in the local sphere, the 'day of the cuarteto.' The selection of that particular day was (supposedly) on account of

June 4, 1934, making the radio debut of the first cuarteto ensemble, the Cuarteto Característico Leo.[2] Adding to this event, the death of Manolito Cánovas on June 4, 2000, the founder of a successful musical band, occurred when the parliamentary project was halfway through. Because of this, according to the statement given in the legislative palace by the author of the project, 'we cannot doubt for a single second in making it a dignified day of collective memory' (Congressman Carlos Pereyra, Legislative Palace. June 7, 2000).

The performance that was set up in the principal premises of the House of Representatives, and where several members of some orchestras, entrepreneurs, and people that had assisted in the dances participated, was for the legislators and the honorees a righteous, necessary, and deserved act.

The author of the project, Congressman Carlos Pereyra from the Vecinalista Party,[3] said at this event:

> This homage was due for a long time, as long as the cuarteto has been an artistic, cultural, and social testimony of Córdoba, born in the crucible of distant rural zones from our provincial land, and arriving later onto the cutting edge of the musical manifestations of the country.
> (Congressman Carlos Pereyra, Legislative Palace, June 7, 2000)

When I got in touch a few days later with the Congressman to interview him about his initiative, and as a way to settle with determination his position, he told me: 'I defend everything that is genuinely from here: the folklore; the indigenous; the gaucho; the tango and also the cuarteto' (Congressman Carlos Pereyra, June 12, 2000). For Pereyra, the validation of the genre—an institutional touch to what already existed according to his words—and the declaration of the cuarteto as (the) folkloric music of Córdoba were movements of a process guiding the exportation of the cultural good of local production, 'at least to Latin America' (Congressman Carlos Pereyra, Interview June 15, 2000). The Congressman wanted to make the cuarteto the characteristic merchandise of Córdoba and therefore integrate it into world music to return money to Córdoba. Pereyra perfectly knew the economic potential present in the world of the cuarteto. He explained in the following speech:

> How many times did the Club Defensores del Oeste, to mention only one very close example to me, summon the Leo, the Cuarteto Berna, Carlitos Rolán and Cuarteto de Oro, and from those summons funds were made available for projects that are now part of the patrimony of Villa Dolores and of each town and city.
> (Interview with Pereyra, June 15, 2000)

The sports institution that Pereyra referred to 'was a club that in the year 70 had 30 years of institutional life.' During that time, his brother, who was the major of Villa Dolores and who occupied, at the time of the interview, a provincial senator's chair, was president of that same sports institution whose patrimony was 'a bag with booties, another bag with shirts, and another bag with soccer balls.' The Congressman continued during the interview:

> we started to work to secure funding to make the club, in the way we made lots of partners. But, do you know what we did? . . . With cuarteto music we made events every Saturday and Sunday, Fridays and Saturdays, and we started to build brick by brick what I can presently say is the most important thing of Traslasierra.[4] And we did it with cuarteto music. [. . .] a little in the democratic period, during the dictatorship, and until the eighties.
> (Interview with Pereyra, June 15, 2000)

Pereyra did not define himself as a 'loyal fan of the cuarteto,' that is, he did not view himself as an agent whose relationship with this artistic genre was established by participating in the balls, and from which a biased point of view could emerge. On the contrary, the Congressman presented himself as someone who adopted a dissociated point of view and conceived the cuarteto 'as a social phenomenon.' To him, this cultural production was

> a means to create employment: hundreds of families from Córdoba live directly from cuarteto music. But all of these efforts, when done during the weekends, require a lot of people. And it is something genuine. And all these cuartetos, who have produced a lot of recordings—you know they have achieved platinum discs, gold discs—are currency that go into Córdoba.
> (Interview with Pereyra, June 15, 2000)

Pereyra saw the cuarteto as a strategy to be a part of modernity and also to live (survive) in (post)modernity.

> We have to use the technology of this global economy, of this globalization policy to, starting from our cultural identity, sell what is ours in a good way, export culture, export music, export idiosyncrasy, export tastes, export traditions. Similar to the case of the jeans by the Yankees. They introduced it to the world.
> (Interview with Pereyra, June 15, 2000)

According to this point of view, to proceed with this task, 'the state had to take all that popular culture, which could be coded, and transmit it to regular customers' (Interview with Pereyra, June 15, 2000) and then develop a political policy that can assure a reconversion and a transformation of the subjects in what is said they originally were. 'To recuperate what is ours but to create a source,' the Congressman confirmed emphatically (Interview with Pereyra, June 15, 2000).

The (re)invention of a local culture was a possibility, in the eyes of the politician, to ensure economic reproduction in times of globalization. This task produced and was anchored in a specialization of different managers in charge of the production of 'what is ours.' In this process, the task of the professional politician was, according to the author of the legislative project, to guide the economy through the construction of strategies that would localize the fluctuating international economical capital.[5] Pereyra knew that industrial development in Córdoba during the second half of the twentieth century through the impulse of the automotive and metal-mechanical industries had assured certain level of development. But, at the same time, he knew that local development was completely dependent because 'big companies are here today, but tomorrow they will be in Brazil, another day they in Europe or get transferred to Hong Kong, Taiwan or Singapore or Southeast Asia or wherever' (Interview with Pereyra, June 15, 2000).

The route to development depended, for politicians like Pereyra, on the sedentarization of international capital. This activity, contrary to the 'nature' of capital, would be possible through the delimitation of certain practices associated with cuisine or music, its isolation and future codification as a 'traditional' feature: 'the Cordobese cuisine' or 'the music of Córdoba.' In this project of dependent development and the fabrication of an 'authentic culture,'[6] professional politicians were responsible for *guiding* the investments of capital toward the production of some merchandises that would only have value when staying 'traditional.' At the same time, the politicians must guarantee the 'authentic' character of these goods.[7]

As part of that policy—which did not discuss the way in which the produced income would be distributed—the state would also have to be responsible for the production of the producers of such merchandise, and consequently develop technical education to qualify an ensemble of future workers capable of integrating themselves in the labor market. 'The government has to train these people by giving them cooking courses and specializing them in those dishes which will identify all that iconography [. . .] for them to be good cooks, good confectioners of those dishes' (Interview with Pereyra, June 15, 2000). Supposedly, there would be private firms that would join forces with this economic movement, accelerating the process further and therefore, in the vision of the Congressman and other agents, Córdoba would develop.[8]

Although these were the motivations behind Pereyra's homage, as confided to me, some congressmen distrusted the initiative and were afraid that it would be seen by civil society as another of the discredited and useless parliamentary practices. On the other hand, the congressmen also had some fear in relation to the proper execution, given the subaltern origin of the cuarteto and its association with bad taste and rude language. The success of the strategy of authentication, as the Congressman knew well, depended on the capacity to generate a representation that was at the height of the circumstances. 'Then, suit, tie, vest, otherwise this would be a disgrace' (Interview with Pereyra, June 15, 2000).

All local media were present and newspaper chronicles, which narrated the homage, always highlighted the rejoicing and order that prevailed in the precinct. The wife of singer Carlos 'Pueblo' Rolán, one of the honorees, stated:

> It was a beautiful reception, very gratifying. It is the formalization of cuarteto. After so many things that we have been through, to be able to reach this instance, the recognition of all social classes. We are all very happy.
> (Laura Rolán. *La Voz del Interior*, June 8, 2000. Section 2C, page 1)

The homage

In the performance that took place in the House of Representatives, two great moments can be identified. First, 'the project of declaration number 3626, in reference to the Homage of the Popular Music of cuarteto' was presented, followed by words from Congressman Pereyra, who justified his project. Later the speeches continued: a brief comment from a congresswoman from the first minority, then two other longer discourses, one from a conservative congressman and another from a representative of the ruling party.

Once the first part of the ceremony was over, during which the representatives of Córdoba spoke on the cuarteto, the ceremony proceeded to hand out plaques and diplomas to those who were considered the most important figures in the genre or those to whom tribute should be paid if the cuarteto was to be honored.

In his speech, Pereyra narrated the story of the genre since its first presentation of the first ensemble of the cuarteto:

> at eleven at night of the fourth of June of 1943, in a cold radio booth up to the multitudinous recitals of La Mona in the Monumental Nuñez Stadium and Luna Park, which marked the glorious entrance of cuarteto cordobés into Buenos Aires.
> (Congressman Pereyra, Legislative Palace, June 7, 2000)

In his version, we find an epic account where a musical form unfolds and develops heroically within time. In this process, prosopopoeia or personification as a discursive trope is used to objectify the cuarteto genre. Different milestones from the development stages are emphasized. First, the birth of the cuarteto on the radio on the night of June 4, 1943, followed by the performance at a rural level in patron saints' and civic festivities, and later at the suburban level with balls in clubs at the outskirts of Córdoba city starting in the mid-1950s. The beginning of the 1970s marked a glorious period with big family dances and production of ensembles. At that time, according to the story, 'the cuarteto, that son, born in Córdoba, of the tambourine and the tarantella, of the piano, the polka, the accordion and paso doble, had turned into a man on its own right' (Congressman Pereyra, Legislative Palace, June 7, 2000). Stories of repression and resistance continued during the period of the last military dictatorship (1976–1983). Finally, the definitive consolidation came with the participation of the Cuarteto Característico Leo in the most important folkloric festival of Argentina in 1987 and the first shows in Buenos Aires. Pereyra's speech seemed to mention, it is time to take over the world and the legislative declaration forms a part of this new era.[9]

The speech ended with some stanzas from 'Nuestro Estilo Cordobés' read out loud. In this song, as in the speech of Pereyra, the cuarteto is (re)presented as a musical type based on the local traditions and part of the combination of dominant symbols (Turner 1968, 80) capable of calling one regional identity that would distinguish the province over the other political-administrative units. Some of the provinces of Argentina appear in the song sang in chorus at the Legislative Palace identified through some musical type already integrated in the national cultural heritage. In this way, the song configured a musical map according to lines that traced the political geography of Argentina. As a result, the cuarteto is localized in spatial terms when it is associated with a specific territory and at the same time it is made as old and original as other mentioned musical genres that originated in the rural world of the nineteenth century or, as in the case of tango, in the suburban stages of Buenos Aires at the end of the same century. In summary, Pereyra's speech started treating the cuarteto as a distant social phenomenon and ended in an appeal, by means of the appropriation of a famous song, to put (one's own) death as the limit of the musical genre and therefore identifying it with life. Dancing the cuarteto (*cuarteteando*) until death was the mandatory sentence of the song.

Following this cheered speech, a congresswoman from the Radical Civil Union expressed her support for the initiative which, in her opinion, 'arrives late because it was an unresolved matter that the Cordobese had with cuarteteros' (Congresswoman Castro, Legislative Palace, June 7, 2000). Immediately after this brief interlocution, a congressman for a center-right party took the floor. His speech stated 'that music which properly and totally represented Córdoba' (Congressman Bustos Argañaráz Legislative Palace, June 7, 2000) as a product of the fusion of several traditions. Among them, he highlighted: the paso doble, which according to him, 'Don Jerónimo Luis de Cabrera surely brought' (Congressman Bustos Argañaráz Legislative Palace, June 7, 2000); the creole waltz with strong reminiscences from Paraguay; the *chamamé* from Corrientes; the southern *milonga*; the cumbia of Afro-American origin; and the tarantella brought by the immigrants from southern Italy.

According to the version presented by this congressman, the cuarteto emerged from a much more heterogeneous mix than the version presented by Pereyra. However, that probably was not the most significant difference. Bustos Argañaráz, an individual identified with the high local bourgeois, in particular with the fraction that establishes the legitimacy of its hegemonic social position with its genealogical connections with the Spanish conquerors of the sixteenth and seventeenth centuries, temporarily separates the Hispanic and Italian components that he recognizes in the cuarteto. The first, represented by the paso doble, came with the conquerors 'four centuries ago' (Congressman Bustos Argañaráz Legislative Palace, June 7, 2000), while the second, distinguished by the tarantella, arrived with Italian immigrants at the beginning of the twentieth century.[10]

According to this presentation, the cuarteto music is characterized by the capacity to articulate different tendencies or forces and therefore by the capacity to represent—'reflect,' according to the congressman—the supposed hybrid nature of Córdoba.

In the fabrication of the cuarteto as 'popular Cordobese music,' Bustos Argañaráz uses a frequent trope in the analysis of the alleged historic singularity of Córdoba. The province—or the city—is considered a privileged stage where the tension between the colony and the republic, tradition and modernity, the interior and Buenos Aires, the countryside and the city, has been played, several times in an anticipative way.[11] In the congressman's speech, Córdoba and the cuarteto work as terms trapped in a metonymic relationship in which the second term works as one of the sowers of the first. The cuarteto appears, according to this allocution, as an allegory in which the unique collective and distinct character of Córdoba is expressed and understood as a product of a process in which the ethnical-racial and the geographical atmospheres are combined.

After this critique, considered by the media to be in an 'academic tone' (*La Voz del Interior* June 8, 2000. Section 2C, page 1), the next speech was by Peronist Congressman José Rufeil. Different from previous presentations, this politician based his defense on the personal knowledge he had of the cuarteto and the friendship that linked him to many of the honorees. Rufeil defined himself as a 'loyal cuartetero' (Congressman Rufeil, Legislative Palace, June 7, 2000) and stated:

> The moment that cuarteto is going through is lovely. I see people from the Cerro de las Rosas, students from the faculties. A social difference does no longer exist in cuarteto, but I would be a hypocrite if I did not remember that those of us who went to a cuarteto ball were discriminated. Even by our own families.
> (Congressman Rufeil, Legislative Palace, June 7, 2000)

The Peronist politician, who was very happy with the ceremony, which he compared to the highly advertised award ceremonies in show business, differed from the rest of the opinions due to his personal tone and automatic identification with the honorees.[12] With regard to the origin of the genre, Rufeil maintained that together with the contribution of European migrations it was necessary to acknowledge the contribution of 'Native American people.'

With that speech the first part of the ceremony ended, and the awards began. First, commemorative plaques were handed out to singers Carlos 'la Mona' Jiménez and Carlitos 'Pueblo' Rolán, composer and lyricist Aldo Kustin, and accordionist Eduardo Gelfo, grandson of the founder of the Cuarteto Característico Leo. Afterward, 13 carton diplomas were handed out to artists and entrepreneurs who participated for a longer or shorter time in the world of the cuarteto. The awardees were announced by the master of ceremonies, who presented the honored artists as well as the congressman who handed out the awards. Later, both subjects found themselves in the space occupied by the president of the House of Representatives and the public applauded.[13]

During the ceremony, each speaker built a place for their enunciation and positioned themselves as progressive politicians who wish to praise a group of local cultural producers and, through that, activate a process of economic development; either as an academic that interprets the cuarteto and attributes to it a determined significance, or as the 'loyal cuartetero' who shares a personal story with the honorees. Beyond these different discursive positions and as they highlighted, all agreed on the act of justice of the homage to a musical genre that they, as representatives of the people of Córdoba, recognized as properly

Cordobese. On the other hand, and as we have also pointed out, each of the speakers attributed a different origin to the cuarteto. Pereyra, based on an academic text, considered the cuarteto as a synthesis of music of the immigrants. Bustos Argañaráz broadened the field by giving way to other musical traditions although first he had to recognize the Hispanic contribution of the city's founder. Rufeil, moving chronologically beyond the conservative congressman, claimed a 'Native American' contribution as mentioned a few months earlier by a local newspaper.

> The cuarteto, that very special music; which we Cordobese feel has to do with indigenous roots. The Sanavirones were very happy, they had ensembles and danced. Compared to the Comechingones, who were much calmer.
> (*La Voz del Interior*, January 5, 2000. Section 2C, page 3)

The parliamentary ceremony (re)told a story very distant from the facts. The performance created a rural and immigrant tradition for cuarteto and built an authenticity in which each of its presenters found a distinguished place. The legislative act also (re)established a hierarchy among the artists depending on who received the rare plaque or the abundant, and therefore lesser distinctive, paper diplomas. Those who received the plaques (Gelfo, Jiménez, Kustin, and Rolán) represented a version of the genre defined as the most 'original': the cuarteto-cuarteto.[14]

To other agents, especially the youths that attended the balls, the importance of the parliamentary act wasn't based on the official recognition of the genre that they danced to. For them the performance was an opportunity to be close to their idols, and take autographs or pictures.

The second time

Years after that homage, in July 2013 and in the framework of the celebrations for the 440 years of the establishment of the city of Córdoba, the Deliberation Council declared the cuarteto the 'Cultural Heritage of the city of Córdoba.' The motion was presented by an initiative of the Municipal Ministry of Culture and had the specific goal of securing the local cultural identity.

Such a meaningful ceremony obligated a change of venue for the sessions of the Council, which in that occasion took place in the distinguished and colonial Red Hall of the municipal town hall. Another distinctive feature was the presence of the media, and of course, of artists and entrepreneurs of the cuarteto. According to the website of the Municipality of Córdoba, 'musical connoisseurs as Eduardo Gelfo and Carlitos Rolán, and young promises as Catriel Argüello' (www2.cordoba.gov.ar/portal/index.php/el-cuarteto-ya-es-patrimonio-cultural-de-la-ciudad/) were present.

After the motion was approved unanimously, the municipal mayor, Ramón Mestre, entered the precinct and addressed those present:

> This is an act of strict justice. For us it is transcendent to recognize cuarteto music for what it means to the culture of our city and our province. Similar

to the way that tango is recognized in Buenos Aires and worldwide, same as the candombe in Uruguay, we hope that this is the first step to find worldwide recognition of cuarteto. The initial kick is the recognition of the Deliberation Council, representing the neighbors, and we think that we should keep working to manage the support of the Legislature of Córdoba and the National House of Representatives and, in that way, obtain the most consensus possible so that UNESCO declares our music a Cultural World Heritage.

(Municipal Mayor, Town Hall, July 4, 2013)

The speech laid out, again, the debt that the state had with the cuarteto in such a way that those municipal cultural policies acquired a reparation character: 'an act of strict justice.' The approved ordinance went further than the previous homage at the House of Representatives as it planned to take specific actions. Together with making the cuarteto musical genre the city's heritage, the ordinance obliged the municipal state to develop actions aimed at 'its preservation and conservation; guaranteeing its dissemination and promotion, fomenting the development of every artistic, cultural, touristic, academic, educational and/or urban activity related with itself' (Ordinance 1528/13). For this, it must find the provincial, national, and international recognition of the new heritage while at the same time entrusting the areas of tourism, culture, and education with the mission of fulfilling the order of the ordinance.

After the speech, the attendees moved to a joint room where the Cuarteto Característico Leo and Carlitos Rolán played classics of the genre and were enthusiastically cheered. The ceremony ended with the official presentation of 'Walk of Fame of the cuarteto,' in a downtown area of the city associated with popular sectors. The project considered sharing a series of architectural interventions, such as piping rain drainage and bettering public lighting, together with the placing of plaques and commemorative sculptures of Cordobese artists who represent the cuarteto.

The official act was well received by the citizens and the media took care to highlight its value. However, the alleged incorporation of the cuarteto to the scholar curricula unleashed a series of discussions and disagreements as well as support and defenses. Was the cuarteto worthy of entering classrooms? Some parents and teachers denounced the musical poverty of the genre, its scarce originality or simplicity, the rude character of some of its lyrics, as well as how some themes addressed marginalization, a bad life, and the world of crime, drugs, and night. But, others argued that it was a good way of effectively approaching students and interviewed high school students maintained that this would finally be a course they could pass.

The middle sectors of the population that did not adopt the cuarteto favorably looked at the symbolic recognition of popular culture and, at the same time, rejected it occupying a space among scholar knowledge. The cuarteto was legitimate music and worthy of becoming heritage as long as it stayed encapsulated in the world of cultural consumption of the popular sectors. That double lecture assured the illustrated and professional urban middle classes a dominant cultural position, in charge of controlling 'good taste' and the legitimate scholar education, while maintaining a subaltern and folkloric place for popular sectors, rooted in local identity or Cordobeity.

The state ordinance and the ceremony identified the cuarteto with all Cordobese and undid, once more, the class identity indicated by the music. At the same time, these actions strengthened the subaltern and folkloric side of the cuarteto and saved the mimesis of 'Fame Boulevard' in Hollywood to a downcast street that served as an open aired popular market. Through the cuarteto, class as a form of social division was (re)created as well as a local cultural identity was (re)built, which joined subjects beyond these separations.

A similar duplicity could be found in the state policies, which on one part promoted the heritagization of the cuarteto and the acknowledgement of its artists, and on the other persecuted the youths that attended the balls. While the life conditions of the popular Cordobese sectors deteriorated and the young cuarteto followers were hunted down and punished as delinquents or dangerous people, their main cultural consumption, the cuarteto, was transformed into heritage.

Given these differential policies with respect to popular sectors and the cultural consumption, one can ponder on the political value of these state-administrative practices referring to culture. If, as this was the case, the policies of cultural acknowledgement were not combined with policies of social or economic redistribution, those processes of heritage formation can become the means for positively accenting a new unequally distributed prosperity. In those opportunities, the cultural identity becomes a spectacle in the sense of Guy Debord (1999) as performed in the 'Camino de la fama del cuarteto': a means for the non-problematic staging of a social economic disparity covered by the protective mantle of culture. Social exclusion combined with cultural inclusion when somebody enjoys economic prosperity while some others have a symbolic recognition. The state, in this case municipal, uses the performative power that constituted it to make heritage, culture, identity, and through them make the inequality it administrated visible.

The municipal state made the cuarteto a heritage and in this process it invented itself through the creation of duties and the forming of new relations of interdependence. As part of this materialization of the state, a series of specialists and cultural managers were put in charge of making the cuarteto 'a World Heritage' according to established regulations by supernational organizations.

The project that the Bureau of Culture established, as highlighted in the speech of the municipal major, was to reach UNESCO. For this purpose, different actions were taken, like the formation of a commission integrated by notable and model members of the community. A technical commission was also constituted to be in charge of the heritagization processes, coordinated by a cultural manager, a municipal employee, and a historian. This commission created a 'Memory' where again the same (hi)story of gender is traced and all of the required paperwork to complete the presentation at UNESCO, which occurred on March 31, 2015.

All these actions were followed by a lobbying effort to get the provincial legislature and the national state to recognize the cuarteto as heritage. As mentioned by the newspapers, the major would meet with the Minister of Education of the Country and the Secretary of Culture worked on a statement project on behalf of the House of Representatives.

As part of that process, the provincial Legislative Power approved on April 14, 2014, law 10.174, which declared the cuarteto as 'a proper, characteristic and traditional musical folkloric genre from the province of Córdoba' and recognized it as 'a component of the provincial cultural heritage in all its manifestations: music, lyrics and dances.' The law declared as 'Provincial Interest' the 'activities related with the development of studies and research on cuarteto and the conservation and reappraisal of documents, places and objects that preserved the oeuvre of its creators and performers.' The provincial law also established June 4 as the 'day of the cuarteto' and January 12 as the 'day of the Piano Saltarín (jumping),' in commemoration of the death of pianist Leonor Marzano, considered as the creator of the genre. Finally, the cuarteto and its creator were officially devoted a day in the calendar of cultural ephemeris of Córdoba.[15]

The materialization of the state

The homage made by a congressman who did not consider himself a 'loyal cuartetero,' but recognized the ability of the balls to create economic resources, was not capable of creating concrete actions beyond the recognition and the (re)consecration of certain hierarchies in the artistic field of the cuarteto. In this opportunity, the state appeared as a beam able to establish, celebrate, institute, and name the cuarteto. Different from this act, the cultural policies carried out by the municipal state defined actions designed to achieve the lined goals. It no longer represented pure statements or words, but proposed putting things in action. The state stated and acted in such a way that the results from its actions became a guarantee of its performative power.

Beyond these differences, the state materialized during the performances several times. First, the state was formed when, with the goal of creating a performance, the relationships of interdependence grew between different agents and, in some occasions, were nationalized. The organization of parliamentary ceremonies that required certain rules of etiquette if they wanted to be happy, according to Austin (1981), connected very diverse agents. Their production involved everything from important lobbying work, conversations between congressmen, inviting esteemed artists, handing out of plaques and diplomas, communication with press, and the fitting-out of the spaces, among other activities. This collaborative work by diverse agents allowed for specific stages to be created where the avatars of cultural distinction and social differentiation could play at the same time as a joint cultural identity was created. For example, joined and separated, those present during the homage called themselves Cordobese while dividing into loyal *cuarteteros* or the *people*, which included artists, at the same time divided hierarchically, their followers, a congressman, and those who, as representatives of the people, awarded them.

The actions taken by the Bureau of Culture of the Municipality of Córdoba allow us to see how the state made itself in the quantitative growth of the number of agents whose economic reproduction depended once more on the incorporation of the state networks. For example, the task of organizing the presentation before UNESCO and producing necessary material meant the nationalization of freelance workers dedicated to the management of cultural projects.

The state was also made in the recognition of 'specialists' who recognized in and by the public powers stop being 'independent managers' and transformed into contractors of the State or even public functionaries. For example, the Secretary of Culture and main promoter of the project was a young man who held several management positions since the beginning of the century at a Cultural Center managed by the Spanish state and the Municipality of Córdoba, all this thanks to his family's resources. Due to his work in that institution, sustained by important European funding, he built social capital and gained knowledge that secured him a specialist position in the area of cultural management. Taking advantage and strengthening that hegemonic position, the subject turned to direct a space of academic formation in the specialty, associating with a private university and with the support of an NGO.

It is interesting to highlight how in the context of a new administration of the municipal state that sought to build itself as effective and efficient under the slogan of 'Ordering Córdoba,' that specialist, whom the state itself created, resulted in an important political capital. In those dynamics, the managers were nationalized while they were integrated in specific administrative networks and gave the state the same materiality produced by itself.

In relation to the cuarteto, the state also materialized through the accumulation of economic resources produced by a higher imposing collection. Exporting the cuarteto, as imagined by Congressman Pereyra, would contribute huge amounts of currency to the depressed provincial economy. The cuarteto could also become a tourist attraction and the collective commercial activities that would be generated around this practice could contribute resources to the state's coffers. On the other hand, by stimulating the production of the cuarteto, the state would transform independent artists that did not pay taxes, because they were sporadic workers, into fiscal subjects that must compulsorily become a part of the current social security protocol. As these sonorities became more successful, massive, and profitable for entrepreneurs and cuarteto artists, the fiscal rent would increase. Through the use of its own performative force, and its capacity to declare and make the cuarteto a glocal artistic genre, the provincial and municipal state could contribute to that process from which they were benefiting.

In other words, the state was materializing when it associated itself with an image that gave it substance. Córdoba was made in and by some sonorities which it legally defined as 'proper, characteristic and traditional of the province, musical folkloric genre.' To that state imagery, as held by Tambiah (1985) in relation to rituals and ceremonies, certain indicial values would be supported and inferred. According to Peirce (1974), it could be said that the legisign cuarteto acquired an emblematic value that derived from its repeated association with the Córdoba legisign. The creation of that relation and its transformation into law was carried out in different

Making heritage 63

actions of the state capable of (re)citing over and over the same (hi)story through which Cordobeity was manufactured as well as the authenticity of the cuarteto. In the ceremonies, the law with which each particular experience of the ensemble of popular sonorities called the cuarteto should materialize was established as a reply to the metonymic association with Córdoba. When finding the cuarteto at balls, in songs, on the radio, TV, movies, or in the 'Camino de la Fama,' subjects found themselves in and with Córdoba. The actions of the state (re)established the emblematic Cordobese character of the genre and iteratively (re)established the metonymic relationship that made the cuarteto one of the semes that condensed in Córdoba (Group (1987).

The metonymic character, a type of synecdoche that made the cuarteto an indicial symbol of Córdoba, was the product of the foreclosure of the metaphoric relationship that both terms maintained. That transformation seemed unthought-of and unthinkable. The actors that participated in these performances of the state did it for different motives and for each of them the acts seemed to have a differential significance. However, everyone said they experimented the emblematic value that the cuarteto had/would have to the agents that identified/were identified as Cordobese. In and through the ceremonies, it was said, experienced, learned, and instituted that the cuarteto was 'Nuestro Estilo Cordobés' (our Cordobese style).[16]

That emblematic value built in and by the performances of the state, was part of the tactics through which Cordobeity, which cuarteto and subjects should/said to have, was generated. In this way, a series of heterogeneous sonorities were objectivized under the form of a specific artistic genre at the same time as some agents subjectivized/subjected as members of the same collectivity.

Last, the state materialized while re(producing) the belief in the capital S, in its power and material. This overvaluation of the state required two somewhat different forms that converged in their productivity. On the one hand, the state presented itself as a being that forgot, disowned, and excluded the cuarteto and popular sectors. Simultaneously, it presented itself as the only, or at least the most important, agent capable of solving the problems it produced. The different performances repeated the debt that the state kept while paying it off at the same time. In this dynamic, the state was self-constituted as a perfectible and fundamental agent in the social process.

In summary, that which was defined as the cuarteto resulted in an excellent resource in the process of the formation of the state as long as it was a new sphere in which state organizations could/should legally intervene. At the same time, through this intervention, the state was given an emblem and heritage that represented it, it constituted itself of a group of nationalized specialists in charge of handling this administration, and it tried to increase tax collections.

The music, and in a more general sense, the culture transformed a resource for the governmentalization of the state while in its name a group of institutions, procedures, knowledge, calculations, and tactics were built, which allowed a particular form of power to be exercised. In the analyzed case, that 'cultural power' or 'force of culture' had specific populations as a goal, particularly the popular sectors, but in a more general way to all of those who inhabited the Cordobese territory, and its most distinguished instruments were ceremonial devices of recognition and creation of heritage.

To make state, or in terms of Foucault, the development of governmentality meant that during the last decade there was an expansion of the government in Córdoba through an ensemble of sonorities, which during the process were transformed into a musical genre and a symbol of identity. The described cultural governmentality was at the same time interior and exterior to the state, because the government tactics allowed defining, in each moment, its limits. These (un)realizable limits of the inside and outside of the state could be observed in the state ceremonies where, in front of media, politicians, artists, entrepreneurs, and consumers mingled. The performances that situated each one in their place also allowed the erasure of those limits, such was the case of Congressman Rufeil and his self-defining as 'loyal cuartetero.'

The paths of the congressman that organized the homage and that of the municipal Secretary of Culture who pushed the heritagization of the cuarteto also show the (un)realizable frontiers of the state. In different ways these subjects, who had the social, cultural, and professional capitals that allowed them to pursue their project, formed part of the government and nongovernment institutions while at the same time trafficking knowledge and influence between them. One based his project in the knowledge acquired while he was president of a sports institution, while the other did it taking advantage of the knowledge he had of the global forms of administration in culture, which he incorporated while administering a cultural institution financed by a European state.

The (trans)formation of cuarteto into a symbol and cultural heritage makes obvious the heterogeneity of the participating institutions and agents and therefore should call attention to that which we call state. This diversity was executed in two planes. On the one hand we find distinct states (provincial, municipal) and supranational organizations linking their actions, and on the other hand we find 'non-nationalized' agents like musicians, entrepreneurs, and cultural managers forming part of this lattice, which meanwhile, with their presence, made state.

With all its apparent banality and kitsch charm, the enactments of the state that made the cuarteto a proper Cordobese musical genre could be described as other mechanisms through which the state was materialized, as nationalized belief, image, and social media in everyday intervention of social life. The magic of the state, in other words, its power to auto-reproduce and represent as a rational agent in social processes in charge of satisfying needs and securing rights of a territorialized population, could be understood as a performative effect of those same performances of the state.

Cases as the one described above allow us to observe the capillarization of forms of domination, their open margins where the state was being made, governmentality, and culture through the action of specific agents.

Notes

1 Several authors have highlighted the importance of considering rituals and performances as practices constituted from the crossing of diverse perspectives and points of view (Cf. Geertz 1987; Gerholm 1988; Gluckman 1958; Rosaldo 1991).
2 Although celebrated, it is possible to suspect whether June 4 is the day of the 'birth' of cuarteto because on the same day a new coup d'etat was produced and the military that took political power declared 'Martial Law.'
3 Pereyra, in his own words, came from 'a rural family, the smallest of nine siblings. I am the youngest and the only one who could study, and my parents were two peasants totally identified with, let's say, the idiosyncrasy of the rural area.' Born in 1954, Pereyra graduated as a lawyer from the National University of Córdoba. He was mayor of a town of his region and this was his third term as provincial congressman. The Unión Vecinalista party, was at that time, the second minority and was defined by Pereyra as 'a party that was born from the small towns and that joins neighbors to give solutions to specific problems' (Interview with Pereyra, June 15, 2000).
4 Traslasierra is a valley in the province of Córdoba.
5 The vision that Pereyra held on the regional economic development justified in tourism picks on a large local political tradition that we cannot analyze here.
6 In his study of North American 'country music,' Richard Peterson uses the concept of 'fabrication of authenticity' with which he wants to point at the socially constructed character of a plan or event that declares itself 'authentic' (Peterson 1992). This fabrication, the author sustains, always has some type of historic infidelity built through a series of permanent adjustments between commercial interests of the producers and the tastes of the public. Peterson's analysis tries to pierce the character of deliberate political manipulation assumed by these concepts and introduce the creation of a public whose reactions, unpredictable at one point, also participate in the self-interested fabrication of the authentic character of determined goods.
7 Additional to this project related to the cuarteto, Pereyra had created a project he called 'Ruta del Paladar' (Route to the Palate), which consisted in organizing the provincial territory in touristic and traditional gastronomic tours based on regional characteristics.
8 For example, on May 31, 2000, a week before the declaration at the House of Representatives, a news story appeared in the *La Voz del Interior* newspaper, which reported about the presence in the city of a famous cook, 'the Gato Dumas,' who recorded a chapter of his television show 'Argentina Genial' transmitted from a channel in Buenos Aires. Dumas invited 'la Mona' Jiménez to his program, and the news journalist registered this encounter where the cook confirmed 'I had a survey made to know where it would be convenient to set a gastronomic school. It was a serious survey; the result claims that Córdoba is one of the best places for the idea' (*La Voz del Interior*, May 31, 2000; Section 2C, page 1).
9 To this metaphysical story that Pereyra (re)cites full of certainties, it is possible to oppose a genealogy of the genre that shows a lot of doubts. It is not only plausible that Leo did not play on June 4, but it is also possible to suspect the rural origin, as all of the musicians lived in the city and had a long career as urban subjects. Either way, the participation of the Sicilian tarantella in the conformation of the cuarteto could probably happen before through radio or recordings than by the contact of Italian immigrants, which were mainly from Piamonte.
10 The anachronism produced by Bustos Argañaráz must be noted, because the paso doble, a Spanish dance in which the dancer imitates the steps of a bullfighter dominating its prey, has a much more recent origin and it became famous in the dance floors during the 1930s decade when it was embraced by the high society of Paris.
11 The local historian Horacio Crespo (1999) made a synthesis of the tensions that are articulated in Córdoba, and proposes a rereading of this trope that describes Córdoba

as a point of encounter through the analysis of thought of José María Aricó and his characterization of the city as 'frontier.'
12 Rufeil confessed he felt like 'I had received a prize together with you, because I consider myself one of you' (Congressman Rufeil, Legislative Palace, June 7, 2000).
13 Together with the dancers and fans of the honorees, students from two elementary schools who were visiting the House of Representatives were present as part of their educational activities.
14 In this group, Gelfo—still active but without much success—was awarded last as the representative of the origin of the genre, while Jiménez—in full activity and fortune—received the award first as the representative of the present-day genre. Rolán and Kustin, already retired, seemed to be there to complete the existing vacuum between the origin and the present.
15 Although since the homage of the year 2000, when June 4 was considered the 'day of the cuarteto,' this ephemeris was a product of the interpretation of the media and was not a part of the declaration on behalf of the House of Representatives.
16 We must recall how the speech of Congressman Pereyra ended with the reading of some stanzas of 'Nuestro Estilo Cordobés' (our Cordobese style), a song by Jiménez that expressed the folkloric and Cordobese character that the cuarteto must have.

References

Anderson, Benedict. 1993. *Comunidades Imaginadas*. México: FCE.
Austin, John. 1981. *Cómo hacer cosas con palabras*. Buenos Aires: Paidós.
Benjamin, Walter. 1989. *Discursos interrumpidos I*. Madrid: Taurus.
Blázquez, Gustavo. 2008. *Músicos, mujeres y algo para tomar. Los mundos de los cuartetos en Córdoba*. Córdoba: Editorial Recovecos.
Blázquez, Gustavo. 2012. 'Fazer cultura. Fazer(-se) estado: vernissages e performatividade de estado em Córdoba.' *Mana Revista de Antropología Social* 18(1): 37–61.
Blázquez, Gustavo. 2014. *¡Bailaló! Género, Raza y Erotismo en el Cuarteto Cordobés*. Buenos Aires: Gorla.
Crespo, Horacio. 1999. 'Identidades/diferencias/divergencias: Córdoba como `ciudad de frontera _. Ensayo acerca de una singularidad histórica.' In *La Argentina en el siglo XX*, ed. Carlos Altamirano. Buenos Aires: Ariel.
Debord, Guy. 1999. *La sociedad del espectáculo*. Valencia: Pre-Textos.
Elias, Norbert. 1997. *Os Alemães. A luta pelo poder e a evolução do habitus no séculos XIX e XX*. Rio de Janeiro: Zahar.
Foucault, Michel. 1975. *Surveiller et punir*. Paris: Gallimard.
Foucault, Michel. 1999. 'La gubernamentabilidad.' In *Estética, ética y hermenéutica*, ed. Ángel Gabilondo. Barcelona: Paidós.
Geertz, Clifford. 1987. *La Interpretación de las Culturas*. Barcelona: Gedisa.
Gerholm, Thomas. 1988. 'On Ritual: a postmodernist view.' *Ethnos* 53: 190–203.
Glukman, Max. 1958. *Analysis of a social situation in modern Africa*. Manchester: Manchester University.
Grupo μ. 1987. *Retórica General*. Barcelona: Paidós.
Hobsbawm, Eric, and Terence Ranger. 1984. *A Invenção das Tradições*. Rio de Janeiro: Paz e Terra.
Lugones, María Gabriela. 2009. 'Obrando en autos, obrando en vidas.' Formas e fórmulas de Proteção Judicial dos tribunais Prevencionais de Menores de Córdoba, Argentina, nos começos do século XXI. Tesse de doutorado em Antropologia. Rio de Janeiro. PPGAS/MN/UFRJ. Retrieved from http://co114w.col114.mail.live.com/mail/–_mso com_1

Macedo e Castro, João Pablo. 2009. *A invenção da juventude violenta. Análise da elaboração de uma política pública*. Rio de Janeiro: E-papers/LACED Museu Nacional.
Navallo, Laura. 2007. Tocando Cultura. Políticas y poéticas del término cultura a partir del análisis de los procesos sociales de creación de la Orquesta Sinfónica de Salta. Undergraduate thesis in Antropología, Universidad Nacional de Salta.
Pacheco de Oliveira Joao. 1988. *O Nosso Governo: os Ticuna e o regime tutelar*. São Paulo/Brasilia: Marco Zero/CNPq.
Peirce, Charles. 1974. *La ciencia de la semiótica*. Buenos Aires: Nueva Visión.
Peterson, Richard. 1992. 'La fabrication de l'authenticité: la country music.' In *Actes de la Recherche* 93: 3–19.
Ramos, Jair de Souza. 2002. O poder de domar do fraco: Formação de Estado e poder tutelar na politica de Povoamento do Solo Nacional. Ph.D. Dissertation, PPGAS/MN/Museu Nacional.
Rich, Adrianne. 1999. 'La Heterosexualidad obligatoria y la existencia lesbiana.' In *Sexualidad, género y roles sexuales*, ed. Marysa Navarro, and Catharine Stimpsom. Buenos Aires: FCE.
Rosaldo, Renato. 1991. *Cultura y Verdad*. México: Grijalbo.
Rufer, Mario. 2010. *La nación en escenas. Memoria pública y usos del pasado en contextos poscoloniales*. México: El Colegio de México.
Sabsay, Leticia. 2014. *Fronteras sexuales. Espacio urbano, cuerpo y ciudadanía*. Buenos Aires: Paidós.
Schechner, Richard. 2000. *Performance. Teoría y prácticas interculturales*. Buenos Aires: Libros del Rojas/UBA.
Silveira Corrêa, José Gabriel. 2002. A ordem a se preservar: a gestão dos índios e o Reformatório Agrícola Indígena Krenak. Ph.D. Dissertation, PPGAS/MN/Museu Nacional.
Souza Lima, Antonio Carlos de. 1995. *Um Grande Cerco de paz*. Petrópolis: Vozes.
Souza Lima, Antonio Carlos de. (org). 2002. *Gestar e gerir. Estudos para uma antropologia da administração pública no Brasil*. Rio de Janeiro: Relume Dumará.
Souza Lima, Antonio Carlos de. and João Pablo Macedo e CASTRO. 2008. *Política(s) Pública(s)*. Rio de Janeiro: Mimeo.
Tamagnini, María Lucía. 2010. Performance y políticas culturales en la inauguración del Museo Superior de Bellas Artes 'Evita- Palacio Ferreyra.' Undergraduate thesis on History, Universidad Nacional de Córdoba.
Tambiah, Stanley. 1985. *Culture, Thought and Social Action*. Cambridge: Harvard University.
Taussig, Michael. 1997. *The Magic of the State*. New York: Routledge.
Turner, Victor. 1968. *The Drums of Affliction*. Oxford: Clarendon.
Vianna, Adriana. 2002. Os limites da minoridade: responsabilidade, tutela e familia em julgamento. Ph.D. Dissertation, PPGAS/MN/Museu Nacional.
Yudice, George. 2002. *El recurso de la Cultura*. Barcelona: Gedisa.

4 Is Spanish our language?
Alfonso Reyes and the policies of language in postrevolutionary Mexico

María del Carmen de la Peza

> When the access to a language is prohibited [...] the access to speech is prohibited [...] to certain speech. But exactly in that lies the fundamental interdiction, the absolute interdiction, the interdiction of diction and of speech. The interdiction of which I speak [...] is therefore not an interdiction among others.
> —Jacques Derrida, El monolingüismo del otro

The agreement of the United Nations Educational, Scientific and Cultural Organization (UNESCO) on the defense of cultural and linguistic diversity, which considers languages as an 'intangible cultural heritage' of humanity, is the result of the fight that different people and communities have put up within conflicts derived from the imposition of the occidental nation-state model as the unique form of political organization. The use of the notion of heritage in the political space of the United Nations as a strategy to defend linguistic and cultural diversity has been, beyond doubt, an important resource of the indigenous peoples in face of the power of the state. However, the fight for the right to culture that is understood as *heritage* is not exempt from ambivalences and contradictions.

In this chapter, I propose some thoughts based on which one can reflect on the conflicts that are obscured behind the policies of *patrimonialization* of languages. In the first part, I briefly recount different moments in the policies of linguistics from the conquest to the present day. In the second part, starting with a critique of the notion of heritage and its uses in the building of the state-nation, I highlight the problems and contradictions that underlie the policies that consider languages —Spanish and other native languages—as *intangible cultural heritage* of the Mexican nation. To achieve this goal, I analyze the ideological-political position of Alfonso Reyes (1889–1959) in relation with Latino culture as well as Spanish in the texts that comprise the anthology *Nuestra Lengua y otros cuatro papeles*[1] by Adolfo Castañón.[2]

I begin with the hypothesis that, in the discourse of Reyes, the ambivalences and contradictions of the postrevolutionary Mexican state are expressed on language and the European colonial culture in relation to other languages and native cultures, tensions, and constitutive conflicts of the policies of languages, and of the mestizo and indigenous contemporary Mexican cultures. The texts that comprise the anthology condense one the most important ideological perspectives that guided the policies of language in twentieth-century Mexico and express, in a more or less explicit form, the different voices of power and other voices—more or less audible—that answer them.

My interpretation of the oeuvre of Reyes is, without doubt, partial and interested. Through it, I intend to offer a glimpse of the conflicts and difficulties that have signified the concomitant process of imposition/appropriation of Spanish as the national language, considered by Alfonso Reyes as 'our language,' and the ambivalences—recognition/negation/prohibition/recuperation—with regard to the native languages.

This work is not a criticism of the literary oeuvre of Alfonso Reyes or of his political thoughts. I consider his discourse as *a knot in a net*, a fragment of the social discursiveness on the language and culture in Mexico, voiced from a legitimate place of enunciation, socio-historically determined. In short, this is a work on the public–political discourse on the Spanish language as the cultural heritage of Mexico.

Community, heritage, and imaginary construction of the nation

> All accounts on the foundational crimes—collective crime, ritual murder, victim's sacrifice—that accompany the history of civilization as a dark counterpoint, don't do anything else but cite the *delinquere* in a metaphorical way ... which keeps us together.
>
> (Roberto Esposito, *Communitas*)

In his book *Communitas* (2003), Esposito suggests that the dominant common sense establishes a synonymy between common and proper, a synonymy that impregnates the notion of heritage in the Mexican nation. The liberal and individualistic conceptions, as much as the community perspectives of the state, share the idea that the national community 'is a good, a value, an essence [...] that which is most proper to us [...] an origin to long for, or a destiny to prefigure.' The citizens belong to a nation and it, at the same time, belongs to them in a circular logic; in other words, 'they have in common what is proper, they own what is common to them,' in such a way that the idea of national community, paraphrasing Esposito, 'is still attached to the semantics of the *proprium*' (2003, 23–25).

Against this interpretation of 'community,' its etymological meaning in neo-Latin dictionaries is 'it is what *not* proper'—in other words, 'what concerns us all ...' (26). Therefore, according to Esposito, what unites a community is not a good or merchandise, but 'a debt [...] an emptiness, partial or integral, of property into its contrary' (31). What joins a community is what is improper—the difference, the conflict—and if we consider the notion of community in that sense, it radically changes the meaning of the notion of national patrimony.

The word 'patrimony'[3] derives from the Latin terms *patri* (father) and from the same root *munus* (community). The root *munus* according to Esposito means gift, but a special type of gift, 'a gift to give [...] something that cannot be kept for oneself,' in other words, 'the obligation that has been contracted with the other ...' (26–31). In this sense, *munus* consists in the reciprocity or mutuality of giving that determines the commitment between the one who gives and the one who receives.

In the same order of ideas, for De la Peña 'the word patrimony means the duty of the father' (*munus patris*), the obligation of the father to inherit that 'which is worth preserving and bequeathing to the next generation: what will allow it to sustain itself materially and spiritually' (2011, 14). Therefore, each new generation is not entirely the owner of the goods received as legacy; it is obliged to bequeath the 'cultural and linguistic heritage'—the inheritance of the father—to the next generation; in other words, patrimony is the duty that compromises the generations with the past and the future at the same time. In the case of postcolonial nations such as Mexico, polemic exists around the linguistic and cultural inheritance that should be bequeathed to the next generation: the native languages (maternal) and/or the language of the colonizer (paternal).

The ideas of community and patrimony understood as property, which sustained the building of the Mexican nation, conceal the violence of the colonization. In terms of Esposito, what remains hidden is 'the fissure, the trauma, the lagoon from which we originate: no the origin but its absence, its withdrawal' (2003, 33). Therefore, behind the notion of national community hide the conflicts derived from the imposition of language and culture of the colonizer[4] to the colonized and the definition of that which constitutes the linguistic and cultural patrimony of Mexico, which has been, historically, a subject of political dispute.

Policies of language: linguistic genocide and castilianization

> When a language dies,
> many others have died
> and many others can die
> mirrors shattered forever,
> shadows of voices
> for ever silenced:
> humanity impoverishes.
>
> (Tlazohcamati Totatzin, *Cuando muere una lengua*,
> Piece translated from Náhuatl)

In Mexico, the strategies[5] of castilianization, assimilation, and integration, implemented in an irregular and intermittent manner by the colonial power first and the modern state-nation later, had a devastating effect on native languages and seriously jeopardized the linguistic richness and cultural diversity of the country. The linguistic ethnocide suffered in the last 500 years has been really alarming: of the 1,241 Amerindian languages that existed before 1519, less than 100 persevere (De la Peza and Rodríguez Torres 2011).

However, the process of castilianization has not been free from conflicts and contradictions. On the one hand, the resistance and fight of the native peoples have hindered the absolute destruction of the nation's linguistic and cultural diversity. On the other hand, internal contradictions within the groups in power, who maintain different perspectives on the role of the inherited cultural heritage of the native peoples, their languages, and culture, in the construction of the new mestizo nation, have had different characteristics in the distinct stages of national history.

In the sixteenth century, although the Catholic kings coercively imposed castilian along with Catholicism in the Iberian Peninsula, they lacked the capacity of doing this in New Spain. In the sixteenth and seventeenth centuries, the process of castilianization was in the hands of the Church through evangelization, in such a way that 'it wasn't until the second half of the eighteenth century that, by order of archbishop Lorenzana, backed by the King Carlos III, that it was tried, with little success, to outlaw the languages of the colonized' (Zavala, cited in De la Peña 2011, 73).

In the second half of the nineteenth century, after independence and once peace was achieved in the country, the governments of Benito Juárez (1867–1876) and Porfirio Díaz (1876–1910) encouraged the cultural integration of the emerging Mexican nation through castilianization and the teaching of the country's history. From the point of view of the dominant classes, either liberal or conservative, the vernacular languages were 'dialects incapable of expressing philosophical or scientific ideas' and therefore an obstacle to the progress and modernization of the country (2011, 74). Despite the efforts of the liberal governments to achieve universal alphabetization and castilianization, the moment when the Revolution broke out, only 5 percent of the population knew how to read or write (De la Fuente 2010).

The policies of alphabetization/castilianization of the country, a priority goal for the postrevolutionary governments of the first half of the twentieth century, were not homogeneous. To José Vasconcelos, secretary of Public Education (1921), the Latin culture, which materialized in Spanish, was the source of modern culture, and the native languages and linguistic diversity were a serious impediment for the progress and unification of the country (De la Peza 2015). According to Ramírez (1928) and Haviland (1982), during that period, Spanish was imposed in schools 'sometimes through drastic measures' (cited in De la Peña 2011, 74). At the core of the anthropological guild, the paradigmatic positions of Gamio in favor of castilianization and of Sáenz in favor of respect for linguistic diversity as different ways to achieve the integration of the indigenous peoples of the nation, clashed.

During the socialist government of President Lázaro Cárdenas (1934–1940), an 'advancement for a greater respect for the indigenous cultures and idioms' took place (González, cited in De la Peña 2011, 76), and the Autonomous Department of Indigenous Affairs (ADIA) was created. The ADIA made an agreement with the Summer Institute of Linguistics (SIL), which contributed significantly to the knowledge and systematization of grammar and writing of various native languages. This policy had no continuity; subsequent governments adopted different positions toward the indigenous languages and cultures: 'During the decade of 1940, the so-called policy of national unity of the Mexican government [. . .] encroached the action of the ADIA (officially suppressed in 1946)' (77). Substituting this autonomous organization, the National Indigenist Institute (INI) was created, which took charge of indigenous affairs, their languages, and cultures, as isolated problems of the national concert. The systematization and conservation of indigenous languages ultimately came down to a particular agreement between the SIL and the Bureau of Public Education (SEP, Secretaría de Educación Pública). From that moment on, the work of SIL was a reason for disputes and entrenched positions, due to its religious proselytism in favor of Protestantism.

During the government of President Luis Echeverria, with the educational reform of 1973, the state insisted again on the creation of a 'common mestizo identity.' This position emerged in the 5th article, fraction III of the education law that proposed the objective of 'reaching, through the teaching of the national language (that is, Spanish) a common language for all Mexicans,' although it added 'without undermining the use of the autochthonous languages' (82). In 1979, the SEP canceled the agreement and the SIL was expelled from the country on account of being accused of espionage for the CIA (77–80).

Within the framework of globalization process of the economy as part of the neoliberal policy of President Carlos Salinas de Gortari (1988–1994) in 1990, 'the Mexican government experienced the influence of an internationalist discourse driven during the last decades by the UNESCO and included in its conception of cultural [. . .] intangible [. . .] heritage the indigenous languages' (14). Within this context, in 1992 two significant modifications of the law were took place. First, 'Mexico adhered to the 169th convention of the International Labor Organization (ILO) by recognizing the right of the indigenous peoples to their languages and cultures [. . .]'; and second, 'reformed the 4th article of the Constitution, to recognize the multicultural nature of the nation 'sustained in the indigenous people' and the obligation of the State to protect their land, cultures and languages' (82).[6]

However, the Law of Education of 2013, agreed by the three majority parties in the Pact for Mexico, effectively ignores the cultural and linguistic differences and has been the subject of repudiation by sections of the union of workers of education in regions with the biggest indigenous populations (Morelos, Chiapas, Oaxaca, and Michoacán) due to its discriminatory and excluding character, unconnected to the reality of the native people, their cultures, and languages. The government of President Enrique Peña Nieto responded to the complaint of the teachers of the Coordinadora Nacional de Trabajadores de la Educación (CNTE)[7] by disqualifying the elementary education teachers through a media campaign of criminalization of the social protest and repressing the protestors (Cruz Montoya and Tadeo Sánchez 2014).

After more than 100 years of educational policies geared toward universal castilianization, the majority of Mexicans have lost their native languages and have no domain of Spanish. Even though the Mexican state has privileged Spanish as the national language for the purpose of public and political interaction, most Mexicans are functional illiterates and do not consider Spanish as their own language (De la Peza et al. 2014).

In summary, the teaching of the language constituted a fundamental tool of colonialism in the process of building the Mexican nation. Spanish was the privileged way to impose Western culture and Christian religion as the only truth through the prohibition, negation, and concomitant devaluation of the indigenous languages and native cultures, which were considered obstacles to progress and modernization.

Linguistic tactics of the indigenous people

> The spectacular success of the Spanish colonization with the indigenous races has been diverted by the use it was given. Submitted, even acquiescent, these indigenous people usually used the laws, practices or representations that were imposed by force or by seduction in very diverse methods from those pursued by the conquistadors; they did something different with them; they subverted them from the inside; not by denying them or transforming them (that also happened), but through a hundred ways of using them in the service of the rules, traditions or foreign convictions of colonization from which they could not escape. They metaphorized the dominant order: they made them work in another registry.
>
> (Michel de Certeau, La invención de lo cotidiano)

Thanks to the struggle of the native nations and to the diverse forms of confrontation, resistance, and cultural negotiation, 68 indigenous languages still exist in the national territory. De Certeau establishes a distinction between the notions of strategy and tactic to distinguish the preconceived and previously designed actions of the institutions of power from the actions of subjects that are in a disadvantageous position in face of the structures of power and domination. Despite the strategies of the powerful to impose Spanish as the national language, the native people deployed different tactics[8] of survival.

Among these tactics used by indigenous people, Aubage highlights first 'the displacement of a Náhuatl diglossia/other indigenous languages for the Spanish diglossia/Mexican languages' (1985, 38). Second are the indigenous cultures, even though they gave up the spaces in which the colonial language was imposed by the colonial power to assure political hegemony:

> The indigenous cultures [. . .] did not abandon commonplace communication, the communication proper to the settlement and that which was intended for community exchanges, the ritual and festive communication, etcetera. (38)

The third tactic developed by native language speakers comprised fencing the conceded spaces to the national language and separating them from the domestic and community aspects, domain reserved for the mother tongue. To contain the invasion that signified the imposition of the national language, the indigenous communities locked them in islets:

> [...] the school islet (when a monolingual education was practiced in the official language), the sanitary islet (if the community possessed a rural clinic), the bureaucratic islet of State (when the representatives of government organisms come to carry out their duties in the community). But all these islets [...] are fenced by another space of institutions. (40)

Native languages were kept alive in local and community spheres as a substantive and carrier role:

> [...] from the ethnic identity, the collective memory, the traditional political organization (system of positions), from the forms of mutual help so much as in collective work as in private work [...] from the cosmogonies and religious systems, from ritual practices and festivities, from traditional medicine, etcetera. (41)

As a result of the tension between the strategies of the powerful and the survival tactics of the communities, even though native languages and cultures have survived, they are isolated: the voices of the indigenous peoples are not heard in the public–political space; the words pronounced in their own language do not have a legitimate place of utterance in the public space. The Mesoamerican speakers were forced to contemporize 'with the relations of force established by the linguistic colonial policies' (38) and the linguistic tactics of negotiation/ resistance/opposition to the national language; they wove themselves surreptitiously 'into the modulations of silence' without showing their face 'in an impertinent matter' to prevent 'the aggressions of power'—colonial and postcolonial— that could not admit to 'be put in doubt or relativized' (41). The indigenous communities—at the same time as they were resisting, consenting, accepting, negotiating—learned the national language due to its potential significance for their economic and political survival.

During the 1990s, in the backdrop of the quincentennial 'celebrations' of the conquest of America, the indigenous peoples raised their voices, saying they had had enough. In a new effort to reverse the silence to which they were historically obliged, the Zapatista movement, together with the other indigenous communities, created a common national and international front and were able to, among other things, enact the General Law of Linguistic Rights of the Indigenous People in 2002. The law considers all native languages as national languages, 'part of the historic and cultural heritage of the country,' and recognizes 'the same rights to use, spread and develop' as Spanish (De la Peña 2011, 83). In the context of globalization and contemporary capitalist expansion, the state of languages— Spanish and native languages—and indigenous and mestizo cultures in Mexico are facing new challenges and possibilities.

The dispute for the language

The linguistic policy of the postrevolutionary Mexican state was characterized by the ambivalence and negotiation necessity while facing the languages—colonial and native—and they are situated in a doubly conflicting position when compared to Spanish from Spain and the native languages. Contradictions and ambivalences that are expressed in a paradigmatic way in the texts of Alfonso Reyes.

The essays gathered in the anthology *Nuestra lengua y otros cuatro papeles*,[9] according to Castañón, can be read 'as a sort of guide, indication or map' of the oeuvre of Reyes. The selected texts were written in different moments of the life of the intellectual Alfonso Reyes; his stance on indigenous languages and Spanish language changed in relation to the events that marked the process of institutionalization of the postrevolutionary Mexican state. The first four essays—Mexico en una nuez (1930, Mexico in a nutshell), Discurso por Virgilio (1930, Discourse by Virgil*)*, Nuestra lengua (1958, Our language), and Visión de Anáhuac (1915, Vision of Anáhuac)—discuss, directly and tangentially, 'the story of the Spanish language in relation with the Hispano-American culture and civilization, in particular from Mexico' (Castañón in Reyes 2009, 9–7) and, from my point of view, in them the ambivalences of the intellectuals and employees of the state against the legacy of the indigenous and colonial past in the conformation of the postrevolutionary Mexican state are expressed.

In the introduction of the anthology, Adolfo Castañón describes the stance adopted by Alfonso Reyes and Marin Luis Guzmán[10] in face of the Royal Academy of language—in two distinct and distant moments in time—as elements of context and keys to the reading of the texts that integrate the anthology. First, it refers to the criticism that Alfonso Reyes made on the Royal Spanish Academy in the reviews Los Mexicanismos and Nahuatlismos y Barbarismos, in which he highlights the value of the works by Darío Rubio.[11] In these reviews, the Mexican playwright describes the explicit rejection of the Royal Academy of Language[12] to include more than half of the proper expressions of Spanish from Mexico proposed by members of the Mexican Academy of Language in the twelfth edition of the Spanish language dictionary. Reyes highlights the importance of the contributions by Rubio, which he considers 'extremely useful' to 'unearth from the dictionaries of Spain so many and continuous errors they contain on American speech' (2009, 13–14).

Second, Castañón emphasizes the position of Martín Luis Guzmán[13] in the First Congress of the Spanish Academies of Languages in 1951. The Mexican writer and politician proposed that 'the American and Philippine Academies, corresponding to the Royal Spanish Academy, quit their association with the latter [. . .] and therefore fully assume the autonomy of no having to abdicate and the integral personality that is inalienable to them' (cited by Castañón, in Reyes 2009, 12–13).[14] Both stances, according to Castañón 'contribute to the valorization of our American ways of using Spanish, clearly against the—frequently—rigid attitude of the Spaniard academics' (14). Both intellectuals express the ambivalent position of the Mexican state, which, on the one hand rejects the colonialism of

Is Spanish our language? 77

the Royal Academy and defends the Spanish of Mexico, and on the other hand adopts an ambivalent position toward the languages and cultures of indigenous peoples which, although it recognizes as part of the past and heritage of the nation, it does not recognize its value as living languages and cultures and actors of the present, and an obstacle for progress. Ambivalences and contradictions that are expressed in the texts of Alfonso Reyes, which I will presently analyze.

In the text Visión de Anáhuac (1915), Alfonso Reyes clearly shows his ambivalence on the conquest of Mexico and the subsequent process of civilization. The young Mexican intellectual who was banished[15] shares the amazement of the Spanish soldiers when contemplating from the cusps of the mountains the City of Tenochtitlan settled between two lakes in the Valley:

> It was then when, in an enviable time of amazement, dazed by the snow peaked volcanoes, the men from Cortés ('dust, sweat and iron'), took a peek over that orb of sonority and brilliance—spacious circus of mountains. Upon their feet in a mirage of crystals, the colorful city extended, all of it emanating from the temple, its radiant streets prolonging the edges of the pyramid.
>
> (Reyes 2009, 116)

From the lecture of the testimonies of the conquistadors on the grandeur of the Empire of Moctezuma, Reyes refers with nostalgia to the prevailing order of the city of Tenochtitlan when Cortés arrived, the material abundance and the indigenous cultural wealth that prevailed before the conquest; the sweetness of the language, the subtlety and harmony of several indigenous expressions:

> The people come and go on the shores of the canals [. . .] Conversations are lively without shouting: the race has refined hearing, and, sometimes, it is spoken in secret. Heard are some sweet clicks; vocals flow, and consonants tend to blend. Chatting is a glad singing. Those 'x's, those 'tl's, those 'ch's that alarm us so much when writing, slip through the lips of the indian with the softness of *aguamiel*.
>
> (118)

Reyes describes the wild beauty of the Valley of Anáhuac—the austere, exuberant, and savage nature—at the same time characterizing and lamenting the devastation of that natural wealth, that is, the 'desiccation of the Valley,' which started in 1449 and partially concluded in 1900:

> Three races have worked in it, and almost three civilizations—there is very little in common between the viceroyal organism and the prodigious political fiction that gave us thirty years of august peace [. . .] From Netzahualcóyotl, to the second Luis de Velasco, and from him to Porfirio Díaz, there seems to run the idea of drying the land. Our century found us still performing the last shovelful and opening the last ditch.
>
> (113)

Reyes points out to the violence in the Spanish conquest that destroyed the indigenous culture and of which only some written documents of 'the most meticulous eponymous legends and also the rules of traditions . . . all poems written in the Náhoa language [. . .] which the indians sang during their festivities . . .' (131)—learned by memory, repeated orally, transmitted from generation to generation—remain. Despite the censure of the church, the 'altered and indirect' testimony of the missionaries over the indigenous poems offer 'a shade of the lustful sensibility that isn't, really, proper to the Spanish missionaries' (132). Nevertheless, Reyes considers that the archeological recovery of such fragments of the indigenous culture will never compensate 'the loss of the indigenous poetry as a general and social phenomenon' (131), a definitive, irreparable, and insurmountable loss.

In the text, Reyes expresses his ambivalence on the pre-Colombian civilization destroyed by the conquest war, refers to the indigenous people as 'graceful and cruel people,' and refers to two moments of his discourse to the practice of human sacrifices that prevailed when the conquistadors arrived: 'Upon them, in some dark gory rite, reached—wailing—the complaint of the shawm and, multiplied by echo, the savage beat of the drum' (117). A few paragraphs later, he adds: 'the exposed skulls, and the ominous testimonies of sacrifice, soon avert the Christian soldier, who in exchange describes the fair with detail' (119).

In Visión de Anáhuac, Reyes characterizes the tragic story of the nation by the recurrent oscillation between authoritarianism and anarchy, and expresses his ambivalence in face of a civilizing process imposed by the authoritarian regimes like the Porfiriato, which he assesses as 'a political fiction that gave us thirty years of august peace' (113) in spite of having contributed to the destruction of the beauty of the valley: 'When the creators of the desert finish their work, the social horror bursts' (114).

The text finishes with his theory on history; he takes distance on the one hand of 'those who dream in absurd perpetuations of the indigenous traditions' and on the other hand on those who insist 'on the perpetuations of the Spanish ones.' What constitutes the nation is a 'common soul' carved by emotion before the natural shared entourage and the evocation of legends and indigenous myths transformed into tradition by an act of political will:

> it joins us with the race of yesterday, without speaking of blood, the community of effort to tame our wild and rough nature . . . we are also joined by the much more profound community of the *everyday emotion before the same natural object*. The clash of sensibility with the same world carves, begets the common soul. The poet sees the reverberation of the moon in the snow of the volcanoes, the specter of Doña María cut out over the sky, stalked by the shadow of the Archer of the stars; or dreaming of the copper ax on which edge lie the heavens; or seems to listen, in the vacant field, the bleak weeping of the twins which the goddess dressed in white carries on her back: let us not deny the evocation, let us not waste the legend. If that tradition was unknown to us, it somehow is in our hands, and only we can dispose of her. (137)

The nostalgia that Alfonso Reyes felt for the pre-Colombian indigenous culture in 1915 changes as the postrevolutionary Mexican state is consolidated.[16] In México en una Nuez, Reyes takes distance from the indigenous civilizations ruled by the Aztecs during the arrival of the conquistadors, and judges them as 'ancient and mysterious civilizations, whose traditions they themselves had started to misunderstand, emptying it little by little of its moral content . . .' (1930, 19).

The indigenous people were defeated due to 'their isolation from the rest of the world' in which they were found during the arrival of the Spaniards, 'which placed them . . . in notorious conditions of inferiority . . .' (19). For Reyes, the conquest, mestizaje and the civilizing process in due course, derived from the colonization, is part of the history of humankind's progress and the tragic fate of the nation:

> Over three centuries the races mix as they can and the colony reigns [. . .] Meanwhile, deafly—the Indians on the bottom, Spaniards on the top, and in the middle the stately and arrogant creoles and the smart and subtle mestizos—the new being of the country spawns.
>
> (22)

The ambivalent judgment on the Spanish conquest expressed in Vision de Anáhuac is diluted in the texts of 1930, where he expresses his conviction over the superiority of Western civilizations, which imposed and depravedly destroyed the Mesoamerican civilizations when the Spaniards arrived—civilizations for which 'we no longer have a moral representation . . . but only a fragmentary vision'; cultures that he considered as disappeared and to which he refers with irony: 'in present day Mexico nobody is willing to sacrifice smoky hearts for the sake of ferocious divinities, smearing hair with blood and dancing to the rhythm of hollow logs' (50).

In *Discurso for Virgilio*,[17] Reyes highlights the importance of the lecture of the classics as a fundamental factor in the conformation of the modern and civilized Mexican nation. Against the indigenist standings that he implicitly refers to, he mentions that 'We should not deceit ourselves any longer or disturb the people with pernicious charlatanism' (50). For him, the autochthonous are not the pre-Colombian indigenous cultures—overrun by Western Latin civilization, which he considers superior—and of which only remains are left: 'a great deposit of raw material, objects, forms, colors, sounds, that need to be incorporated and dissolved in the fluid of a culture . . .' (49–50).

The autochthonous is the mixture of the substrate of the native cultures and the Latin-European culture to which he refers metaphorically as the crescent of a river—that washes but also tows and razes what it finds on its path—that runs over land in its path toward the sea:

> up until today the only waters that have washed us are—derived and shaded in Spanish up where history wants—the Latin waters . . . the Mexican spirit is in the color of the Latin water, just as it reached us, it acquired here, in our home, while running during three centuries licking the red clays of our land.
>
> (50)

Tributary to the European ideas of Herder and Vico, Alfonso Reyes claims Latinity as heritage and as a project for the postrevolutionary Mexican nation. He criticizes the dominant positivism, instituted with the secular education in public schools that, in the interest of development of scientific thought, 'uprooted every plant from the humanities' and the liberal standings—in other words, most university academics, a group in which he includes himself—that reject Latin because they consider it 'religious archaism,' controlled by the church and nurtured in 'schools full of priests' attended by the conservative sectors and that are referred to as 'the defeated classes of politics' (47). Reyes proposes as an education policy 'to return to ones' own, to what is Castilian' and to the profound knowledge of Spanish through Latin, 'the language of Virgil' that exists 'in the origin of our language,' and consequently to the study of etymologies:[18]

> the roots of the words—substrates of the mental experiences of a whole civilization . . . this decent from the hidden deposits of our collective psychology, that immersion into the communicating vessels of the subconscious where each man is a graft of ancestors.
>
> (54–5)

The roots of the words for Reyes, as much as for Herder, are a privileged track to access the origin of our own thoughts, feelings, and creativity (Herwitz 2012, 44–45). They consider the national language as a 'bank' of the archive of cultural values collected in time and which are transmitted from generation to generation, a privileged device of memory through which citizens gather around traditions, symbols, and rituals that celebrate and bestow a sense of unity to the national community of the present (47–48). His stance on Latin culture in his Discurso por Virgilio is in contradiction with that which he postulated 15 years earlier in his Visión de Anáhuac. Contradictions and ambivalences are expressed in the linguistic policies of different postrevolutionary governments, insisting on the unification of Mexicans around Spanish as a national language.

Spanish, our language

In El español, nuestra lengua,[19] Reyes expresses in a more finished way the evolutionist and neo-colonial theory of languages and Spanish as a national language through which the linguistic politics of Mexico have been sustained. The text is structured in four sections: Generalities; Latin and Romances; Spanish; America and Mexico. In the first part, Reyes raises his theoretical conception about language; he defines, describes, and explains the human faculty of language, its manifestation in the diversity of languages that exists and have existed, its relationship with thought and with scientific and popular knowledge, and its variations in each time and place. Here, he returns to the metaphor of the river used in previous texts to speak of language:

> This variability of language is not a unique consequence of the variability of time and space; language, running like a river through different streams

(different natural environments, regions where residuals of previous different languages remain, or that suffered invasions from different people with a diverse idiom, or simply contacts or vicinities with different foreign groups) carry diverse flavors and nuances in its way; either in the construction of phrases, or in the form of the words, or in pronunciations, accents, tonalities and ways of speaking.

(Reyes 2009, 94)

In the next sections, he presents an evolution of Spanish from its origins—as a Romance language derived from the confrontation between imposed Latin by the Roman Empire against local languages—and its subsequent consolidation as a 'universal' language due to the imperialistic expansion of Spain as much in the Iberian Peninsula as in the Colonies, which gave way to the particular forms of Spanish in America and in Mexico:

From 1525 forward, we enter the Golden Century, and the great imperial expansion of Spain reflects itself in the new musculature of the language. Spanish has become a universal language [. . .] As a result of emigration and conquests, the Spanish language—other than being spoken in the Peninsula—is presently spoken in our continental and insular Americas.

(100)

In the last section, Reyes talks about the specificity of Mexican Spanish, highlighting some distinctive features of pronunciation, vocabulary, phrasal construction, and stylistic tendencies among which he emphasizes:

the tendency to soften the j . . . the tendency of converting the ll and the y into a sonorous French g . . . and to articulate with excessive difficult pronunciations . . . The use and abuse of diminutives. . . the abominable vice of pet wording 'este' everywhere.

(105)

Mexican Spanish is a 'mixture'[20] resulting from different ways of speaking peninsular Spanish imposed by the conquest, which displaced the distinct indigenous languages and cultures that left their mark not only in the vocabulary but in other forms of Mexican speech, 'more social than linguistic' like:

[. . .] the predominant desire to speak in mid-tones without raising the voice so much . . . the natural tendency of having a very strong position in phrases and their coherent construction . . . a *je ne sais quoi* of the national courtesy that has managed to save itself in spite of violent social transformations.

(106)

In the last part of the text, Reyes assures 'the linguistic conquest of Mexico has not finished yet'; nevertheless, he does not assume the opinion as his own.

Through the phrase 'it has been said,' which precedes this opinion, he attributes the phrase to a subject of general and indefinite enunciation, giving voice to the common sense of the epoch in his text. He also highlights the existence of a *duel* among 'the academic' and 'the colloquial' common in all languages.[21] Reyes emphasizes the exaggerated efforts of some Hispano-American speakers to 'speak with decency up to gentility' and a major resistance to 'neologisms' than 'the public and the Spaniard readers', and questions himself: 'Could it be, that as assured, America feels less of an owner of Spanish than Spain?' (107). A hypothesis that, although it may seem farfetched, would be very useful to consider the relationship between Mexicans and the Spanish language.

As a conclusion

The texts united in the anthology *Nuestra lengua y otros cuatro papeles* reveal the intermediate and ambivalent inscriptions of the Mexican[22] intellectual Reyes on metropolitan colonialism, languages, and local culture. Employing the metaphor of the river—recurring in Vision de Anáhuac (1915) and Discurso por Virgilio (1930), where he refers to the Latin civilization and Spanish as the inheritance of the Spanish conquest—he synthesizes his theory of language and the evolution of languages. His theory on Spanish as our language—the language of Mexicans— is drawn on the conception of Western history, Kantian and Darwinist, and at the same time, universal, lineal, and evolutive of the *progress* of humankind. Though it describes the conflicts between the colonial and creole elites (represented by the clash between the Royal Spanish Academy and the Mexican Academy of Language and between the colonial language and local languages) derived from the wars of conquest and colonization, he simultaneously possesses an evolutionary perspective that considers the life of the languages—particularly the domain of Spanish compared to indigenous languages—the result of *natural selection*. From his point of view, indigenous languages, dominated by Spanish, would be destined to disappear.

The ambivalent position of Alfonso Reyes on Latin culture and Spanish as a national language in relation to native languages and cultures is a paradigmatic expression of conflicts and ambivalences of the postrevolutionary Mexican state on the policies of patrimonialization of languages.

As shown throughout the discussion, considering the mother tongue as a natural, intrinsic property is a polemical subject. Even though it is true that an essential alienation of language exists, that the language always comes from outside, that it is always the language of some other, 'from it we cannot deduce that all exiles are equivalent' (Derrida 1997, 82).

The question deliberated by Reyes whether Americans, specifically Mexicans, feel *lesser* ownership of Spanish than Spaniards, is without a doubt very keen and pertinent. Even though, as pointed out by Derrida, languages are not owned by anyone, as a result of the violent and despotic army of the colonial power, that language, which is always the language of some other for everyone, appears as the language of the master. The master, the colonial power, 'does not possess as its own what it notwithstanding calls *its language*; . . . because language is not a natural good, it can historically by itself through violence and cultural encroachment . . . *fake that it appropriates it to impose it as its own*' (38). Spanish, the 'silent and silenced' heritage of the father, the conquistador, supplants the native (maternal) languages and establishes in the mother tongue but as the language of the other, from that absolute other: the colonizer.

In summary, the evolution, growth, and disappearance of languages is not a *natural process*; it is part of the global, national, and local political history. The tacit or explicit prohibition of native languages in the scholastic apparatus and in the different spaces of public life 'represents . . . so much of a cause as an effect of the growing futility, of the organized marginalization of these languages' (57).

The weakening of the indigenous languages has been an explicitly sought-out effect from, first, the Spanish colonial policies and, later, by the neo-colonial policies of the Mexican state. At the same time, the exclusion and discrimination of the indigenous languages and the dialectal varieties of popular Spanish has hindered the complete existence of Mexican Spanish. The expansion or disappearance of languages has been the result of the conquest, the colonization, and the prolongation of internal colonialism.

Notes

1 Published by the National Council of Culture and Arts in 2009, 50 years after the death of the author. The anthology includes five essays written between 1915 and 1958: *Visión de Anáhuac* (1915), *México en una nuez* (1930), *Discurso por Virgilio* (1930), *Memorias de cocina y bodega* (1945), and *Nuestra lengua* (1958).
2 Adolfo Castañón is one of the many academics and great experts of the oeuvre of Alfonso Reyes. Among his works, we distinguish *Caballero de la voz errante* (2012).
3 Heritage and patrimony are used indistinguishably from one another throughout the text (TN).
4 The colonial policies of language consisted in 'reducing the languages to One, in other words, to the hegemony of the homogeneous' (Derrida 1997, 58).
5 'I call strategy the assessment (or manipulation) of the relations of force that are made possible when a subject of will and power (a corporation, an army, a city, a scientific institution) turns to be isolatable. The strategy proposes a susceptible circumscribed *place* as something *proper* and for as being the base to administrate the relationships with an *exteriority* . . . of goals or of threats' (De Certeau 1996, 42).
6 It seems fitting to point out that this law is dead letter. The Mexican Congress, in September 2013, approved, in spite of the opposition of the left, secondary laws on energy that gave absolute right to the President to deprive the indigenous peoples of their lands in favor of national or transnational corporations to exploit the mineral resources as well as petroleum and natural gas.
7 Independent union organization, dissident from the National Union of Education Workers (SNTE, Sindicato Nacional de Trabajadores de la Educación), which pertains to the corporative structure of the Institutional Revolutionary Party (PRI, Partido Revolucionario Institucional).
8 According to De Certeau: 'The tactic is 'an art of the weak' [. . .] it is a movement at the inside of the field of vision of the enemy [. . .] they are procedures with value due to the pertinence they bestow upon time: in the circumstances where the precise moment of an intervention transforms into a favorable situation, in the speed of the movements that change the organization of space, in the relationships between

84 *María del Carmen de la Peza*

successive moments of a dirty trick, in the possible crossovers of duration and heterogeneous rhythms' (1996, 40). The bets on the place (the strategies) and on time (the tactics) distinguish the ways of acting of the powerful and of those found in a weak position in face of the former.

9 Published by the National Council of Culture and Arts in 2009, 50 years after the death of Alfonso Reyes.
10 Members of The Athenaeum of Youth.
11 Mexican playwright and member of the National Academy of Language.
12 In the year 1884, of the 1,285 proposals by the Mexican Academy as contribution to the twelfth edition of the Dictionary, 'the Spanish Academy rejected 633, and the 652 remaining entered the Dictionary through modification, therefore the definitions are inexact' (cited by Castañón, in Reyes 2009, 13–14).
13 Member of the National Academy of Language since 1940, 'friend and ex-companion of Alfonso Reyes at the Ateneo group' (Castañón, in Reyes 2009, 12–13).
14 The speeches that were announced on April 27 and May 5 and 8 were collected under the title *Batalla por la autonomía* (Battle for autonomy), in his complete oeuvres (12–13).
15 The text *Visión de Anáhuac* was written in Madrid in 1915. In note 12, Castañón summarizes the historical context during which Reyes wrote the text: 'barely two years have passed since the Decena Trágica; two other years still have to pass for the Constitution of 1917 to be promulgated, and we are off by several years so that since Plutarco Elías Calles the 'parenthesis or anarchy' is closed and the process of institutionalization starts' (140). In 1913, he witnessed the death of his father Bernardo Reyes—of which he felt personally responsible. The General from the Porfirio Díaz regime fell during the battle of the coup d'etat driven by General Victoriano Huerta, who participated against President Gustavo Madero. There was personal and national drama, which he expressed in his theater work 'Ifigenia Cruel' (1924). The participation of his father in the coup marked his political and intellectual career. In 1914, Alfonso Reyes was obligated to take exile in Spain (1914–1924) where he eventually started incorporating into the national political life as a diplomat during several governments that emanated from the revolution. Between 1924 and 1939, as part of the diplomatic team of the Mexican government, he continued doing his literary work and became an essential figure of the intellectual sphere of Latin America. When he returned to Mexico in 1939, by order of President Lázaro Cárdenas, he established the Casa de España which later—due to a nationalist dispute—changed its name to El Colegio de México.
16 'Since 1920 a clearer idea of the national reconstruction is glimpsed, and the governments succeed in a more continuous fashion. Uprisings fail and there are more often lead by less prominent figures. The use of new constitutional precepts gives way to trials, conflicts, misunderstandings in the country and abroad, which little by little calm themselves and take, approximately, the way of law' (Reyes 2009, 37).
17 Written for the homage of the poet Virgil in the second millennia of his birth and organized by the SEP under the order of Commander in Chief Plutarco Elías Calles, who he mentions indirectly in the text: 'The president exposed me . . . and insisted in the urgency of showing the advantages and pleasures of the agriculture of our peasant people, addicted first by the exclusive attention that the Spanish Conquest gave to the working of the mines, and intimidated later by the practical slavery to which they were reduced in the system of big haciendas [. . .] This is how the spirit of Virgil seems to beat amongst the most vivacious concerns of Mexico and sheds light on our agrarian policies' (56).
18 In the context of the procedure of modernization and facing the anguish of the loss of the religious values that was generated by the process of secularization, philology and science, which search for linguistic roots of the words tracing back the genealogic tree

of languages, achieved a key role in the recovery of the common lost origin, as foundation of the nation.
19 Mature text by Alfonso Reyes, written in 1958, a year before his death on December 27, 1959.
20 Originally 'mezcolanza' (TN).
21 In this context, he moderates the critical position he had adopted during other times on the conservative stance of the Royal Spanish Academy. He approves the caution of the Academy 'in face of neologisms, regionalisms, and Americanisms' and opposes those who 'desire a dictionary with fully open doors to everything that is said and spoken' (107). Even though it is true that in democratic societies, just as the languages and laws 'of the sovereign people always has a right to be modified or changed for others,' 'if it is done everyday they would never live according to civilized policies' (108).
22 Mexican from a family that supported Porfirio Díaz, he studied Law at the University of Mexico in the Western tradition and continued his literary formation in the Spanish metropolis with the famous Hispanic philologist Menéndez Pidal.

References

Aubage, Laurent. 1985. 'Las estrategias de resistencia de las lenguas precolombinas en México'. *Comunicación y cultura en América Latina* 14 (Julio): 37–44.
De Certeau, Michel. 1996. *La invención de lo cotidiano. 1. Artes de hacer.* trans. Alejandro Pescador. México: Universidad Iberoamericana. 1990.
De la Fuente, Juan Ramón. 2004. 'Presentación' In *Discurso inaugural de la Universidad Nacional*, ed. Justo Sierra. México: UNAM.
De la Peña, Guillermo. 2011. 'La antropología, el indigenismo y la diversificación del patrimonio cultural de México'. In *La antropología y el patrimonio cultural de México*, ed. Guillermo De la Peña. México: CONACULTA.
De la Peza, Ma. del Carmen, and Lilia Rebeca Rodríguez Torres. 2011. 'Políticas de la lengua en México: del plurilingüísmo y la multiculturalidad al monolingüismo.' In *La investigación en didáctica de la lengua y la literatura: situación actual y perspectivas de futuro*, ed. Ma. del Pilar Nuñez Delgado, and José Rienda. Madrid: SEDLL.
De la Peza, Ma. del Carmen, Lilia Rebeca Rodríguez Torres, Iliria Hernández Unzueta, and Ricardo Rubio. 2014. 'Evaluación de competencias de lectoescritura en alumnos de primer ingreso a la Universidad Autónoma Metropolitana-Xochimilco'. *Argumentos* 27(74) (Enero-abril): 117–49.
De la Peza, Ma. del Carmen. 2015. 'El cantinflismo como síntoma: pensar la nación desde sus márgenes'. In *Nación y Estudios Culturales. Debates desde la poscolonialidad*, ed. Mario Rufer, and Ma. del Carmen de la Peza. México: Itaca/UAMX.
Derrida, Jacques. 1997. *El monolingüísmo del otro.* trans. Horacio Pons. Buenos Aires: Manantial.
Esposito, Roberto. 2003. *Communitas. Orígen y destino de la comunidad.* trans. Carlo Rodolfo Molinari Marotto. Buenos Aires: Amorrortu.
Herwitz, Daniel. 2012. *Heritage, culture, and politics in the poscolony.* New York: Columbia University.
Montoya, Cruz, and Tadeo Sánchez. 2014. *Magisterio en Movimiento 2013: métodos de comunicación y ataque mediático'.* Tesis de Licenciatura de Comunicación. México: UAMX.
Reyes, Alfonso. 2009. *Nuestra lengua y otros papeles.* ed. Alfonso Castañón. México: CONACULTA.

5 Cultural management and neoliberal governmentality
The participation of Perú in the exhibition *Inca—Kings of the Andes*[1]

Gisela Cánepa

Introduction: the case study, the approach, and the questions

In October 2013, the exhibition *Inca—Kings of the Andes* was inaugurated at the Linden Museum Stuttgart, the Staatliches Museum für Völkerkunde, Baden–Württemberg, Germany. The exhibition displayed pieces that belonged to collections of several European museums, Peruvian public and private museums, and private collectors. As I will discuss in more detail later, the exhibition was a success in many aspects, which can not only be attributed to the particular interest that the German public might have for the Inca, which is rooted in German colonial imagination on South America (Onken 2014), shaped by academic and public discourses since the nineteenth century to the present (Gänger 2014; Noack 2015). Instead, I want to argue that its success can be explained by the way the exhibition was conceived and managed, which followed the mandates imposed by the cultural policies that have emerged in the frame of neoliberal governmentality and that count for the fact that in the context of globalizing forces, museums increasingly operate as business corporations (Karp et al. 2006). These promote the design of collaborative enterprises that imply the exchange of museum artifacts, experts, and knowledge; and entail requirements of efficacy in terms of cultural and institutional representation and visibility, and of economic efficiency. Therefore, one can argue that as an instance of neoliberal governmentality, the Inca exhibition proved to perform efficaciously and efficiently.

Furthermore, cultural regimes in general and heritage regimes in particular are becoming increasingly neoliberal (Yudice 2003), instituting new regimes of power that operate as new 'politics of truth that produces new forms of knowledge and expertise that govern new domains of regulation and intervention' (Coombe 2012, 382). In that regard, I want to argue that the Inca exhibition invites us to ask questions regarding (i) a particular form of dealing with heritage and knowledge that can be drawn from the exhibition; (ii) the way neoliberal governmentality operates as a cultural regime; and (iii) the possibilities and restraints that such regime imposes upon differently positioned participants to renegotiate their place within local, national, and international power relations.

The largest part of the artifacts that were displayed at the Inca exhibition belonged to the Linden Museum, which was founded in 1889 by the Society for Trade and Geography. In 1973, the museum was passed over to the Landesmuseums of the federal state of Baden–Württemberg, which are under the jurisdiction of the Ministry of Science, Research, and Art (Ministerium für Wissenschaft, Forschung und Kunst). The Linden Museum, as well as European museums in general, is heir to a colonialist tradition that governed the formation of archaeological and ethnological collections in Europe at the end of the nineteenth century and the beginning of the twentieth. These collections were acquired through purchases, donations, or expeditions that were organized by the museum in the late nineteenth century, allowing the narration of grand histories that were further instrumentalized by the propaganda apparatus of the colonial states.

Such an undertaking, intersected by scientific, commercial, and political interests, transformed Europe into the host and custodian of a worldwide and diverse cultural legacy, which was considered to be in danger of extinction, and in need of proper study. For the purposes of this article, and following on (Said 1978), I understand the colonial relationship between Europe and Latin America in terms of knowledge production and institutional arrangements, a field in which the creation of archaeological and ethnological collections and their management to date have played a central role.

Today, European ethnological museums are reviewing their agendas in the context of a globalized world where intercultural relations have acquired centrality both for thinking the cultural and political reality within Europe, as well as Europe's relationship with the world. In that sense, they have started to design new initiatives using the language of cultural diversity, inclusion, and participation. The Linden Museum is a member of the International Ethnographic Museum Network[2] and participates in the Sharing a World of Inclusion, Creativity and Heritage Project,[3] which are both cultural initiatives supported by EU programs.

The goal is to work across networks while developing reflective and inclusive museum practices that should contribute to the cultural and political reconfiguration of Europe, as well as to the promotion of a global intercultural dialogue. These initiatives, which can be framed within ongoing debates in the field or museum studies and museum practitioners (Karp and Levine 1991; Karp et al. 1992), seek to overcome the colonial bias of museum practices, working in a collaborative and participatory manner through the flow and exchange of experts, knowledge, and objects.

> This project includes ten European ethnographic museums, which have started to reflect on the need to redefine the role that museums play today. Created in the context of colonization, after independence they had to abandon their original function as showcases of exotic artifacts and as political propaganda [. . .] RIME, [. . .] has among its objectives the fight against exclusion, racism

and xenophobia, [...] while promoting intercultural dialogue. It is clear that museums, especially museums dealing with the cultural richness of other cultures, have a responsibility to preserve a shared heritage.[4] (Translated by the author)

However, following on Coombe s argument, efforts like those undertaken by the International Network of Ethnographic Museums involve new politics of truth, which 'legitimize new relations of power and knowledge as it creates new subjects positions for individuals and social groups, while fostering the articulation of collective subjectivities holding possessive relations to culture' (2012, 380). In that regard, the Inca exhibition of the Linden Museum constitutes an interesting case study that poses further questions, for example, regarding the implications that participating in such exhibitions has for those countries from which the exhibited artifacts originate. One might ask, what are the potentials, restraints, and paradoxes of such participation in terms of decolonizing processes in the context of global relations?

My aim in exploring *Inca: King of the Andes* is to focus less on the exhibition itself and more on the participation of Peru in it in order to inquire more specifically on the ways in which the terms of participation are defined and on the responses of Peruvian public and private institutions to the challenges posed by these emerging forms of heritage management. I also intend to discuss how collaborative enterprises operate in terms of neoliberal governmentality within Peru as well as internationally.

* * *

My interest in discussing the museum exhibition *Inca: Kings of the Andes* is part of a broader project where I am interested in reflecting on the formation of public subjectivities, the reinvention of national narratives and national projects, the process of defining and negotiating the terms of citizen participation, the constitution of political legitimacies and leadership, as well as in the emergence of new forms of knowledge and expertise. More precisely, I am trying to problematize on an emerging cultural regime, paying special attention to the way it is operating in Peru since the neoliberal reforms implemented by Alberto Fujimori in the early 1990s and in the postwar context.

I identify three principles that articulate new narratives and performativities in current Peruvian society, being constitutive of neoliberal governmentality. These are entrepreneurship—as a discourse and as pragmatics—and the imperative to participate that articulate new narratives and performativities in Peruvian society; *city branding* and *nation branding* that have become politics of state allowing the translation of the logics marketing and corporate management into forms of government; and the experiencing of citizenship and public interest. Working on two case studies and focusing on city branding (Cánepa 2012) and nation branding (Cánepa 2013), I have been trying to advance the discussion of neoliberalism as a cultural regime, exploring the way it operates at a local and a national level respectively. The Inca exhibition constitutes a third case study that allows me to locate the discussion within an international context.

For the staging of the Inca exhibition at the Linden Museum in Stuttgart, Peru was invited to participate in the exhibition at various levels: through the temporal loan of archaeological artifacts that belong to national and private collections, the internships of two Peruvian archaeologists at the museum, and the collaboration of Peruvian archaeologists as authors in the exhibition catalog and presenters in the international seminar organized as part of the exhibition program. Finally, the logo of the Peruvian nation brand was printed on different items like banners and the credit sheet of the exhibition catalogue. The exhibition itself, as well as the museum's facilities, were used to organize events where Peru was marketed as a tourist destination.

Peruvian participation in the exhibition involved the engagement of government and private institutions, as well as private agents, such as the Museum Directorate of the Ministry of Culture (*Dirección General de Museos del Ministerio de Cultura*), the National Museum of Peruvian Archaeology, Anthropology and History (*Museo Nacional de Arqueología, Antropología e Historia del Perú*— MNAAHP), the office for the promotion of Peruvian exports and tourism, of the Ministry of Foreign Trade and Tourism (*PromPerú*), and the private Museum Larco.

I will particularly focus on the participation of Peru in the exhibition by analyzing the relations and negotiations it engaged in with German institutions and actors, but especially by comparing the distinct performances of Peruvian public and private institutions. By doing so, I hope to analyze the impact that such international performance has at a national level. Furthermore, I will address these negotiations and different responses by paying attention to the particular issue of the exchange and loan of collection items, since I consider it a critical instance where knowledge about and possession of culture can be performed nationally and internationally. Following Clarke's (2012) discussion on the work of governing, I see these performances as critical sites where one can observe neoliberal governmentality operating through heritage management.

The Inca exhibition: defining new domains and terms of performance

The Inca exhibition was an initiative of the Linden Museum Stuttgart in partnership with the Lokschuppen Ausstellungszentrum—Rosenheim—Bayern, which is a public private initiative of the city of Rosenheim, managed by the Veranstaltung & Kongress GmbH. Rosenheim. Due to the huge number of visitors that attend their federal exhibitions (Landesausstellungen), Lokschuppen has established itself as one of the 10 most successful exhibition halls in Germany. On its web page one can read:

> The exhibition center in Rosenheim is also famous for its national exhibitions and special exhibitions which combine sound scientific knowledge with elaborate, attractive displays.

The exhibition center has built a good career for itself, turning from an engine shed in 1858 into the successful, nationally significant crowd puller which focuses on quality that it is today.[5]

The partnership of the Linden Museum with the Lokschuppen exhibition center has allowed having two main exhibitions sites, as well as to reach a public that is already acquainted with and loyal to the cultural offer of the latter. *Inca: King of the Andes* was inaugurated on October 12, 2013, at the Linden Museum where it remained until March 16, 2014, and was then moved to Rosenheim for a second period that lasted from April 11, 2014, to November 23, 2014. Such collaboration permitted a longer exhibition period, as well as obtaining a larger space, which facilitated access to a wider public. Both institutions also shared the costs of a full color illustrated catalog. Additionally, the project included a large number of public and private sponsors, and involved public authorities of the highest level. The Inca exhibition was under the umbrella of the mayor of the city of Stuttgart, the president of the federal state of Baden–Württemberg, and German President Joachim Gauck.

According to statements by museum director Inés De Castro, exhibition curator Doris Kurella—also responsible for the Latin America section of the museum—as well as many other actors involved in the exhibition, which I collected from informal conversations and media coverage, *Inca: King of the Andes* was the first and most comprehensive exhibition presented in Europe, devoted exclusively to the Inca. What is emphasized by the organizers of the exhibition when making this statement is that no previous exhibition had focused entirely on the Inca, since previous museum exhibitions had used the name 'Inca' but displayed archaeological pieces of other Andean civilizations that developed before the Inca.

The goal was to fill a knowledge gap among the European public regarding the Inca civilization by assuring an exhibition with high academic standard and up-to-date knowledge on the topic. Although the Linden Museum owns an important and valuable collection of Inca material culture, the curators agreed that museum artifacts of other European and Peruvian collections had to be included to meet the goal. The exhibition entailed the loan of archaeological artifacts from nine German museums, six European museums, three Peruvian museums, and one Peruvian private collector.

Collaborative work not only involved the flow of objects but also of people and knowledge. Thanks to a scholarship from the German Academic Exchange Office (Deutscher Akademischer Austauschdienst, DAAD), two young Peruvian archaeologists had an internship at the Linden Museum during the time the preparation of the exhibition began. Both of them and a German graduate student who was doing a professional internship are listed as research assistants in the credits of the catalog. European and Latin American experts participated as speakers at the symposium *New Perspectives on the Incas*, held from March 3 to March 5, 2014, at the Linden Museum, or as authors of articles included in the catalog. Some also contributed to the program of cultural activities that ran parallel to the exhibit.

Nevertheless, the academic goal had to be fulfilled in accordance with the mission statement of the museum. Two statements from the mission statement, for example, are: 'We provide a forum for dialogue between people of different cultures. Our visitors are the life of our museum. We strive to make it attractive to them.'[6] These pose a set of different imperatives on the museum that go beyond the foundational principles that defined the museum as an institution advocated to the production of scientific knowledge and its dissemination, thus redefining it as an institution in the service of the community and its development (Borea 2006).

So, for example, the need to borrow exhibit objects of other museums has to be problematized beyond the academic argument. Looking at the Inca exhibition and its beautiful and colorful catalog, one recognizes a museographic design that foregrounds a visual and sensory experience, aimed at high aesthetic and recreational standards, which requires the display of unique pieces. In this regard, it is not always clear if a certain artifact was chosen because of its aesthetic value or its expositive value in order to communicate new knowledge about the Inca society. Although this aesthetic turn within ethnological museums continues to challenge several of its foundational principles and give rise to unpleasant debate, it has proved effective for the ethnological museum to compete within a broader and more productive art and heritage industry. And this has been the commitment of the Linden Museum, which also is in tune with the fact of have chosen the Lockschuppen Ausstellungszentrum.

Furthermore, in accordance with the goals from the mission statement of the museum, two cultural programs were organized (October–December 2013 and January–March 2014), which were offered to visitors in parallel to the exhibition. These programs included lectures, activities for children, concerts, Peruvian food, and guided visits addressed to diverse audiences. These were designed with the intention of attracting a broad public through not only a visually appealing proposal but also a sensorial experience of Inca society. Various special travel packages to visit the exhibition were offered, which included travel discounts with the German Railway (Deutsche Bahn) to reach Stuttgart, museum entrance tickets, and hotel accommodation. On the web site of Arbeitsgemeinschaft Lateinamerika (Arge-LA), a platform that promotes and supports tourism to Latin America, the following can be read:

> Likewise, you can book special guided tours that can be nicely complemented for example with the Peruvian national drink Pisco Sour or supplemented by a potato tasting. Also exciting is the combination package with a visit to the Zoological and Botanical Garden 'Wilhelma Stuttgart,' to see the resident vicuñas and alpacas after the exhibition, which is led by the Zoo curator. Also, exclusive evening tours are available.[7]
>
> (Translated by the author)

The exhibition was not only announced and promoted through the museum's web site,[8] but also through newspapers and magazines. Magazines like *Geschichte* and *National Geographic-Germany* devoted their front pages to the Inca exhibition. Andreas M. Gross, president of Arge-LA, lamented that the Inca exhibition did not make it to the cover of *Der Spiegel* in its edition of the week October 14, 2013:

> In October, the Inca almost made it to the front page of the 'Der Spiegel'—were it not for this bishop with his freestanding new bathtub. At the last minute he managed to appear on the front page of the Hamburg magazine, but Matthias Schulz six page long fascinating story 'The sons of the Andes' still was an absolute highlight of this Spiegel edition.
> (América Latina. Das Magazin für Lateinamerika 2013, 65)[9]

The planning of the media coverage was enhanced by the collaboration between Linden Museum and Arge-LA. The museum is a cultural partner of the Arge-LA, and could count on the long-term relationship that the latter holds with PromPerú, which contributed to negotiating the terms of the collaboration. In exchange for the funding of a press trip to Peru that included a specialized press team and the director of Linden Museum, PromPerú and Arge-LA could organize a series of activities within the framework of the exhibition and in the museum building, in order to promote Peru as a tourist destination and to offer information and advice to representatives of travel agencies.

Several features of the exhibition can be outlined: (i) its emphasis on collaborative work that enables public/private partnerships; the circulation of objects, persons, and knowledge; interdisciplinary work and the itinerant character of the exhibition; (ii) its reliance on innovation, creativity, and commercial vision; (iii) the positioning or branding of the exhibition as per marketing criteria, which implies wide media coverage, itinerancy of the exhibition, and offering of a diversified cultural experience that might be appealing to a diverse public.

Further, this expresses very well the new mandates governing cultural management today, which can be identified as constitutive of a performative order where principles of planning and evaluation results are privileged, while the cultural objects and repertoires are mainly defined as resources (Yudice 2003). With regard to heritage management, Coombe (2012, 378) says:

> Certainly we are witnessing a new dominance of market ideologies in heritage management and in its means of 'valuation' with an increasing emphasis on *investment* in cultural resources and human capital so as to yield economic returns, adding value to them so as to encourage tourism, foster foreign direct investment, encourage product differentiation, and promote new commodification of 'cultural resources.'

The exhibition exceeded the expectations of the organizers. In words of Inés de Castro reported by the local newspaper *Oberbayerisches Volksblatt Heimatzeitung* (OVH) on November 24, 2014:

The success is the result of a professional and collaborative working partnership of two experienced and successful institutions. More than a quarter million people in Stuttgart and Rosenheim have visited the exhibition. The topic has been sensible to the taste of the audience.

(Translated by the author)

In informal conversations with officials of the cultural sector in Germany, I noted admiration as well as caution regarding the actions of the director of the Linden Museum for undertaking what has been considered a mega-project. On the one hand, his courage for taking several risks was highlighted and interpreted as an effort to transform the museum and cultural management itself, which resulted in an achievement in a context when many cultural institutions are facing cuts in their budget and human resources. On the other hand, certain decisions were questioned in the sense that they affect the very nature of the modern museum and its practices, considered to be principally an institution dedicated to the generation and dissemination of knowledge, and committed to the search for truth. The grand commercialization of the exhibition has been criticized, since it allowed for the repetition of a mystified tale, in which a series of clichés and stereotypes about the Inca civilization have been reiterated, and further replicated in the media (Noack 2015).

With regard to the last concern, which is also seen in the light of the goal of the exhibition to fill a gap regarding the knowledge of the German public about the Inca, I want to highlight two observations gathered during my fieldwork. The first refers to the last room of the exhibition, which is labeled *Descendants of the Inca*. It is a dark room where photographs of contemporary southern Andes as well as handicrafts are exhibited. The room is dominated by a screen on which images that document testimonies in different languages (Quechua, Spanish, and English) and of people of different origins currently living in Cuzco are projected. Their testimonies appear to answer the question about the value the Inca legacy has for them today. In these testimonies, the validity of the Inca heritage and the need to take responsibility for its preservation is exalted. While the images present us with a multicultural world, one supported by testimonies in three different languages and the voices of various subjects, the content of the testimonies recall a stereotyped interpretation of Inca society and legacy, which has been brilliantly summarized by Cecilia Méndez (1995) in the phrase *Incas yes, Indians no* (Translation by the author).

In the same vein, I was able to gather some opinions regarding the international seminar held at the end of the exhibition at the Linden Museum. It was argued that it should have been held before, since it presented new findings and debates on Inca society that could have enriched the exhibition itself. It is interesting to note that in the guided visit that I participated in during the last days of the exhibition in Stuttgart, the person in charge pointed to the fact that she has been updating her libretto in light of the latest contributions on the Inca that had been exposed at the seminar held just some weeks before.

These observations reveal a tension within the Inca exhibition, the curatorial work, and its management. On the one hand, there is the scientific purpose of communicating rigorously and at the highest standard the latest findings about Inca society, and on the other, the desire to reach a broad public with an attractive proposition. Since it is a public that is mainly familiarized with a preexisting and essentialized European ethnographic imagination, it is difficult to avoid repeating a number of clichés and stereotypes about Inca civilization when one tries 'to touch(ed) the taste of the audience' (OVB November 24, 2014). In other words, the efficacy of the museographic narrative derived from the reproduction of old narratives.

On the other hand, there is the tension resulting from the need to respond to the new requirements of performativity that government bodies such as ministries, or the culture committee of the EU imposed on museums in general and ethnological museums in particular, compromising the negotiation of scientific, commercial, and diplomatic agendas. The managing of these tensions as well as the paths that the realization of concrete projects will take depend on a number of circumstances that have to do with the availability of resources (the value of the museum's collections, budgets, institutional linkages, projects course); as well as with the expertise and backgrounds of its employees who must work increasingly in an interdisciplinary and collaborative manner, and who are ultimately the ones carrying out the projects. In that regard, it is worth mentioning that Dr. Inés de Castro has both an academic background as well as professional experience in the tourist sector.

Nevertheless, beyond the mentioned controversies about the Inca exhibition, for the people in charge of the Linden Museum and its collections, it had been worth taking the risk, since the success of the exhibition marked the repositioning of the museum in the state of Baden–Württemberg and in relation to German and European ethnological museums. The renowned newspaper *Stuttgarter Zeitung* gives credit to this achievement with the headline 'The Inca exhibition was the driving force in 2014':

> 'The exhibitions have attracted great interest from the public, the Inca exhibition was a success,' says the director of the Linden Museum, Inés de Castro. The Incas were previously scantly considered in ethnological museums; the Stuttgart exhibition was one of the first in Europe. Sixty percent of the museum visitors had come in the past year especially for the Inca exhibition to the city, says de Castro. 'This is an incredibly high praise for our house. Finally, the Linden Museum gets the recognition which it is entitled to,' says museum director (January 27, 2015).
>
> (Translated by the author)

The success of the exhibition, which was measured in terms of media coverage, public attendance, and institutional performance to achieve visibility and lead collaborative projects at national and international levels, had a demonstrative function, that argued for the viability of the museum in a globalized world, which is increasingly governed by principles of economic rationality. What is at stake in a museum project like the one I am discussing here is no longer the need to respond only to the mandates of rigor and scientific value that have governed the modern museum in general and ethnological museums in particular, but the ability to perform with success under a new legal, economic, and political order, as well as under new regimes of legitimacy and value. In this context, for example, management, design, and marketing, appear as new fields of knowledge and expertise.

In other words, the success of the exhibition stems from the ability and possibility to dramatize management itself, since such performance is constitutive of the very terms of valuation and legitimation that are put into play. Through such performance, the domains of regulation and action are not only defined and standardized, but acquire normative force. Within such logic, one can understand the efforts invested by the Lokschuppen Ausstellungszentrum, in order to get press coverage each time they reach a new milestone in terms of audience. This is linked to Clarke's (2012, 3) argument regarding the need of governments to perform.

> So, governments need to perform like governments, and this increasingly involves performing 'performance'—as something to be measured, managed and evaluated (thus creating new forms of governmental work: inspecting, auditing, measuring and data managing).

While the mandates ruling these new forms of management are dictated through a set of definitions and regulations by various governmental institutions at the local, national, and transnational level (the city of Stuttgart, the Ministry of Science, Research and Arts of the state of Baden–Württemberg, the EU, and UNESCO), museums are another instance of transnational governance through which these institutions exert their regulatory power. To the extent that the performativity of museums is evaluated and legitimized through quantifiable criteria such as media exposure or audience size, while their very performance works increasingly as a constitutive force that normalizes such principles, it can be argued that these performances operate under principles of economic pragmatics.

It is in this sense that we can understand this new management as an instance of neoliberal governmentality. Cultural management as neoliberal governmentality further implies the operating of a set of performativities that match the requirements of *efficacy* in terms of cultural and institutional representation and *efficiency* in terms of economic sustainability. The public recognition of the success of the Inca exhibition configures the Linden Museum as a referent and measure for what counts as high performance: a model to be followed. It is through such performance that the domains of regulation and action are not only defined and standardized, but acquire normative force. Thus, I want to argue, the Inca exhibition, allows the Linden Museum to perform *cultural possession*, while disputing its leadership in the world of museums.

I am drawing here on the notion of *possessing culture* as discussed by Coombe (2011). According to the author, distinct communities emerge and shape their political agencies through identity politics that are based on claims of authenticity and for cultural repertoires and resources. In that context, he argues performing cultural possession constitutes a 'field of transnational politics in which, concomitantly cultural properties are asserted and new political identities and agencies are forged' (2011, 107).

In that regard, I consider the *Inca—Kings of the Andes* exhibition and the manner in which it was fashioned, as a way through which the Linden Museum aims to perform its legitimate possession on the Inca collection. This occurs in a context in which the ethnological museums have been in need to review their own colonialist tradition, while nations and local communities are demanding the return of what they consider their cultural legacies. Within the same line of thought, I think that to respond to the invitation to participate in the exhibition implies engaging in an arena where cultural possession can be disputed. The following sections of the article will deal with the question about the implication that the participation in *Inca—Kings of the Andes* has for Peruvian national and private institutions.

Discussion: disputing cultural possession

1 Collaborative work: paradoxes between public and private efforts and the legitimacy of European collections

In the Inca exhibition, museum artifacts on loan play a central role for *performing and disputing cultural possession*. To carry it out efficiently means having control over the collection in terms of its material possession, as well as mastering it as a source of knowledge. According to the statements of the director of the Linden Museum and the curator of the exhibition, using only the collection items of the Linden Museum would not have allowed the presentation of an innovative and original narrative on the Inca. Additionally, the fact of working with artifacts of other collection offers the opportunity to demonstrate a good knowledge of their own collection as well as of the content and potential of others. Only then is one in the capacity to identify and select those pieces that create an unedited version of the Inca, both in terms of new knowledge and of the visual and aesthetic proposal. Finally, it also involves the administrative and logistic capacity to effectively accomplish the loan and transfer of the items of these other collections.

In order to proceed, I want to discuss the differentiated performances of the MNAAHP and the private Museo Larco, in terms of the loan of their collection items to the Linden Museum.

Although the loan of museum artifacts is an old practice, today the loan policy of a museum and the efficiency of the procedure have become main criteria for evaluating its institutional performance and occupying a position in the global world of museums. Within this logic, in the last decade, the Museo Larco has implemented a series of changes that have allowed for international recognition, not only attracting a large number of visitors but also being recognized as a reliable and efficient partner to carry out collaborative projects that include the loan of museum artifacts as well as participating in the curatorial and museological design of national and international temporary exhibitions, which are listed on its web page. The entire museum collection is inventoried, cataloged, and accessible to researchers and the general public through the museum's web site. It also has a loan policy that is clearly established and systematized so that the procedures are streamlined and transparent. The bottleneck appears when the procedure reaches the Peruvian Ministry of Culture. Since the collection of the Museo Larco belongs to the cultural heritage of the Peruvian nation, for the collection items to leave the country, the signature of the Peruvian president is required. Such bureaucratic procedures are complicated and slow, and are subject to contingencies.

In regard to the MNAAHP and the Museum Directorate of Ministry of Culture, a number of deficiencies in the management of its collections have been specified by different people that I have interviewed, both from outside and from within the government. Such deficiencies result in difficulties in working collaboratively with public museums. Thus the opportunity to have a successful international performance, measured according to the management principles as established internationally and by exhibitions like the *Inca—Kings of the Andes*, is very unlikely, while the capacity to *dispute cultural possession* globally is very weak.

From the perspective of the museums, like the Linden Museum, that are working in the logic of collaboration and internationalization, the collaborative approach offers an opportunity for emerging nations to overcome old colonial relations and gain a position in the globalized world. In that sense, performances like that of the MNAAHP and the Museum Directorate are seen as an obstacle to advance in this direction. From this perspective, these institutions that are perceived as inefficient and reluctant to change also jeopardize their moral status since they do not deploy efforts to manage the national cultural heritage in terms of the new opportunities that the globalized world and neoliberal governmentality offer.

On the contrary, the Museo Larco—which has been managing its collection effectively and efficiently, conducting a transparent administration, as well as taking over a series of public tasks in the framework of corporate social responsibility like offering free access to its collection through its website, conducting research projects, offering workshops, engaging in work with schools, and promoting the image of Peru as a destination for cultural and historical tourism—emerges as the desired partner to work with, since it not only knows how to perform internationally, but understands the advantages of doing so.

Here I want to pose a first argument. In terms of the *dispute over cultural possession*, it is a private institution and its business management of cultural heritage, which stands out as the most competent and morally solvent custodian of the national heritage. The Museo Larco and its business management model gain legitimacy because of the bad performance of state institutions. Through this process, the idea of cultural heritage management as a technical issue gains predominance together with the idea that its administration might more efficiently and transparently be accomplished by private institutions. This way the political dimensions of cultural policies end up being invisibilized and neglected, while cultural heritage loses its power as a discursive and performative tool for imagining and arguing over a political community. Being rather defined as a cultural resource, it serves for packaging a tourist offer, which will further contribute to promote the nation brand in the global tourism market.

The production of *Inca—King of the Andes* involved in the exhibition is another instance where the *performance and dispute of cultural possession* between nations and institutions occurs. It is significant that the curator of the exhibition and the director of the Linden Museum have both emphasized in interviews to the media the fact that they had personally traveled to see the collections *in situ* in order to find the relevant artifacts for the Inca exhibition. One can interpret that the exploration trips of the nineteenth century have been replaced by trips for scientific exchange, inter-institutional contacts, and media reportages, while the temporary loan of artifacts have replaced the permanent acquisition of them.

Here I want to make a second argument. As it is suggested by the case of the Inca exhibition, in terms of the *dispute over cultural possession*, hegemonic knowledge about other cultures does not require any more the exclusively owning of original items gathered in a collection. I want to argue that in this emerging regime, archaeological and ethnographic knowledge is not solely a matter of *patrimonial possession* but of *performativity*. The *performance of cultural possession* obtains its efficacy from the ability to make these artifacts perform, by having a leading role in the temporary gathering of them in order to arrange them in a design that can be proclaimed to be a novel, comprehensive, and updated representation of the Inca. The exhibition organizers repeatedly argued that although the German public is familiar with the word Inca, it does not really know what it means. So the aim of the exhibition was to fill this gap and such a task required an innovative step that allowed the museum to transcend its own collection on the Inca.

In this regard, it is worth mentioning that the Inca exhibition was inaugurated the same year Peru was celebrating the centenary of the discovery of Machu Picchu by Hiram Bingham. This celebration occurred in a special context, since a significant part of archaeological artifacts that Bingham collected and delivered to Yale University had been recently returned to the Peruvian government. The devolution was achieved after several legal and diplomatic efforts brought forward by the Peruvian government. Additionally, in 2014, three textile pieces of the Nazca culture that belonged to the collection of the Museum of World Cultures in Gothenburg were returned by the Swedish Government to Peru.

The origin of archaeological and ethnological collections in Europe remains a sensitive issue, and the claims of the countries where the artifacts come from still compromise legal, scientific, and diplomatic domains, where the *dispute over cultural possession* is also performed. In that regard, one can state that to participate in the Inca exhibition through the loan of museum items of patrimonial value implies a sort of concession and tacit agreement about the legitimacy of the Linden Museum as legitimate custodian of its Inca collection. One might argue that the collaborative model and the participation of Peruvian public institutions configure a perfect scenario to perform such legitimacy. In this sense one might also wonder whether the limited capacity of the Ministry of Culture and the MNAAHP of engaging in collaborative projects is only due to the inefficiency of its administrative structure or to the resistance of its officials to change. Or is it rather possible to argue that it could be related to an understanding that the terms in which the performance of cultural possession is regulated are defined by others, while underperforming operates as a strategic stance.

2 The Inca as cultural heritage and the Inca as a nation brand

From the perspective of some officials of the Ministry of Culture and the Ministry of Foreign Affairs, the Inca exhibition in Japan, inaugurated in March 2012, had been of greater significance for Peru than the exhibition in Germany. Japan's exhibition, which lasted until February 2014, was showcased in nine Japanese cities and already in the first four months, 460,000 visitors attended it (Peru Embassy in Japan, 2013). The exhibition titled *The Inca Empire show: 100 years after the discovery of Machu Picchu*, which was attended by the Peruvian Minister of Culture the day of its opening at the Museum of Natural History of Tokyo, was carried out in the context of trade negotiations between Peru and Japan, which sought to attract major investments to the country and to increase the number of tourists. Additionally, the exhibition, which was organized on the occasion of the centenary of the discovery of Machu Picchu, was done in collaboration with an archaeological project in Machu Picchu in which both countries participated. It was an initiative in which commercial, scientific, and cultural agendas were very tightly articulated.

According to the opinions that I have been able to gather on the exhibition in Japan, it can be argued that in terms of the *dispute over cultural possession*, this exhibition was perceived as a more interesting scenario for Peru. Since the exhibition placed emphasis on Machu Picchu as the site of Inca society and cultural heritage, the performance and dispute over cultural possession was not defined in terms of the possessing of a collection or a museographic narrative, but rather in terms of the sovereignty of the Peruvian nation-state on an archaeological site. As such, Machu Picchu embodies the material traces of the Inca culture and is the place where new knowledge on Inca culture through collaborative projects is being produced. It is interesting to note the enthusiastic account of an employee of the Ministry of Culture who witnessed the event in which Japanese tourists visiting Machu Picchu recognized one of the Peruvian archaeologists that they had seen in the documentary film screened during the Inca exhibition in Japan. They immediately took a picture of him as evidence of their visit to Machu Picchu and their encounter with the people who have knowledge about the place. Through photographic and playful devices, they are contributing to the configuration of Machu Picchu, while they participate in its shaping as a sovereign site in terms of the performance of cultural possession.

Following this line of argument, I will argue now that the *dispute over cultural possession* in the context of the Inca exhibition in Japan does not occur here between Japan and Peru. Rather, it does tell us about the emergence of two different conceptions regarding the legacy of the Inca as well as of two regimes of cultural management: the Inca as *cultural heritage* and the Inca as a *nation brand*. At this point one may ask what are the conceptions that are gaining supremacy in Peruvian governmental institutions and which are the conceptions that are governing cultural policies in the Ministry of Culture in Peru. Additionally, one may want to know if the fact of conducting cultural management of the Inca heritage in the logic of *nation branding* will allow for the design of cultural policies that encourage a sense of belonging, and politicized and historicized debates on national identity, as well as strengthening democratic institutions and practices— or, as I have discussed in the previous sections, contribute to the depoliticization of cultural heritage.

Heritage management of the Inca in terms of *nation branding* has to do mainly with the administration of Machu Picchu as a tourist destination, and it is a mission that has been entrusted by the Peruvian government to PromPerú. As part of this effort, PromPerú launched a campaign that consisted of supporting the candidacy of Machu Picchu to be nominated as one of the New Seven Wonders of the World in 2007. The nomination as the fourth New Wonder was achieved after an open voting process online.[10] Since the Inca exhibition at the Linden Museum seemed to work better as a platform for nation branding, than the one for cultural and scientific exchanges between Germany and Peru, one can understand why the participation of PromPerú had been more enthusiastic and aimed for more visibility than that of the Ministry of Culture. Two additional arguments to the present discussion can be made here.

The first refers to a tension between the agendas of the Linden Museum and PromPerú. Although PromPerú considered it convenient to participate in the Inca exhibition in Stuttgart, it is important to point out that it has a broader agenda. According to officials I have interviewed, at the present moment, PromPerú has the challenge to promote other archaeological destinations in order to diversify the Peruvian touristic offer, as well as invest efforts and resources to gain other markets such as Asia and the Arab Emirates. In that sense, it struggled to maintain its participation in Stuttgart and Rosenheim within the margins of its own agenda. One critical issue was the negotiations regarding the amount of investment PromPerú was ready to put in for the press trips to which several journalist were invited in order to guarantee a good coverage of the exhibition. At first, PromPerú was not entirely convinced of covering costs of the whole group that was to travel to Peru. From the perspective of the institution and people involved in the Inca exhibition, the reluctance of PromPerú was understood as the expression of the unawareness of Peruvian officials about the importance of the museum exhibition to position Peru in the German tourism market, as well as of the relevance of Inca society for human history.

As can be followed from the previous discussion, the first interpretation does not take into account the fact that the Inca exhibitions constitute only one context where PromPerú promotes the country as a tourist destiny. There are several other platforms where PromPerú has been already working for some time, like the main tourism fairs in Germany. On the other hand, the German market is not the only one PromPerú has on its agenda. The second interpretation misses the point that as PromPerú personnel argue, it is not its duty to assume responsibility for the historical and cultural contents or promotion of the different manifestations of national cultural heritage.

The second argument refers to the contradictions that arise between the management of Machu Picchu as the nation brand's image by PromPerú, and the management of Machu Picchu as a cultural heritage included in the Human Heritage list by UNESCO. The latter requires assuming a series of compromises established by UNESCO regarding the protection and conservation of Machu Picchu. So while Machu Picchu is still used as one of the main referents of the Peruvian nation brand, for the promotion of the country as a touristic destination, the Ministry of Culture and its regional office in Cuzco find themselves in the dilemma to have to restrict number of visitors to the site, since there is a lot of pressure to prioritize economic income over cultural preservation. Drawing on Kirshenblatt-Gimblett's (2006) discussion on the production of world intangible heritage by the authoritative power of UNESCO, the case I am discussing here falls into the kind of tensions that occur precisely because the rights of global consumers are prioritizes over the right of local and national heritage custodians.

Furthermore, these tensions are due to the fact that each governmental agency gets assigned different agendas, specific areas of action, and limited budgets. I have recorded very clear statements from PromPerú officials in regard to the fact that although they consider having a say in relation to the national identity discourse, they are not responsible for the preservation or dissemination of cultural heritage. For that reason, their participation in the Inca exhibition in the Linden Museum, cannot be mistaken for an initiative in the same line as the collaborative and reflexive museum that the network of ethnographic European museums seeks to develop.

These tensions are additionally influenced by the approaches and expertise that are put into work by the staff that works in PromPerú and in the Ministry of Culture respectively; while the former are mainly communicators and designers, the latter have a background in archaeology, anthropology, or history. These differences are not irrelevant, since as Clarke argues government workers 'need to be understood as having social characters, position and dispositions that are formed in social relationship and trajectories' (2012, 4).

Finally, within this constellation of agendas and expertise and the fact that PromPerú focuses rather on nation branding allows the Linden Museum to engage in a partnership with a Peruvian institution without challenging its say on Inca society as the hegemonic cultural institution it seeks to be.

Conclusive remarks

Through the case of the *Inca—Kings of the Andes* exhibition, I aimed to inquire about the constraints and institutional frameworks governing the management of cultural heritage under the neoliberal regime, at a local and transnational level. I also intended to discuss the transformation that such regime allows regarding the colonial relationship between European ethnological museums, and the museums and cultural legacies of the countries from which their collections originate.

Key principles that govern this new order respond to the imperatives of efficacy and efficiency, and are aimed at ensuring the competitiveness of the museum for the sake of its economic viability. For this, it is necessary to conduct a distinctive performance of cultural possession that, in the same logic of building a brand, can result in the distinguishing feature of the museum. On the other hand, within such order, it is required to implement collaborative strategies that facilitate interaction and mobility between people, objects, and knowledge that operate in favor of the sustainability of the museum. The imperatives of effectiveness and efficiency are, moreover, subject to results-based evaluations that require quantifiable criteria, such as media exposure, number of visitors, as well as minimizing costs. Thus not only the imperative of efficiency but also the imperative of efficacy is subject to an economic rationality.

What is at stake within this emerging order, which I have considered to be constitutive of a neoliberal governmentality, is the establishment of a new regime of knowledge and legitimacy within which cultural heritage is managed, compromising the very nature of the ethnological museum in the contemporary world. This regime of cultural management, which I understand as constitutive of a neoliberal governmentality, creates a set of tensions. The present case study allows me to highlight two of them. A first tension operates at the intersection of knowledge and consumption, in other words, between the validity of the museum as an institution of knowledge and its economic viability. In this new regime, the modern ethnological museum as an institution dedicated to critical thinking and the search for new knowledge is thus challenged by the need to offer services that have to be competitive in the market. Achieving the latter implies emphasizing aesthetic and sensory aspects of museum objects and their display at the expense of contextualization and analysis. On the risk of de-contextualization and de-historization through processes of aestheticization has been written critically (Kleinman and Kleinman 1996). On the other hand, within the sensory turn in anthropology, it has been argued that sensorial experiences also offer the possibility of critical exploration and reflexive apprehension of the world (Pink 2006). However, the second option requires work that needs to be properly based on the theories and methodologies of anthropology of art and of anthropology of the senses, especially if one's aim is to break with an aesthetic language that naturalizes and reproduces common-sense knowledge and the prejudices that go with it. This has certainly not been the case of the Inca exhibition.

The second tension I observed is between two different forms of performing cultural possession. In one form, ownership over the collection's artifacts takes predominance, while immobility is imposed on them; while on the other form, what counts is the ability to manage the flow of them. The second implies in turn the move from a representational system, where objects operate as data and are valued in terms of the place they might occupy within a classificatory order, to a performative one that is governed by principles of accessibility and connectivity, and where objects function as resources. In this regard, it is interesting to note, for example, that it has been crucial for the Museo Larco to become globally competitive, to have their collection objects not only inventoried, but allocated in their digital version on the website of the museum. The accessibility and connectivity that digital objects allow are a condition for its material mobility and visibility. As I have discussed above, this implies a tension between two different principles that govern the production of heritage. That is, the tension between the principle of owning a collection and therefore drawing knowledge and power from its objectified, immobilized, and particularized form; and the principle of managing a collection in such terms, that knowledge and power derive from the capacity to make the collection artifacts perform.

In any case, this case study shows that the tensions I identified involve the intervention of new actors, ideas, and actions, as well as a number of new conditions and possibilities. As the performance of the Museo Larco indicates, these changes open up a number of possibilities for the museum to reposition itself in the global context. Nevertheless, this has to do with fact that due to its condition as a private initiative, the Museum Larco has been in the condition to carry out the reorganization of the museum, introducing very easily a corporate management model, and with it new forms defining and managing heritage. Having done this reorganization, the museum has assured for itself the means and capabilities to respond properly and successfully to the challenges that transnational heritage management put on museums.

Nevertheless, the same is not true for the MNAAHP, since specific constraints like agendas and budgets, as well as the forms in which the state conceptualizes heritage and institutionally organizes its management, play a part in the difficulties to introduce corporative logics. Although, through offices like PromPerú and its marketing logic, the conceptualization and management of heritage as resource is gaining terrain at the state level, it is possible to observe that such an approach operates in tension with others where sovereignty over heritage continues to be a guiding principle. This is the case of the MNAAHP and the Ministry of Culture, which for that reason make a strategic distinctions and decisions regarding their collaboration with the Linden Museum or with the Japanese museums, universities and diplomatic corps.

The case shows us the complexities of collaborative and participative work at a national and transnational level. These include the tensions that operate within Peruvian government institutions itself; between public and private institutions and between governments and museums of different countries; and between two different models to produce and manage cultural heritage. For that reason, I argue for the fact that the decolonizing and democratizing possibilities that neoliberal governmentality offer in terms of heritage management need to be approached critically. Participation and loan of museum artifacts go along with a series of paradoxes that in certain circumstances help rather to define new forms of distinction and hierarchies, while facilitating the reproduction of old colonial relations.

As I have discussed, the Linden Museum gains recognition as a legitimate custodian of its Inca collection; the Museo Larco loan policies and PromPerú s

Cultural management 105

nation branding contribute to the gaining of supremacy of private initiatives, forms of management, and interest over public interest and sovereignty; and technical solutions are valued over political struggle when it comes to cultural heritage management.

So for example, the Museo Larco and PromPerú have proven to be good partners for the Linden Museum, in the sense that their participation in the Inca exhibition aims principally to positioning themselves in the market, without constituting a challenge to the legitimacy of the Museum as custodian of its Inca collection, nor as a producer of authoritative knowledge on Inca society. Since their participation in the project does not challenge the Linden Museum politically, neither does it contribute to any decolonizing process. On the contrary, the partnership with Peruvian academic and public institutions that could eventually allow for a critical participation in terms of redefining old colonial relations do not seem to be fully in the interest of Linden Museum. The Inca exhibition, whose management follows a collaborative model that facilitates mobility of objects, people, and knowledge, as I have tried to show, involves the installation of a new order in terms of the performance of cultural possession, for which Peruvian public museums lack the conditions to successfully negotiate or dispute the terms of its participation in a politically relevant manner that could contribute to redefine old colonial relations.

In this context, the participation of the private Museo Larco in the Inca exhibition stands out above the public museum because of a more transparent and democratizing management of its legacy, and its willingness to engage in international projects. So, its participation contributes in legitimizing a technical and business-like vision of cultural heritage management of cultural heritage, while obscuring its political dimension. One should not forget that archaeological and ethnological collections of European museums, as well as private collections in Peru, have been set up in the context of colonial relations either globally between Europe and Peru, or locally, between aristocratic landowners, the illustrated bourgeoisie, and the indigenous population (Gänger 2014). In that sense, the contradiction lies in the fact that at the same time that the Museo Larco initiates a democratic process regarding the management of the national heritage, becoming the legitimate custodian of its collection, it silences a political and cultural history inhibiting the opportunity to reflect on the conditions of national identity and citizenship formation in Peru. So, as it can be seen, while neoliberal heritage management presents itself as operating exclusively at the level of technical expertise without political compromises, it rather constitutes an ideological tool, that reproduces and legitimizes old relation of domination and exclusion.

Thus, more collaboration seems to lead to less intercultural dialog and less opportunities for a politically relevant public debate. In my analysis of the case, I could further argue that Peru achieves a better performance of cultural possession when it comes to its archaeological sites, like Machu Picchu. As I have stated above, this better performance of Peru is strongly defined by a heritage management that falls under the logic of nation branding, which submits cultural heritage to market imperatives. In this context, the management of Machu Picchu as a resource prevails over its management as a source of knowledge. I have the overall impression that in Peru, a model of cultural politics that understands culture as a resource and nation branding as the proper approach to manage our cultural heritage is prioritized. Perhaps it will allow Peru to gain a better position in the global market. But being a country where cultural institutions are weak and public political culture lacks a democratic tradition, I rather envisage that cultural heritage management as neoliberal governmentality implies the risk of endangering the cultural heritage in a material sense, while it restricts the potential of cultural heritage as a source for historic and political imagination and reflection.

Finally, I want to comment on a last point mentioned in the introductory section regarding the idea of neoliberalism as a cultural regime. My argument is that in the current context, culture has to be understood beyond the idea of a set of narratives constituting an ethos, or a complex of meanings in constant redefinition. In the current order, cultural repertoires have come to play a central part in identity politics as a main arena where political rights are being claimed and fought for, and in which post-Fordist capitalist culture as an intangible resource has become central to the production of economic value.

Within this context, when I refer to neoliberalism as a cultural regime, I rather mean that the work of governing occurs through the staging of cultural repertoires, which are operationalized in a productive and strategic way. This process is further carried out by implementing knowledge of new fields of expertise, which in turn respond to the performative principles of effectiveness and efficiency, not the search for truth. This operates in correspondence to the postmodern order where according to Lyotard (1984), knowledge is used in terms of its productive and transformative potential, and legitimized by its applicability. In other words, cultural repertoires and its management have turned into a field where corporate pragmatics can be experienced and rehearsed, as well as played with, in fields other than the economic. Following on this argument, what the analysis of the Inca exhibition shows us is the complexities and historical contingencies through which neoliberal governing, institutional arrangements, public agendas and citizenship are being shaped through emergent forms of local and global cultural management.

Notes

1 This study has been possible thanks to the Georg Forster Research Fellowship that I was granted by the Alexander von Humboldt Foundation, in 2014–2015. The grant allowed me to spend a research period in Germany and therefore I was able to visit the Inca exhibition in Stuttgart and in Rosenheim, to attend different promotional events in Germany where PromPerú has a participation, to conduct interviews and informal conversations with different actors, and to get acquainted with the debate around ethnological museums. I had also the opportunity to discuss some preliminary versions of this article with my colleagues in Germany in the context of workshops and lectures.
2 http://modymus.blogspot.de/p/red-internacional-de-museos_21.html (last visited April 2, 2015).
3 www.lindenmuseum.de/ueber-uns/forschung-und-netzwerk/ (last visited July 22, 2014).
4 www.lindenmuseum.de/ueber-uns/forschung- und-netzwerk/ (last visited July 22, 2014).

5. www.lokschuppen.de/en/lokschuppen-exhibition-centre.html (last visited June 3, 2015).
6 www.lindenmuseum.de/ueber-uns/leitbild/ (last visited March 20, 2014).
7 www.lateinamerika.org/index.php/presse/aktueller-pressedienst/37-lateinamerika-veranstaltungen-in-deutschland/792-linden-museum-inka-austellung-in-stuttgart (last visited April 3, 2015).
8 www.lindenmuseum.de/inka/.
9 www.lateinamerika.org/index.php/presse/aktueller-pressedienst/24-in-eigener-sache/834-arge-inka-ausstellung.
10 Educacionenred www.youtube.com/watch?v=MQeJ69yENZg (last visited June 7, 2015).

References

Arbeitsgemeinschaft Lateinamerika. e.V. 2013. 'Somos Latinoamérica. Lateinamerika daheim und unterwegs erleben.' *América Latina. Das Magazin für Lateinamerika* 65.

Arbeitsgemeinschaft Lateinamerika. www.lateinamerika.org/index.php/presse/aktueller-pressedienst/37-lateinamerika-veranstaltungen-in-deutschland/792-linden-museum-inka-austellung-in-stuttgart. Seen April 3, 2015.

Borea, Giuliana. 2006. 'Museos y esfera pública: espacio, discursos y prácticas reflexiones en torno a la ciudad de Lima.' In *Mirando la esfera pública desde la cultura en el Perú*, ed. Gisela Cánepa, and María Eugenia Ulfe. Lima: CONCYTEC.

Cánepa, Gisela. 2012. 'Gestión municipal como marca: identidad, espacio público y participación.' *Cuadernos. Arquitectura y ciudad*. Lima: Revista del Departamento Académico de Arquitectura—PUCP, no. 16: 41–85.

Cánepa, Gisela. 2013. 'Nation Branding: The Re-foundation of Community, Citizenship and the State in the context of Neoliberalism in Perú.' *Medien Journal* 3: 7–18.

Clarke, John. 2012. 'The work of governing.' In *Governing Cultures: Anthropological Perspectives on Political Labor, Power, and Government*, ed. Kendra Coulter, and William R. Schumann, 209–32. New York: Palgrave Macmillan.

Coombe, Rosemary J. 2011 'Possessing Culture. Political Economies of Community Subjects and their Properties' In *Ownership and Appropriation*, ed. Mark Busse and Veronica Strang, 105–27. London: Berg.

Coombe, Rosemary J. 2012 'Managing Cultural Heritage as Neoliberal Governmentality.' In *Heritage Regimes and the State*, ed. Regina F. Bendix, Aditya Eggert, and Arnika Peselmann, 375–87. Göttingen: Universitätsverlag Göttingen.

Educacionenred. www.youtube.com/watch?v=MQeJ69yENZg. Seen June 7, 2015.

Embajada del Peru en Japon. 'Exposición sobre el Imperio de los Incas replica exitosa acogida en Fukuoka.' http://embajadadelperuenjapon.org/exposicion-sobre-el-imperio-de-los-incas-replica-exitosa-acogida-en-fukuoka/. Seen March 12, 2015.

Gänger, Stephanie. 2014. *Relics of the Past: The Collecting and Study of Pre-Columbian Antiquities in Peru and Chile, 1837–1911.* Oxford: Oxford University.

International Ethnographic Museum Network. http://modymus.blogspot.de/p/red-internacional-de-museos_21.html. Seen April 2, 2015.

Karp, Ivan, Christine Mullen Kreamer, and Steven D. Lavine, eds. 1992. *Museums and Communities: The Politics of Public Culture*. Washington: Smithsonian Institution.

Karp, Ivan, Corinne Kratz, Lynn Szwaja, and Tomas Ybarra-Frausto, eds. 2006. *Museum Frictions: Public Cultures/Global Transformations*. Durham, North Carolina: Duke University.

Karp, Ivan, and Steven D. Lavine, eds. 1991. *Exhibiting Cultures: The Poetics and Politics of Museum Display*. Washington: Smithsonian Institution.

Kirshenblatt-Gimblett, Barbara. 2006. 'World Heritage and Cultural Economics.' In *Museum Frictions: Public cultures/global transformations*, ed. Ivan Karp, Corinne Kratz, Lynn Szwaja, and Tomas Ybarra-Frausto. Durham: Duke University.

Kleinman, Arthur, and Joan Kleinman. 1996. 'The appeal of experience; The dismay of images: Cultural Appropriation of Suffering in our times.' *Daedalus* 125(1) (Winter): 1–23.

Linden Museum. www.lindenmuseum.de/ueber-uns/leitbild/. Seen March 20, 2014.

Lockschuppen Ausstellungszentrum–Rosenheim. www.lokschuppen.de/en/lokschuppen-exhibition-centre.html. Seen June 3, 2015.

Lyotard, Jean-François. 1984. *The Postmodern Condition. A Report on Knowledge.* Manchester: Manchester University.

Méndez, Cecilia. 1995. *Incas si, indios no: apuntes para el estudio del nacionalismo criollo en el Perú* 2. Lima: IEP.

Noack, Karoline. 2015. 'Buscando un Inca de aquí y de allá: los Incas de nuestro tiempo, Alemania y Lima, Perú.' *Tribus Sonderband/Special Edition: Perspectives on the Inca*, Stuttgart, 16–37.

Onken, Hinnerk. 2014. 'Südamerika: Ein Zukunftsland der Menschheit. Colonial Imagination and Photographs from South America in Weimar Germany.' In *Weimar Colonialism. Discourses and Legacies of Post-Imperialism in Germany after 1918*, ed. Florian Krobb, and Elain Martin, 145–66. Bielefeld: Aisthesis.

OVB (Oberbayerisches Volksblatt. Heimatzeitung). Platz unter Top Ten gefestigt; November 24, 2014. www.ovb-online.de/rosenheim/platz-unter-gefestigt-4475594.html. Seen March 12, 2015.

Pink, Sarah. 2006. *The Future of Visual Anthropology: Engaging the Senses*. London: Routledge.

Said, Edward W. 1978. *Orientalism*. New York: Vintage Books.

Samerberger Nachrichten. Aktuelles von Chiemensee und aus Bayern 1. http://samerbergernachrichten.de/100–000-besucher-bereits-bei-inka-ausstellung-im-rosenheimer-lokschuppen/

Samerberger Nachrichten. Aktuelles von Chiemensee und aus Bayern 2. http://samerberger-nachrichten.de/150–000-besucher-bei-inka-ausstellung-in-rosenheim-dauer-bis-23-11/

Samerberger Nachrichten. Aktuelles von Chiemensee und aus Bayern 3. http://samerberger-nachrichten.de/inka-ausstellung-hat-schon-25–000-besucher/

Sharing a World of Inclusion, Creativity and Heritage project. www.lindenmuseum.de/ueber-uns/forschung-und-netzwerk/. Seen July 22, 2014.

Stuttgarter Zeitung. Bilanz der Stuttgarter Museen 2014. 'Linden Museum ist der große Gewinner.' January 27, 2015. www.stuttgarter-zeitung.de/inhalt.bilanz-der-stuttgarter-museen-2014-linden-museum-ist-der-grosse-gewinner.c9f4e7b5-2f74-4a91-9077-c2b632e9fbf5.html. Seen February 20, 2015.

Yudice, George. 2003. *The Expediency of Culture: The Uses of Culture in the Global Era*. Durham: Duke University.

6 Commemorate, consecrate, demolish

Thoughts about the Mexican Museum of Anthropology and its history

Frida Gorbach

To commemorate

The book *Museo Nacional de Antropología: 50 años* (*National Museum of Anthropology: 50 years*), published in September 2014, was recently presented by the National Council for the Culture and Arts. It is a large—even huge—format book, as if its size was intended to emulate that of the celebration, full of color and attractive illustrations, and in which, without knowing exactly how, I ended up participating (Gorbach 2014). Just one more piece of information: the 'popular' edition of the book costs 2,500 pesos (about 160 dollars), and the 'deluxe' one more than 75,000 pesos (about 4,700 dollars).[1]

The day the book was presented, in the museum's auditorium, five high ranking officials delivered speeches; they were, with the exception of the President, the same individuals who wrote the book's multiple forewords. In strict hierarchical order: first, the President ('I celebrate the publication of these valuable volumes and I encourage the reader to penetrate into this wonderful tour, to witness all that Mexico offers humanity'); after him, the Minister of Tourism ('This Museum safeguards the Mexican native peoples' legacy, not just to be inherited and transmitted to the future generations, but also to remember and reassert our identity as Mexican'); then, the director of the National Council for the Culture and Arts ('Mexico's indigenous past is an unyielding part of its present: to remember and to study it is to understand ourselves'); the director of the National Institute of Anthropology and History ('The Museum opens its doors to Mexicans looking for their roots and to all citizens of the world interested in a pluriethnic country with an extraordinary cultural diversity'); the director of the Museum ('we are talking about pages that, tacitly of explicitly, celebrate [the Museum] even when the historian's trade advices to leave the praises to other literary genres'); and finally, the president of the Museum's Board ('This book testifies to the tenacity of a group of scholars and, at the same time, to the multitudinous fervor of those who visit the halls where yesterday's, today's and eternity's Mexico meet').

110   *Frida Gorbach*

As I listened to these speeches, I felt that something was out of place. I thought about the paradoxes involved in the publishing of such a colossal book in a time in which it is widely recognized that Mexican anthropology is in crisis, when anthropologists have spent decades criticizing the historical link that their discipline has built with the state. I couldn't help but reflect on the fact that this commemoration, so respectful in the presence of hierarchies, occurred in a moment in which the idea that we are living in the ravages of a 'failed state' can be heard, insistently and everywhere. Therefore, I can say that the cause of my uneasiness was not the book itself but its context: the homage book was presented in an act that repeated an old practice that aimed to affirm the survival of the pre-Columbian past and, above all, to guarantee the durability of the alliance between anthropology, the museum, and the state. It was not easy to discern if the event was the last simulacrum of the state as society's hegemonic center, or rather a small demonstration of today's incapacity to create practices capable of reproducing a coherent mythology of a state able to impose itself with effective authority over the population (Hansen and Stepputat 2001, 16).

Nonetheless, the *50 years* book and its public presentation ceremony have only triggered what I would actually like to propose in this paper. After this commemorative event, I went back to the history of the Museum of Anthropology—the book's subject—not to review its contents but to reflect on its fundamentals. Above all, I was interested in circling, once more, the relationship among anthropology–archaeology, the museum heritage, and the nation-state, amazed at my confusion[2] of these concepts, examining its origins and why it is so difficult to distinguish them analytically. I decided to challenge this apparent symbiosis, to unravel its terms, and understand in more detail how they are articulated.

However, in this attempt to separate that which is confused, I had to ask myself a question about the present. Let's say that the motivation behind approaching the concepts' genealogy came from the need to answer a question about 'us,' that is, about the ways in which we, archaeologists, anthropologists, or historians, write from within this symbiosis, trapped, engaged—without even noticing it—with the state and its institutions, hierarchies, and identity forms. Moreover, my efforts to separate scientific disciplines, the museum, and power required, in order to make room for the difference, a methodological process: to break with the disciplinary frameworks. Therefore, this text is also an attempt to *historicize* anthropology, and to *anthropologize* history, as a strategy to mobilize time, differentiate concepts, and open up a space for critique.

To monumentalize

Whenever the Museum of Anthropology's history is narrated, the day on which the 'Monument of monuments'—as the Public Education Minister called it—was inaugurated is unavoidably mentioned, and rarely is the following quote, extracted from the president's speech on September 17, 1964, missing: 'The great austere building, with its sober lines and noble spaces, whose construction was waited for years, opens its gates this morning. And it does so in September in Chapultepec' (INAH 1964, 16).

Paraphrasing the president, one could say that what this story is about is the sequence of episodes that constitutes those years of waiting. In this sense, both anthropologists and historians that have rescued the Museum of Anthropology's history agree that 1964 represents the culmination of a long process, the final realization of 'an ancient project, a yearning of identity with the past that crosses almost a century and a half,' that constitutes 'the synthesis of a great ideological, scientific and political feat' (Florescano 1993, 161–162). This long process, in terms of its institutional fulfillment, began in the years after the independence war, at the moment in which Agustín de Iturbide crowned himself Emperor of Mexico and decreed the creation, in the University, of a Conservatory of Antiques, and a Cabinet of Natural History; continues for almost two centuries with decrees, good wishes, false starts, many efforts, promises, failed attempts, and many names for the same museum (The Mexican Museum, National Museum, Mexican National Museum, Public Museum of Natural History, Archaeology and History); and finally culminates, with a sudden twist, in 1964 (Fernández 1987).

However, this is actually a history written in hindsight, which projects backward an idea conceived in the twentieth century, an idea that shows how, since forever, archaeology has been the nation's original substratum (López Caballero 2011).[3] The origin, mythic as every origin, dates back to 1790 and outlines what, in the twentieth century, would take its true form. According to the historians' version, in that year, the Creole Jesuit Francisco Xavier Clavijero, in his *Ancient History of Mexico*, imagined a 'museum as useful as curious in which ancient sculptures, existing or to be discovered in the excavations, could be stored.' This is why a historian such as Florescano considers that the Museum of Anthropology represents the realization of Clavijero's dream, the first Creole that paused to 'consider the indigenous past as a strange one, and turned it into the past of those born in Mexico' (Florescano 1993, 147). The anthropologists' version of this history locates the origin in that same year, but at the moment when the Aztec calendar stone and the Coatlicue were discovered underneath the Templo Mayor ('Great Temple') and were publicly exhibited (De la Peña 2011).

In any case, 1964 constitutes the heart of the history. So far, we have only reviewed the sequence of the precedents, the chain of episodes that had to happen so that the archaeological remains from the pre-Columbian world could become the authentic representation of national identity. It is as if history were a distilling work, as if time could only move forward by recovering its original vocation. And this is how history narrates the way in which the nineteenth-century collections of natural history, anatomy, teratology, and *historia patria* ('history of the homeland') disappeared as the space solidified the alliance between archaeology and the 'cultural heritage created by the Mexicans' (Florescano 2011, 11).

Anthropologists tell a slightly different version of this story. 1964 represents not only the culmination of a long historical process, but also the announcement of a new phase. That year, social anthropology made an entry into a museum that was devoted, up to this point, to exhibiting archaeological remains, and occupied the second floor of the new building. The 'value of all living cultures' is maintained over 'the value of the monumental archaeological remains'; the contemporaneous

112 *Frida Gorbach*

ethnographical indigenous presence—'living heritage' of the world destroyed by the conquest—is placed above the archaeological collections (Peña 2011, 14).

In the end, this second perspective splits the origin because it calls attention to an event neglected by official history: in 1790, after the Coatlicue was unearthed and exhibited in one of the university's courtyards, it was once again buried because the Indians from the city and nearby towns started to worship it, leaving offerings and lit candles at her feet (Peña 2011, 57). This second version ends up splitting the idea of cultural heritage because, if the Aztec calendar stone and the Coatlicue's exhibitions mark the beginning of the heritage created by the state, then the moment the state buried the Coatlicue and the Indians congregated to worship it marks the rise of 'popular heritage.' If, in the first case, the heritage is seen as an *archive*, as the sacred storehouse of the identitarian principle, in the second case its romantic vein turns it into the evidence that a lost, neglected, and different cultural origin can be salvaged through it.

At the same time, these two conceptions of heritage correspond to two stances that have long been debated in Mexican anthropology: on the one hand, there are those who emphasize the role of dominant groups in the conceptual conformation and symbolization of the past and its remains (Florescano), and, on the other, those that are identified with anthropology's *critical* school,[4] who emphasize the role of subordinate groups in the creation and appropriation of the past, argued that 'the indigenous groups have created alternative collective identities, complementary or parallel to the dominant national vision' (2011, 15). It could be contended that these positions corresponded to two ways of conceiving the state and of relating with it. While some tell a sequential story of its consolidation, others, using a different time frame, center around the moments in which society resists power. In one case, the state is consecrated as the entity in charge of regulating social life; in the other, it is resisted by imagining that a relationship with it is indeed established but from the outside.[5]

In the end, even with these divisions, the historical time form is still the same. Determined by the origin and with only one possible path to traverse, this story, in any of its versions, intertwines the idea of heritage with that of the nation-state in a way that the state is at the center of the narrative while heritage becomes a tool that ensures its future perdurability. Perhaps it would be better to rephrase all this as a set of questions: How can it be that both definitions of heritage reproduce the same idea of history? To what extent do cultural heritage and anthropology remain trapped in the history of nationalism? Could it be that the past is no longer deduced from the principles of human nature, while heritage constitutes its most tangible evidence? Finally, what possibilities for analysis are opened up by this idea of an evolving state entity in whose presence obeying and resisting are the only viable options?

To order

In the above discussion, 1964 represents, on the one hand, the culminating moment for indigenist and revolutionary anthropology,[6] 'the climax of a way of understanding and making anthropology' (Téllez 1987, 305), the most tangible embodiment of the symbiosis between the ruins, anthropology, and the state. On the other hand, it marks the beginning of a new critical distance. Before 1964, Mexican anthropology lived its 'golden age' splendor, a phase in which anthropological practice matured and professionalized, abundant with economic resources and important dates: the founding of the National School of Anthropology and History (1938) and of the National Institute of Anthropology and History (1939), the first celebration of the Indigenist Congress (1940), and the founding of the National Indigenist Institute (1948). The following year, the discipline's contradictions would 'overflow' (Méndez 1987, 358; Téllez 1987, 305–206), marking the beginning of the critique directed toward the indigenist policies and, therefore, toward the relation that anthropology had built with the postrevolutionary state. This critique went so far that indigenism, the heart of 'golden' anthropology, is seen today as the project in charge of expropriating indigenous groups' social memories in the name of science and nationalism (Navarrete 2009, 10).

My interest is not so much in the different moments of that critique but in the place that history has had in the discussion. The starting point won't be the sixties, but the eighties, when the history of Mexican anthropology became a field of scholarly interest.[7] We cannot properly talk about a historical reflection before *La quiebra política de la antropología social en México* (1986), a book that aimed to recover 20 years of discussion in an effort to foster a new establishment for Mexican anthropology, or before *La antropología en México* (1987), a collective work in 15 volumes that recovers the discipline's history from the colonial times to the present.[8] According to Raymundo Mier, in the previous decades, anthropology's Marxist school, fashionable at the time, did nothing more than 'involuntarily extend the dehistoricizing project' that had characterized anthropological work (Mier 1996, 277). Until then, according to anthropologists, nobody had had enough time to reflect on the debates, schools of thought, methods, and rules of their own discipline: the discipline's imperatives had been too instrumental, the political urgency to intervene in the country's reality and contribute in the search of solutions for the 'great national problems' too demanding.[9] In Mier's opinion, this interventionist vocation explains why anthropology had excluded its own history from its reflections (1996, 275).

Nevertheless, in relation to history, what we should be wondering about is to what extent the beginning of such reflection meant a transformation in the way anthropology was conceived and made, that is, if the idea of *historicizing* knowledge led to different ways to think about 'the other' and to relate with him. This is the central issue because, I think, the idea of history contains within itself a way of conceiving the nation and the state, and, in the same sense, the image we create about the state compromises in many ways the idea about the subjectivity of the 'other.'

It is interesting to notice that many texts focused on analyzing anthropology from its own history continue an old project: the emphasis is still on making the engagements between the discipline and state visible, in highlighting the collusion

114 *Frida Gorbach*

between anthropologists, archaeologists, and state officers, as if it is necessary to continue to measure their effects on the discipline or as if it is now important to review the events of subordination and reveal the names of those who, giving in to their fascination with power, 'betrayed' their original critical stance (Nhamad 2008). But, above all, what these texts keep unaltered are the foundations on which the historical reflection stands. Because, it could be argued, this historiography reproduces in general terms the most orthodox forms of historical discourse.

Let's look closely at *Recursos ideológicos del Estado mexicano: el caso de la arqueología* (Ideological resources of the Mexican State: the case of archaeology), a paper by Ignacio Rodríguez (1996), in which the author demonstrates, in an almost schematic fashion, the discursive strategy of many texts, including those that make up the 15 volumes of *La historia de la antropología*. In this case, Rodríguez narrates the recent history of Mexican archaeology following the succession of the six-year presidential terms: 'the impact of Cardenism,' 'archaeology during the transition to civilian rule,' 'the ideological take-off (1958–64),' etc. Following closely the episodes that make 'national history,' he narrates how the different archaeological projects were set in motion according to the whims of the president in office: López Mateos and the Teotihuacan project, Díaz Ordaz and Cholula, Luis Echeverría and the recovery of Cuauhtémoc's bones, López Portillo and the Templo Mayor project. As if the subordination always came from outside, the author proposes to analyze 'the external conditions that have left a mark in Mexican archaeology and shaped her into her particular physiognomy' (84). The author separates the interior from the exterior in such a way that the country's 'economic and political situation' is mirrored in the discipline's interior, as if the academic and political worlds—especially in Mexico—ever had sharply defined boundaries.

In the paper we are reviewing, as in many others, archive and history seem to be synonymous, and so the second is seen as the repository from which evidence that directly informs about the events of the past is extracted. Narration is organized following the succession of episodes that constitute 'national history,' a prefixed context, a stable reference framework that, from the outside, determines the sense of the events, and so, the history of the discipline ends up telling how the Mexican state and its institutions formed and developed, while the anthropologists represent themselves as victims, pressured by the state but located on its periphery. In this sense, the state appears as an entity that, from outside, imposes itself over society, and this is why Rodríguez is able to recommend a 'cultural reorganization' that could originate in the 'civil society,' a term that, since the 1985 Mexico City earthquake, has been used to blend everything that is not the 'state.' In fact, it is at this frontier between the inside and the outside that the main questions arise:

> Just how capable are we of organizing to confront a State accustomed to impose his ideological visions over the academic needs? How capable are we to politically subsist without the cyclical endowment of financial

resources? Would we have the capacity to structure with the civil society a non-political-ideological alternative to the uses of archaeological remains?
(1996, 102).

It would seem that the historical reflection is still trapped in the ever-present urgency, dominated, as Alejandro Araujo says, by the question of what should anthropology be in the face of the nation's problems. Still the political urgency logic ousts the interest in analyzing the rules of knowledge and the historical conditions of its production (2014, 6). What is true is that it is necessary to theoretically reformulate the idea of history itself, and, by means of that, to rethink an old attachment to the origin, an origin in which the discipline was legitimized as the most useful social science in the task of finding solutions for the national problems. If the idea of history is not reformulated, how can we stop reproducing the thread of continuity that Araujo observes between Manuel Gamio's *Forjando patria* (*Forging a Fatherland*) (1916), one of the founding books of Mexican anthropology and the most representative of indigenist anthropology, and *México profundo* (*Deep Mexico*) (1987), the finest book of what was known, by the end of the sixties, as anthropology's critical school? This continuity would be crystallized in the '*indio*,' an essential entity that, therefore, is in no need of discussion; synthesis of a different way to conceive the world, history, and civilization, whose origin is in the pre-Columbian world and holds motionless across history (2012, 360). This means that, by keeping as a substratum the essentialist idea that the indigenous civilization is the denied base of the national culture, anthropology keeps thinking of the *indio* as an intellectual contemplation and administrative reform object, and of the anthropologist as the expert who possesses the truth about that object.

If the task at hand is to escape from the tentacles of indigenism, we should disassemble the traditional ways of making history as well as mobilize concepts so that they stop being universally valid reference points that require no discussion. Have we, by chance, asked ourselves thoughtfully how did we create categories such as history, science, heritage, nation-state, or *indio*? Have we seriously thought about how the notion of the state was historically created, in each moment and in each situation, how was it that it became the center from which the fiction of the lineal conception of historical time emerges? Hansen and Stepputat consider that as long as the state is seen as a universal entity, the source of social order and stability, as the agency capable of creating the authorized space of a nation materialized in geographical frontiers, infrastructure, monuments, and institutions, will remain fundamental in our image of what society is (2001, 2).

To explain why we are still clinging to this idealized image, we have to face epistemological difficulties and many political reasons. After all, we can't forget that disciplinary history does not have a different origin from that of the national formations, and that the birth of anthropology is connected to both the postrevolutionary Mexican state and the scientific and developmentalist ideas. Even considering all this, we should ask ourselves to what degree those decades dedicated to denounce the complicity between scholars and officers did nothing more than foreclose the reflection about the relationship with the other: Why that effort to unmask the relationship between anthropology and power avoided the critical revision of the relationship between anthropology and the *indio*? How is it possible that the historicizing of their own practices failed to lead anthropologists to analyze the social space that authorizes or makes their representations thinkable? (De Certeau 1993). In this sense, for Navarrete, the

> dialectic relationship between the research object (the pre-Columbian past, seen as exceptional) and the subject that studies it (the modern scientist that claimed to be equal to archaeologists all around the world) has been key to the justification of State's monopoly over archaeological heritage.
>
> (2009, 12)

I think that is what Lomnitz means when he says that to get out of the crisis in which Mexican anthropology currently is, and to allow it to regain a seat at the public debate table, it is necessary to reflect about ethnography, that practice of interaction that involves the body in the process of generating social data (2015). What he is proposing, I think, is to foster an 'ethnographic turn,' like the one that took place in the eighties in the United States and brought with it a radical change in the ways of thinking and doing anthropology. We could say that it is because of that turn that the anthropologist-ethnographer had to begin wondering about his own place of enunciation: Who provides the authority to speak on behalf of the others' identity or authenticity? Through which operations can he proclaim himself an expert? In short, to what degree and in which ways has he been an accomplice to domination? (Clifford and Marcus 1986). To historicize one's own practices would then mean to analyze the ways in which we, social researchers, have inhabited the scholar, professor, and intellectual positions, the ways through which each one of us, from his own trench, has contributed to that 'imaginary relationship' where one class dominates another.

To consecrate

After all this, what do we have to say about the Museum of Anthropology? Because, if the trajectory of the discipline's knowledge seems to depend on its possibility of exhibition, and if the museum exists only to commemorate its relationship with power, how should we consider the specificity of the museum device?

We could begin with the idea that the museum and scientific discipline are not the same, that the contents of the former are not a mirrored reflection of the discussion that has taken place in the scholarly sphere. For some, the actual crisis in Mexican anthropology is precisely due to the fact that the discipline came to be frozen there, in the pieces, display cabinets, and mannequins of the Museum of Anthropology, despite the museum not being its representative anymore. In the case of the Museum, heritage plays a key role, to the point of determining even its specificity as composition and texture of time. Let's say that heritage is in charge of articulating the different discursive forms that circulate within it (history, biology, aesthetics, anthropology . . .), of unifying the discourses by fixing them in time and by making culture a fact of nature. Its materiality allows the transformation of the 'ruins' into the evidence of an unquestionable gift that we received directly from the past, and so its function is to blur the distinction between knowledge and power by means of two actions: on the one hand, disguising as natural something that belongs to the realms of culture, on the other, turning a 'culture problem' into a problem of state character. Bennett called this the 'exhibition complex' referring to the great nineteenth-century museums where objects, exposed *in situ*, stripped of all context and joined with nature in a relationship of continuity, served as vehicles to inscribe messages of power and disseminate them across a wide audience (2004, 74).

If we go back to history with this, it would be necessary to retell it in a different fashion. From the perspective of heritage, understood as the set of assets and traditional practices that identify us as a nation, the museum's origin would be situated in the eighteenth century, not in an unearthing event (the Aztec calendar stone and the Coatlicue) or in a dream (that of the Creole Jesuit Clavijero), but in the disposition of that first Natural History Cabinet, the one that José Longinos created with the collections of 'the three realms of nature' gathered during the 1787 Botanical Expedition but that were never sent to Spain (Constantino 2010, 2). It could be argued that this cabinet, a private museum, open to the public to foster its education and supported by the imperial authority, constitutes a matrix over which archaeological and ethnographical layers would later be superimposed. In this sense, Bennett shows how modernity was construed in natural history museums, how these spaces worked as a 'laboratory' in which the disciplines were in charge of providing the necessary context to build a new past (2004). And so, while the enlightened New Spanish Cabinet naturalized a certain classification, it appropriated the territory on behalf of the empire and, at the same time, opened a space for the Creoles' demand to speak of nature in the name of a nation of their own (Gorbach 2014).

The history of the Museum of Anthropology could be then conceived from a long duration viewpoint, which dates back to the nineteenth century and even further back, to the eighteenth century, when the imperative of ordering nature by means of the language of science enters the stage. What I am arguing here is that the naturalization of a certain classification, a certain hierarchy, and also a certain pedagogy (Findlen 1996, 403),[10] founded in the original indistinctness between the real (the object), the power (of the state), and the knowledge (of natural history) over which the Natural History Cabinet was structured, constitutes the matrix over which the first nineteenth-century National Museum, and later the Museum of Anthropology, would be erected. It is a colonial matrix that the Museum of Anthropology has tried to cover up. Because even though its construction is obligated to a desire of erasing the colonial times, that dark phase identified with the empire, colonialism, and foreigners' hegemony that constitutes a hindrance for national history, the builders of the new museum, in the words of Roger Bartra, reclaimed without noticing 'the preservation of supposedly pre-Columbian customs that are, in fact, almost all of them, of colonial origin' (2004, 345–346; Rozat 2002).

This matrix is colonial and modern at the same time because it is a mechanism that extracts the object from its history and turns it into heritage, that is, in natural evidence of the past. It consists of an operation by which the 'museum piece' is extirpated from the link with the subjects that use it daily; torn out from history by erasing the violence of the conquest and of 'all the differentiation processes in which the racialized gaze rests' (Rufer 2014, 113). In this sense, it could be argued that the ethnographic collections that entered the museum in 1964 represent not so much an interpretative turn but the 'material' evidence of that old ideological construction in which contemporary indigenous groups are reduced to pieces of a heritage petrified in display cabinets, dioramas, mannequins, and scenes, recognized only as remains of a disappearing culture (Dorotinsky 2002; García 2009; Navarrete 2009; Peña 2011; Rufer 2014).[11] The abovementioned colonial matrix refers to the origin of a discipline that has been historically constituted and constructed through the encounter between a sovereign European observer and a non-European native in which the first affirms itself as the representative of a superior civilization (Clifford 2008; Rosaldo 1991, 35–51).

Maybe this is the place where anthropology dwells, trapped in the spatial gap that opens between the archaeology halls of the Museum of Anthropology's first floor and the ethnography ones of the second. Maybe anthropology is nothing but a ghost, the one that, as Bartra would say, allowed the indigenist ideology to enter the halls of the museum (Bartra 2004).

To demolish

But then, what to do with the Museum of Anthropology? How can it be detached from an evolutionist and nationalist gaze founded in a theory about the natural superiority of a group over another?

To escape this, Bartra proposes to rethink the relationship between archaeology and ethnography; that is, to review the link between the ancient and the modern, and, in that way, go through the conquest, the colonization, and the Christian space until we reach modernity. Instead of limiting ourselves to the description of marginal and 'primitive' cultures, he suggests undertaking an 'ethnography of modernity,' an ethnography of the hegemonic culture (2004, 347). Whatever is necessary to show that history is neither evolutionary nor pacific; to open the discipline to diverse perspectives and points of view; to show that heritage is a historical object, full of internal contradictions, center of political conflicts, producer of exclusions, and that its conceptualization overflows the limits of the 'great national problems' (Martín-Barbero 2005, 4). A way must be found to dismantle the monolithic time of the nation and show that the museum is constituted by a combination of times, of multiple pasts articulated in ways that are not those of the successiveness. Something should be done to transform the museum into an act of memory and present not relics but objects linked with the living reality of contemporary indigenous groups (Rufer 2014, 107). Maybe one of these ways is to recognize how the museum, in its present form, stands on this colonial-Creole-scientific-indigenist matrix, so that this acknowledgement allows us to imagine other time cuts and to experiment with new beginnings and new ways of relating to the past.

Nonetheless, there exists another possibility, the one proposed by Eduardo Abaroa in a 2012 artistic installation titled Destrucción total del museo (Total destruction of the Museum). There, he presented a work of 'destructive engineering': by means of the description of a merely physical process, he sought to shatter matter, to show its underground passages, to separate its parts, to dismember the building piece by piece, to demolish it and expose its remains, and this as a way to undo meanings and 'symbolically crack national identity.' Isn't it true—the exposition curator asks—that 'we are tempted to demolish it, at least in this way?' (Cruzvillegas 2012).

Notes

1 This special edition, which I was able to glance over on the day of the presentation with the aid of special gloves, will be included in the Christmas baskets that the President gives out in December, or so I have heard.
2 The author wrote an untranslatable word game, in which the word 'confusión' (confusion) is separated with a dash to form 'con' and 'fusion', which means 'with [the] fusion [of]'. (TN)
3 Tomás Pérez Vejo would look at it this way: the Museum of Anthropology's history is conditioned by 'anthropology's triumph as the science of the regime, and that of indigenism as State ideology' (2012, 74).
4 In the sixties and seventies, anthropologists like Guillermo Bonfil Batalla, Rodolfo Stavenhagen, Salomón Nahmad, and Leonel Durán opposed the elites' 'imaginary Mexico' and showed that indigenous cultures had a creative and civilizing role. See, among others, Bonfil Batalla (1989) and Nahmad (2008).
5 It is the case of Ricardo Pérez Montfort, who considers that official culture did not generate 'cultural identities' but 'false identities, shoddy and glittery' by manipulating and denying the plurality and versatility of local cultures (2011, 247). In this sense, he seems to reject the possibility that these stereotypes can produce cultural identities.
6 Salomón Nahmad defines indigenism as follows: 'more than a theoretical corpus, indigenism constitutes a conceptual and political position, a set of theoretical and adminstrative practices that combined cultural relativism theories with paternalistic policies for the indigenous populations' defense, development, and assimilation. Seen from the contemporary theories about race and culture point of view, indigenism resembles an eclectic grouping of theories that go from racial inferiority ideas to indigenous culture issues, which aim to the idea of indigenous civilization as of national culture's base' (Nahmad 2008).
7 This reflection space continues today. See, among others Araujo s/a. Rutsch (1996), Krotz (1987), and Vázquez León (2003).
8 The goal of this work was, in the words of Enrique Florescano, at that time Director of the National Institute of Anthropology and History, 'to fill out a void: the lack of a critical and systematic record of the anthropological task in and about Mexico' (1987, 9).
9 *Los grandes problemas nacionales* (*The great national problems*) is the title of a book by Andrés Molina Enríquez published in 1908, two years before the Mexican Revolution started.

10 In the Natural History Cabinet, exhibiting specimens of the three kingdoms of nature wasn't as important as showing the classification in itself. Not the singular, exotic, or unknown, as happened in the cabinets of curiosities, but the regular, that which orders nature. Following Linnaeus's classification, the Cabinet sought to order nature, by class, order, genre, species, and variety; in shelves, stands, drawers, signs, catalogs, according to its uses in medicine, industry, and economy.

11 In a research about communitarian museums in Mexico, Mario Rufer argues that even though the current rhetoric of heritage is still using the logic of the exhibition complex, the mechanisms and the ends pursued are different, because if in the nineteenth century the goal was to exhibit the great feats of the modern nation-state to a population that had to be educated, now it is more about a poetic of return, that is, allowing tradition to escape its archaic character in the Museum of Anthropology and to be produced in the town or village's spatial remoteness (2014, 97).

References

Araujo, Alejandro. 2012. 'Guillermo Bonfil Batalla. *México profundo* (1987).' In *México como problema. Esbozo de una historia intelectual*, ed. Carlos Illades, and Rodolfo Suárez. Mexico City: UAM–Siglo XXI.

Araujo, Alejandro. 2014. 'Mestizos, indios, extranjeros: lo propio y lo ajeno en la definición antropológica de la nación. Manuel Gamio y Guillermo Bonfil Batalla.' In *Aproximaciones contra el racismo*. https://contraracismos.files.wordpress.com/2014/10/alejandro-araujo-bonfil-y-gamio.pdf.

Bartra, Roger. 2004. 'Sonata etnográfica en no bemol.' In *El Museo Nacional de Antropología. 40 Aniversario*. Mexico City: Consejo Nacional para la Cultura y las Artes – Equilibrista.

Bennett, Tony. 2004. *Past Beyond Memory. Evolution, Museums, Colonialism*. London – New York: Routledge.

Bonfil Batalla, Guillermo. 1989. *México profundo*. Mexico City: Consejo Nacional para la Cultura y las Artes.

Certeau, Michel de. 1993. *La escritura de la historia*. Mexico: Universidad Iberoamericana.

Clifford, James. 2008. *Itinerarios transculturales*. Barcelona: Gedisa.

Clifford, James, and George E. Marcus, ed. 1986. *Writing Cultures. The Poetics and Politics of Ethnography*. Berkeley – Los Angeles – London: University of California.

Constantino, Ma. Eugenia. 2010. 'Los gabinetes novohispanos: espacios de exposición, catalogación, discusión y validación de la historia natural'. *Paper presented in the XII Congreso Mexicano de Historia de la Ciencia y la Tecnología*. Mexico.

Cruzvillegas, Abraham. 2012. 'Eduardo Abaroa: destrucción total del Museo de Antropología.' In *Artishock: revista de arte contemporáneo*. www.artishock.cl/2012/03/17/eduardo-abaroa-destruccion-total-del-museo-de-antropologia/.

De la Peña, Guillermo. 2011. 'La antropología, el indigenismo y la diversificación del patrimonio cultural mexicano,' In *La antropología y el patrimonio cultural en México*, ed. Guillermo de la Peña. Mexico City: Consejo Nacional para la Cultura y las Artes.

Dorotinsky, Débora. 2002. 'Fotografía y maniquíes en el Museo Nacional de Antropología.' *Luna Córnea* 23: 60–5.

Fernández, Miguel Ángel. 1987. *Historia de los museos en México*. Mexico: Promotora de Comercialización Directa.

Findlen, Paula. 1996. *Possessing Nature. Museums, Collecting, and Scientific Culture in Early Modern Italy*. Berkeley: University of California.

Florescano, Enrique. 1987. 'Liminar.' In *La antropología en México*, vol. 1, ed. Carlos García Mora. Mexico City: Instituto Nacional de Antropología e Historia.

Florescano, Enrique. 1993. 'La creación del Museo Nacional de Antropología y sus fines científicos, educativos y políticos.' In *El patrimonio cultural de México*, ed. Enrique Florescano. Mexico City: Fondo de Cultura Económica.

Florescano, Enrique. 2011. 'Preámbulo.' In *El patrimonio histórico y cultural de México*, Pablo Escalante Gonzalbo (coord.). Mexico: Consejo Nacional para la Cultura y las Artes.

García Canclini, Néstor. 2009. *Culturas híbridas. Estrategias para entrar y salir de la modernidad*. Mexico City: Debolsillo.

García Mora, Carlos ed. 1987. *La antropología en México*, 15 vols. Mexico City: Instituto Nacional de Antropología e Historia.

Gorbach, Frida. 2014. 'El Museo olvidado.' In *Museo Nacional de Antropología. 50 Aniversario (1825–1964)*. Mexico City: Consejo Nacional para la Cultura y las Artes.

Hansen, Thomas Blom, and Finn Stepputat. 2001. 'Introduction: of imagination.' In *States of Imagination. Ethnographic Explorations of the Poscolonial State*, ed. Thomas Blom Hansen and Finn Stepputat. Durham – London: Duke University.

INAH. 1964. *Boletín del Instituto Nacional de Antropología e Historia*, September.

Krotz, Esteban. 1987. 'Historia e historiografía de las ciencias antropológicas: una problemática teórica.' In *La antropología en México*, ed. Carlos García Mora. Mexico City: Instituto Nacional de Antropología e Historia.

Lomnitz, Claudio. 1999. *Modernidad indiana. Nueve ensayos sobre nación y mediación en México*. Mexico: Planeta.

López Caballero, Paula. 2011. 'De cómo el pasado prehispánico se volvió el pasado de todos los mexicanos.' In *El patrimonio histórico y cultural de México*, ed. Pablo Escalante Gonzalbo. Mexico City: Consejo Nacional para la Cultura y las Artes.

Martín-Barbero, Jesús. 2005. 'Patrimonio y valores. Desafíos de la globalización a las herencias y los derechos culturales.' In *Patrimonio y valores: claves de articulación en el marco de la Convención de Patrimonio Mundial*. Paris: Place de Fotenoy.

Méndez Lavielle, Guadalupe. 1987. 'La quiebra política (1965–1976).' In *La antropología en México*, vol.2, ed. Carlos García Mora. Mexico City: Instituto Nacional de Antropología e Historia.

Mier, Raymundo. 1996. 'Las taxonomías del desprecio. Vicisitudes en la historia de la antropología en México.' *La historia de la antropología en México*, ed. Mechthild Rutsch. Mexico City: Universidad Iberoamericana-Plaza y Valdés-Instituto Nacional Indigenista.

Nahmad Sittón, Salomón. 2008. 'Mexico: Anthropology and the Nation-State.' In *A Companion to Latin American Anthropology*, ed. Deborah Poole. India: Blackwell.

Navarrete, Federico. 2009. 'Ruinas y Estado: arqueología de una simbiosis mexicana.' In *Pueblos indígenas y arqueología en América Latina*, ed. Cristóbal Gnecco and Patricia Ayala Rocabado. Bogotá: Banco de la República – Universidad de los Andes.

Pérez Montfort, Ricardo. 2011. 'Nacionalismo y representación en el México posrevolucionario (1920–1940). La construcción de estereotipos nacionales.' In *La idea de nuestro patrimonio histórico y cultural*, ed. Pablo Escalante Gonzalbo. Mexico City: Consejo Nacional para la Cultura y las Artes.

Pérez Vejo, Tomás. 2012. 'Historia, antropología y arte: tres sujetos, dos pasados y una sola nación verdadera.' *Revista de Indias*, LXXII(254). http://revistadeindias.revistas.csic.es/index.php/revistadeindias/article/viewFile/887/960.

Rosaldo, Renato. 1991. *Cultura y verdad, Nueva propuesta de análisis social*. Mexico City: Consejo Nacional para la Cultura y las Artes – Grijalbo.

Rozat, Guy. 2002. *Indios imaginarios e indios reales en los relatos de la conquista de México*. Mexico: Universidad Veracruzana – Instituto Nacional de Antropología e Historia.

Rufer, Mario. 2014. 'La exhibición del otro: tradición, memoria y colonialidad en museos de México.' *Antítesis* 7(14). July-December. Londrina: Universidade Estadual de Londrina.

Rutsch, Mechtild, ed. 1996. *La historia de la antropología en México*. Mexico City: Universidad Iberoamericana-Plaza y Valdés – Instituto Nacional Indigenista.

Téllez Ortega, Javier. 1987. 'La época de oro (1940–1964).' In *La antropología en México*, vol.2, ed. Carlos García Mora. Mexico City: Instituto Nacional de Antropología e Historia.

Vázquez León, Luis. 2003. *El Leviatán arqueológico. Antropología de una tradición científica en México*. Mexico City: Centro de Investigaciones y Estudios Superiores en Antropología Social.

7 Going back to the past or coming back from the past?
Governmental policies and uses of the past in a Ranquel community in San Luis, Argentina

María Celina Chocobare

Between 2006 and 2009, the government of the province of San Luis carried out some initiatives specifically for a part of the population known as Ranquel.[1] Regulations were created, and lands, houses, a school, a hospital, and other benefits were given to 22 Ranquel families. These families that lived in the cities of Villa Mercedes and Justo Daract now moved to the new lands. On May 30, 2009, the Ranquel town was officially founded and obtained the minimum and temporary status (till the nation makes a decision) of municipality. This area is located approximately 180 km from Villa Mercedes to the south of the province and the nearest city is Batavia, located at a distance of 27 km.

During 2009, after the foundation of the Ranquel town, official actions were widely implemented at a provincial level (also regional and national). In different sectors of society (meetings with family and friends, staff rooms, comments in *El Diario de la República* newspaper,[2] and in the sessions of the provincial legislature), some doubts or suspicions were raised about the authenticity of those who claimed to be Ranqueles. These were some statements heard among the people: 'these are not real Indians'; 'those are not Ranqueles'; 'they are lazy and opportunistic'; 'the Ranqueles are not Indians from San Luis.' Some people were also afraid that the sovereignty of the province could be affected in the sense that 'all the Indians would move to this place.' Other people thought that *malones* (Indian raids) would start again, or that criminals would hide in the Ranquel town because the police had no jurisdiction there. These situations aroused my interest in understanding how the 'recognition' is carried out, and have also raised some questions about the way in which these constructs about these indigenous people are created. As Briones suggests, the common sense statements could be used as a way to look for possible lines of historical consistency (2004, 74).

In the present work, my aim is to reflect upon the different uses of the past, which were evident in statements of agents belonging to the ruling party, opposing parties, and the general public. I understand that in the disputes that are generated due to the implementation of governmental actions for the families recognized as

Ranqueles, the said families are defined as a separate group belonging to the interior of the society of San Luis, occupying a specific place in the history of the province. The Ranqueles are defined as a group that belongs to the past, in tension with the rest of the society of San Luis.

According to the abovementioned information, this investigation focuses on a perspective that analyzes the relations between the state actions and the populations that receive them. Therefore, the state is considered as 'an administration' as described by Adriana Vianna and Juliana Farias in their work about the relationship between violence and gender in Rio de Janeiro, taking into account the ideas of Souza Lima who 'considers the state in its routine and institutional action and in its continuous process of formation, as an action which is always incomplete and that is exercised over the territories and populations through time' (Souza Lima quoted in Farias and Vianna 2011, 93). This point of view allows us to recognize the tutelary action undertaken by the government. In this sense, the Ranqueles are defined as people that deserve the protection of the state, since they cannot change their unfavorable situation by themselves (Souza Lima 1995). The Ranqueles would be in a situation of 'vulnerability' caused by social exclusion and the absence of social and political recognition.[3] Through a set of actions that seek reparations for historical injustices, the provincial state has become a protector–provider of this community, being responsible for the 're-emergence of the indigenous identities.'[4]

An interpretation of the past by the provincial government has been made concrete in regulations, big buildings, ceremonies and touristic projects. These uses of the past create social meanings that are disputed according to the interests that belong to the present time (from the perspective of the Ranquel families, government agents, opposing parties, and from the different viewpoints of individuals), and also enable a more complex analysis of the idea that the memories imposed from this position of power of the government are fixed, considering them 'an unstable configuration of meanings, characterized by uncertainty, impermanence and contradiction' (Rufer 2010, 121–124). At the same time, these memories could enable the reconfiguration of those established differences, causing instability in the historical constructions of *otherness*[5] to the interior of the province.

The purpose is not only to observe the public representations of the past, which are made concrete in documents, shows, exhibitions, buildings, etc., but also to reflect upon the processes through which they are constructed, investigating the disputes, contradictions, and different meanings that are assigned to them. The work of Mario Rufer has been inspiring in analyzing the relationship between the uses of the past and the state actions, since he deals with the issues of the 'artifacts of memory' in the public domain. Rufer indicates that when we discuss the representation of the memory in the public domain, it is important to take into account the way in which 'the past time is reproduced, told and integrated in a present time which is characterized by relationships of power and difference.' According to this, registering the processes of debate and disputes for public representations of the past allow us to understand 'the different locations of the memory' that come into conflict, and the ambiguities that exist in what Rufer calls 'the public domain of the uses of the past.' The author detects two processes in the ambiguities mentioned: on the one hand, the state that becomes a symbolic representation of the past in the present, and on the other hand, this power would be 'experimented, understood and answered' in different ways by certain social groups (2010, 120–121).

In August and September 2009, in the Chamber of Deputies of the province, there were discussions among some deputies with regard to the adhesion of the Chamber to the tribute for the anniversary of the foundation of the city of San Luis and the approval of 'an emergency act' (without prior Congress approval), which conferred the expansion of the cession of lands with a minimum status of municipality to the 'Ranquel community.' In order to analyze these discussions, I would like to focus on the contributions of Shore, who considers the government policies as 'tools for intervention and social action that regulate and change the society' (2010, 32). One of the most important characteristics of these government policies is that they help to construct 'new types of subjectivity,' that is to say, they help to classify people as 'citizens,' 'professionals,' 'immigrants,' 'criminals,' or 'perverts.' Therefore, these policies provide individuals and groups with certain identities, and while they help to construct them actively, they establish different ways to regulate, control, and act upon the populations (36). As I mentioned earlier, these debates took place while the state actions toward the Ranqueles were being widely implemented due to the foundation of the Ranquel town and the relocation of families to this place. This situation helped to visualize the indigenous presence and a change in the way the state acted toward 'the native communities of the province,' and at the same time generated disputes for the meaning of those actions in relation to the 'history and identity of the province.'

The birthday of the city ... Who are the *Sanluiseños*?

> On August 25, 1594, the Conqueror founded the city alongside the river Chorrillo and in the side called Punta de los Venados of the hills of San Luis, exactly the same day consecrated to Saint Louis King of France, patron saint of the city.
>
> In this tribute project, we would like to adhere to the commemoration of the 415th anniversary of the foundation of the city of San Luis, and also adhere to the ceremonies related to this commemoration.[6]

This is how the project for the adhesion of the Legislature of the Province of San Luis to the tribute for the commemoration of the 415th anniversary of the foundation of the city was presented. But in 2009, following the actions carried out by the provincial government for the Ranquel families, some deputies started to reconsider the reason for the commemoration. I am interested in analyzing the way in which the past is evoked due to a possible change of sense in the provincial history, which alters the certainties related to the commemoration. In the discussions chosen, the tensions due to the implementation of governmental actions toward the Ranqueles are evident, and thus the meanings of said tribute are under dispute. As Adriana Vianna and Mauricio Parada state, the commemorations imply the 'suspension' of everyday life, which would account for the intensity of the commemoration, since it is in that 'emptiness of meaning' that new forms of social orders can be taught, practiced, and can become significant for most part of the population (2002, 86).

The actions carried out by the provincial government toward the Ranquel families were accompanied by an accusation speech against the colonial violence, while in the project of adhesion to the tribute, the 'conqueror' was presented as the founder of the city and responsible for leaving a legacy. This contradiction is observed by one of the deputies who expresses the following idea:

> in order to adhere to this project, [. . .] I would like to know ¿Which is the opinion of the ruling party about the history of this province? On the one hand, we have all these tributes to the Ranqueles, native communities, we have public documents issued by the ruling party itself, in which it [. . .] condemns the genocide [. . .] suffered by this native community called Ranqueles. On the other hand, [. . .] today in this tribute project, which I can read in the corresponding part, that heritage, the goods received, the essential and permanent values in which we have to include the catholic religion, the language and the culture of the past . . .[7]

In the deputy's statements, colonial violence is doubted as there were suspicions with regard to the possible victims—'that community called Ranqueles.' Even though the interventions of the deputies can be considered controversies among opposing political groups, I would like to concentrate on the disputes to define the past, and how this process helps to order the positions in the present, which seek to settle the differences under the idea of 'San Luis unity.' The celebration, which has been shaped during these 415 years since the Spanish foundation, is intended to maintain the unity of the Sanluiseños. The alteration of the provincial history due to the accusation of colonial violence against the 'native communities' (apart from the presence of Ranquel families) could put the unity founded (among other components) in the Spanish 'heritage' in danger. Therefore, it was necessary to unify the controversies in the 'melting pot.' This idea is expressed by the following deputies:

> [. . .] now that we are celebrating this period of the foundation of the province of San Luis, of the interpenetration of two cultures which were completely different and that clashed; one is the culture brought by the Spanish conquest, and the other one is the culture of the native communities. In that clash of the two cultures, we should find a harmony which can be positive for the entire province of San Luis . . .[8]

The deputy who started the debate said:

The history of San Luis, like the history of this country [...] is what it was once called a 'melting pot.' San Luis does not only include the first Spanish people, but also the Italians, the Turkish, the Jewish, the Polish, all of them, including the mestizos. This mingling of races, first between Spanish people and native communities ... we are all puntanos.[9]

Following the same line of thought, deputy Quiroga added that

> in the end, the aim today is to remember a special day, August 25, which many of us have celebrated along the years, maybe with some differences, but for all the Sanluiseños, or for most of them, this is another anniversary of our beloved San Luis.[10]

In this way, we start a new 'cancellation of the memory of the nonwhite people' (Segato 2010, 26) that coexists in contradiction with the 'recognition.' As Hale indicates, although the mestizo project as a government ideology is in decadence, the measures implemented in the last years imply new ways of governing the citizens that can reinforce or exacerbate racial hierarchies' (2004, 2). Therefore, the *mestizaje* would be a

> comfortable third position, since it allows us to repudiate the European invaders of the past, but at the same time does not prevent programming the existence as we were part of them, in the same way that the exaltation of the Indians from the past does not prevent the segregation of the present Indians.
> (Colombres 2006, 318)

The opposing positions that generate the discussion disappear with the idea of the 'melting pot,' which is the 'origin of the sanluiseño.' There is a strong need to 'harmonize' the opposing 'versions' and in this harmonization, once again, the recently recognized 'native communities' are sent to the past, to the 'point of origin' of the foundation of the province. After these discussions among the deputies, the tribute project was approved unanimously in spite of the declared differences, and the sense of continuity of the celebration was protected. The intentions of the ruling party were not as important as the desire to celebrate the foundation of the city once again. The 'native communities' should be part of the interior of the provincial history, emphasizing the idea of unity in the celebration of the Sanluiseños. The analysis of Blázquez (2012) about the 'patriotic performances' that celebrate the May Revolution of 1810 in Argentina can be useful to analyze the discussions generated as a result of the celebration of a new anniversary of the city of San Luis. Blázquez (2012, 127) defines the patriotic performances as

> forms of restored behaviors [...] or actions carried out always for a second time, that every time that they are carried out, the same thing (or more or less) is said and the same stories (almost all) are presented. These

characteristics are part of the poetics of the performative force that helps to imagine a nation and create individuals who are capable of doing it.

In this sense, it was important to protect the meaning of unity that implies the anniversary of the city. As Blázquez indicates: equivalent to May 25 in Argentina, August 25 would be an 'inaugural event' for the Sanluiseños, and 'if it is repeated again and again the idea becomes a fixed one' and allows the Sanluiseños to recognize themselves as a community that 'believes in' August 25 as an inaugural ceremony for the Sanluiseños and 'becomes the protagonist' of this event (2012, 128).

Coming back from the past or going back to the past?

The governmental actions carried out for the Ranquel families in San Luis are included in a broader process of recognition of the indigenous rights, which goes back to the last decades of the twentieth century. This process is linked to a historical event related to the formation of a language of differences, of the creation of certain places and policies that can block others, possibly generating inequalities and producing tensions that can make hegemonic classifications unstable (Grimson 2013, 11–19). In a context where the negation of the cultural difference is being modified by its 'celebration,' new ethno-national borders are being created that place emphasis on the value of this difference (Boccara and Ayala 2011). As Segato states, 'the important role of the national state as the creator of diversity is not over' (2002, 106). On the contrary, the idea that 'the state could take advantage of 'administering the ethnicity' (instead of) working for its elimination' has prevailed since the 1980s (Gros 1997, 32; quoted by Segato 2002, 106). Argentina, as a signatory country of international agreements, incorporates in the constitutional reform of 1994, the recognition of the ethnic and cultural preexistence of the indigenous communities (Article 75, Section 17).[11] However, the provinces do not reproduce the national policies in a similar way; they recreate in its interior different ways of administering their local formations of otherness, while at the same time specifying them in relation to the 'national identity' (Briones 2008, 17).

According to some governmental agents from San Luis, the Ranqueles are being recognized as a population from the past. In pictures published in official pamphlets, in the buildings and houses that simulate indigenous huts, in the initiative of relocating them in a rural and isolated area, the Ranquel families are associated with the characteristics of rural life, nature, and traditional clothes that relate them to the characteristics of their ancestors, which the descendants do not necessarily maintain. This fact helps generate doubts in relation to the authenticity of the descendants. These characteristics are identical to the way in which the Ranqueles are presented in local historical productions (Núñez and Vacca 2011; Pastor 1942). These productions place emphasis on the problematic relationships between the Ranqueles and the Hispanic-Criollo society of San Luis. The people of San Luis are presented as victims of the Ranquel tribes, which stalk them continuously, while the Ranqueles are characterized by their bravery. These stories create the idea of a heroic San Luis, a poor province with a small population, due to the fact that a lot of men were sent to the independence wars in Spain, and then the province suffered the Ranquel attacks. After the 'Conquest of the Desert' that took place at the end of the nineteenth century,[12] the literature says that the Ranqueles were apparently annihilated and then made 'invisible' as part of the population of the province.[13] I consider that these statements help to reinforce ideas about certain characteristics that the Ranqueles should possess, and generate doubts about their 'existence' and authenticity,[14] as they were dispersed in different sectors.

The ordinary session No 17 of the Chamber of Deputies of the Province (September 16, 2009) treated the approval of the 'emergency act' (without prior Congress approval) N° 2884-MGJyC-2009, which conferred the expansion of the cession of lands with a status of municipality to the Ranquel community. The discussions that took place before the session consolidate representations of the past that come into tension when there are different opinions with regard to the 'place' that the Ranqueles are assigned as a different group, in the interior of the society. By drawing upon the past, the Ranqueles are accepted as a community that belongs to that period. In such a case, their recognition should be related with that period and not with the present or future. The past becomes unstable and controversial, and different deputies suggest whether or not to accept the current presence of the Ranqueles.

Among the different points to consider for the approval of the mentioned decree, some opposing deputies suggest that the provincial sovereignty could be lost due to the recognition of a 'Ranquel nation' in the interior of the province. The cession of lands to the Ranquel families is also considered a 'misuse' of the economic assets of the province, especially due to the doubts related to the authenticity of those families. Some deputies call them 'supposed Ranqueles.' Other deputies indicate that these families are not 'native' of the province of San Luis, but nomadic indigenous peoples. I am not interested in discussing the different interpretations among the deputies, but the ways in which the past is evoked to command positions in the present. By drawing on quotes of academic and legal literature, different versions are presented to construct different entities: the Ranqueles, the provincial state, and the Sanluiseños. In the words of deputy Estrada Dubor:

> If you had to pay attention to the reality of the time, in the past of the province of San Luis, we remind you that it is called reaction, going backwards. And we [. . .] have the obligation to act now and in the future.
>
> Mr. President, this topic about the native communities [. . .] should be taken into account by all the Argentinians [. . .] it is a non-virtual drama, it is real, and it exists in the provinces of Neuquén, Río Negro, Salta, Jujuy, Formosa, Chaco [. . .] but [. . .] this problem does not exist in the province of San Luis. We have to concentrate on that seriously. We know that it involves ecosystems, natural resources [. . .].

Mr. President, I ask myself again: ¿where are we going? ¿how is this going to continue? [...] and what will remain [...] to the Sanluiseños of the twenty-first century? Because this sounds very nice in the virtual sphere of the past and history, but Mr. President, we need to concentrate on the present San Luis.[15]

In this lengthy quote, there are certain issues that could also be heard outside the sessions hall: the lack of Ranqueles in the province makes the 'indigenous problem' an 'issue' that belongs to other Argentinian provinces, and also the idea that it is acceptable to recognize them as communities from the past, but without affecting the economic assets of the province. According to these statements, the Ranqueles are a 'threat' to provincial sovereignty. Therefore, their recognition would only be accepted in the 'virtual and past' sphere to which the 'Indians' belong, which would also be 'very nice.' As a result of these ideas, it is important to reflect on the way in which the Ranqueles are being defined as a community from the past, occupying a place in the historical narrative of the province, in which the indigenous past would perpetuate itself as a 'point of origin' in the time of the nation-state (Taussig 1995, 58).

One of the opposing deputies also said that the Ranqueles were a nomadic community, which means that they had not settled in the current territory of San Luis. In response to this statement, Julio Braverman, deputy of the ruling party and in charge of presenting the project, stated an opposing view:

> what we want to do is to generate a broad social policy that includes everybody equally. The Ranquel nation has lived in these lands, regardless of the fact that they had belonged to them or not. This is a legal act which will help the Ranquel nation to develop, live in peace, in freedom, with all their rights and with the possibility of growth.[16]

This counterview does not include the idea of permanence and proposes the idea of 'preexistence' of the Ranqueles in the current territory of the province of San Luis. This is related to one of the characteristics of the actions carried out toward the Ranquel families. These are presented as 'natural' based on the ethnic and cultural preexistence of the Ranqueles, so a disagreement would be considered inappropriate (Shore 2010, 34). In this way, a previous past to the Spanish conquest is mainly evoked, blurring bigger processes of oppression and negation of the indigenous presence in Argentina.[17] At the same time, the deputy relates the actions intended for the Ranqueles with governmental policies that seek to 'generate a wider social policy,' considering the state a facilitator of a group of benefits for the Ranquel families, which will 'help' them to develop, live in peace, with freedom, with progress, and with all their rights. Due to criticism from opposing deputies, the deputy decides to expand his idea by reading a prologue written by the governor, Alberto Rodriguez Saá, for a compilation of laws that the Senate of the Province would be enacting.[18] According to the deputy, this prologue would serve to clarify to all deputies about the process initiated in the province 'with the recognition of the Ranquel community.' Following the deputy s ideas, progress should be understood as economic development and inclusion in the 'technologies of the modern world'; he proposes the following:

> a community must have economic viability [. . .] it must have an economic organization that allows the community not only to live, nourish itself and meet its needs, but also to obtain capital to invest so that the community can be part of progress. At the moment, the Ranqueles have chosen horse breeding, rural activities [. . .] once we have signed a final treaty with the Ranqueles, our idea is to add cold-storage industries, leather industries, digital industries and craftwork. Also, we will include tourism and all the activities that are related to this industry.[19]

By signing a 'treaty' with the provincial government, the Ranqueles would finally enter the 'world of progress' moving from rural activities to industrial ones, which will allow them to accumulate capital. These actions of state 'recognition' could be analyzed through the hypothesis of Taussig about the 'magic of the state' during his study of the mountain of María Lionza in Venezuela. Taussig emphasizes that it is important to recognize that 'primitivism' is not the origin lost in the darkness of time and history but, on the contrary, remains as a vital force in the rational discourse of the modern state (1992, 514–515). The idea of primitivism would be represented by the relationship between the Ranqueles and nature and their relationship to the land, as opposed to the idea of civilization progress provided by the state. In the Ranquel town, the past is reproduced in an esthetic way that is reflected in the presence of the state, which is made concrete in the big buildings built in town (apart from building houses, a school and a hospital, the government also built a floating stage in one of the lakes belonging to the community) that stand out in a dry, flat, and deserted landscape. This allows us to think of the need of the state to create 'a fair and undeniable aura' (Taussig 1992, 516). Consequently, the state sovereignty is not limited but extended to the Ranquel community. The way in which the state actions are presented situates the Ranqueles as recipients of those actions. This is expressed in the prologue in question, that 'we have two cultures' (Ranqueles and Huarpes; also the de Comechingones culture is taken into account). They are not defined as people or communities, but as cultures. It says that we 'have returned' the lands to the Ranqueles and:

> We are working now to rebuild the past, because it is evident that the Ranqueles as well as the Huarpes have suffered a cultural breakdown and cultural control [. . .] There is a lot of evidence that allow us to verify this, especially during colonial times, when these communities were not allowed to speak their language, recognize and practice their religion, to have their own religious and pre religious views and their spiritual thoughts. We should return, allow, and provide all these things to the communities mentioned.[20]

The cultural distance as well as temporal distance is emphasized. The time of the Ranqueles is a past that needs to be rebuilt (this would allow them to 'recover their culture'), because it has been 'broken' by colonial domination. In this way, 'the point of origin' in which the indigenous would be situated can converge with the progress that has characterized the destiny (now offered to the Ranqueles) of provincial history. The Ranqueles are recognized as a part of a past that has been overcome and now they should be 'incorporated' into a 'world of progress.' The aim is that they can keep their traditions and show them as evidence of the past, which is now 'rebuilt' with the help of the provincial state. In this way, the past, which is represented as a point of origin, and progress, which is represented by the actions 'offered' by the state, come together. Shore (2010), inspired by the observations of Malinowski (1926) on the role of the myth in the Trobiand society, points out that public policies offer rhetoric narratives that serve to justify or condemn the present and to legitimize those who occupy positions of authority. These rhetoric narratives also 'provide the means to unify the past and the present,' giving 'coherence, order and certainty to actions carried out by the government, which are often illogical, disorganized and uncertain.' These narratives also 'provide an alliance zone, a way to unify people in order to have a common aim or objective and a mechanism to define and maintain the symbolic borders that separate 'these people' from "us"' (Shore 2010, 32). There is protection dynamics that organizes the state actions by ordering, separating, and classifying Ranqueles and Sanluiseños, and identifying progress with state actions and the 'traditional customs' with the Ranqueles. The inclusion of the Ranqueles in the 'world of progress' is thought to be related with the role of the state, which, as Souza Lima indicates, becomes 'a group guardian, space controller, and an entity in charge of maintaining the differences in their niches' (2002, 16).[21]

Shortening distances

Due to this set of governmental actions intended for the Ranqueles, a debate arose that allowed to experience a public memory in relation to the indigenous populations and their controversial position among past, present, and future. In this, different suspicions related to the presence of the Ranqueles gain importance. A 'negative recognition' is brought up once again as a result of the presence of the 'other,' which would threaten the provincial-national sovereignty. A double game of negation takes place: on the one hand, the recognition of the Ranquel presence and, on the other hand, the recognition of 'the other' that 'would come back' (or rather belongs to) from the past.

The way in which the past is represented with the initiative of relocating Ranquel families to a place isolated from others and situated in a rural area, with the clear intention that they could 'recover' their culture and rebuild their past with the 'help' of the provincial government, not only implies the idea of culture and identity as static (Cuche 2002) but also involves a great motivation to define, administer, and exhibit the difference. However, the families in the Ranquel town are probably reappropriating the past in a different way. The past is evoked to establish continuity with their ancestors, but the present-future dimension is emphasized. In relation to this, a Ranquel woman stated that her decision to move to the lands was based on the idea of 'what they have always been, what they are and what they will be.' Further, with regard to those who visit the town and look at them in a strange way, other women that live in the town say: 'some people have asked us: What type of clothes do you wear? They think we are not like them! We are urban Indians!'[22] In this way, they do not situate themselves in the past nor do they consider themselves separated from the society of San Luis. While identifying themselves with their ancestors by recognizing their origin as indigenous, they emphasize their urban nature, which gets rid of the rural and detached representation and creates a discontinuity between that 'remote past' and the present of the families. Taussig's idea about violence and resistance in the Americas is useful while thinking how these women would be 'promoting accepted essences again,' destroying the myths around the image of the 'Indians' as a population from the past (1995, 52–72).

The way in which the Ranquel families are 'recognized' by the provincial government generates suspicions, while questioning the idea of their nonexistence and challenging the historical discourse of the province, but without deconstructing it. In fact, it coexists in a controversial way as it is used by the ruling party, the opposing parties, the Ranqueles, and other public expressions.

In the local sector, the historiographical productions situate the indigenous in a distant past, in conflict with the Hispanic-Criollo society of San Luis. This idea is in contrast with the actions recently carried out by the provincial government. These governmental actions used the national and international policies of recognition toward the indigenous communities as points of reference, but they defined their actions on the basis of the attributes that the indigenous communities may possess according to local historical literature. Therefore, we can reflect on how the 'recognition' policies help to create asymmetric relationships that go back to the past, building a narrative that situates the Ranqueles inside the official history of the province. This narrative transfers them from a remote past to the present, incorporating them as a primitive component, as an aboriginal culture. According to the way in which the Ranquel families define themselves, we could ask ourselves if this process that joins the celebration of the difference with the official history, could be re-read through memory practices that situate the construction of identities in the 'between' and not in the 'distance.'

Notes

1. The Ranqueles were one of the indigenous tribes that have been registered as inhabitants of the Pampa–Norpatagonian territory since the middle of the eighteenth century.
2. Provincial newspaper belonging to the government, which disseminates news on the actions carried out by the provincial government. It is the only printed newspaper that is sold in the entire province. In the digital version, readers can write comments below the news.
3. This contact would not have been possible without the conversations between María Gabriela Lugones and the research project team: 'The protective dimension of state actions in three cases, Córdoba 2012–2013' run by María G. Lugones.
4. Executive power of the province of San Luis, letter of commitment, November 9, 2006, provided by the Centre of Ranqueles Studies of Villa Mercedes City.

134 *María Celina Chocobare*

5 By analyzing the national configurations of diversity, Rita Segato indicates that inside each national society 'unification strategies implemented by each state are produced, and the reactions created by these strategies are reflected in special ruptures in the national societies.' Therefore, according to her, a 'national formation of diversity' takes place in each national history. Inside this formation, 'the 'historical otherness' are the social groups, and their way to be 'the other' derives from that history and it is part of that specific formation (Segato 2002, 114–115).
6 Vallone, Andrés Alberto, provincial deputy, Chamber of Deputies of the Province of San Luis, report of parliamentary proceedings No 14, August 19, 2009.
7 Laborda Ibarra, Juan José, provincial deputy, Chamber of Deputies of the Province of San Luis, report of parliamentary proceedings No 14, August 19, 2009.
8 Estrada Dubor, Eduardo Luis, provincial deputy, Chamber of Deputies of the Province of San Luis, report of parliamentary proceedings No 14, August 19, 2009.
9 Laborda Ibarra, Juan José, provincial deputy, Chamber of Deputies of the Province of San Luis, report of parliamentary proceedings No 14, August 19, 2009.
10 Quiroga, Augusto Cecilio, provincial deputy, Chamber of Deputies of the Province of San Luis, report of parliamentary proceedings No 14, August 19, 2009.
11 This recognition is the result of a process that started around the 1980s, when the following factors were combined: the democratic transition that generated new spaces of discussion to direct the demands that the indigenous populations had been asking for, and an international context that recognized the indigenous populations (Mandrini 2008, 271).
12 Military campaign carried out by the Argentinian state between 1878 and 1885, with the intention of occupying the territories inhabited by indigenous communities.
13 It is important to point out that there are no local historical productions that deal with the situation of the Ranqueles after the Conquest of the Desert, which took place at the end of the nineteenth century.
14 This same line of thought appears in textbooks for the primary level.
15 Estrada Dubor, Eduardo Luis, provincial deputy, Chamber of Deputies, Legislative Branch of the Province of San Luis, report of parliamentary proceedings No 17, September 16, 2009.
16 Braverman, Julio Saúl, provincial deputy, Chamber of Deputies, Legislative Branch of the Province of San Luis, report of parliamentary proceedings No 17, September 16, 2009.
17 The Ranqueles maintained their autonomy until the military actions that took place at the end of the nineteenth century. However, in different statements of governmental agents, they make reference to the colonial violence and, to a lesser extent, to the one carried out by the Argentinian government. I consider that this association between a remote past of domination and a present of recognition creates suspicions of the Ranqueles in the present, since they may not have similar characteristics as their ancestors. This way of 'recognition' is similar to the reparation way studied by Lazzari (2007) for the Rankülche case in La Pampa.
18 The prologue read by the deputy during the session is similar to the prologue of the book *San Luis, los dueños de la tierra*, 2009. Gente 1 ed. Buenos Aires: Atlántida.
19 Braverman, Julio Saúl, provincial deputy, Chamber of Deputies of San Luis, report of parliamentary proceedings No 17, September 16, 2009.
20. Braverman, Julio Saúl, provincial deputy, Chamber of Deputies of the Province of San Luis, report of parliamentary proceedings No 17, September 16, 2009.
21 Souza Lima draws attention to the etymological unit between 'gestar' and 'gerir' (develop and manage). 'Develop' refers to the constitutive and educational function of teaching how 'to be,' and 'gerir' refers to daily control in administrative terms (Souza Lima 2002, 16). I consider that the distinction made by Souza Lima can explain different

practices carried out by the state power that combine this educational and administrative dimension. This is present in the intention of guiding an interpretation of the past and the destiny of the Ranqueles. This community is established as a population different from the rest, while the state presence is expanded in its continuous process of formation.

22 Interviews carried out by the author, November 9, 2010, Ranquel Town, San Luis.

References

Blázquez, Gustavo. 2012. 'Las fiestas mayas una y otra vez. Performances patrióticos y performatividad de estado en Argentina.' In *Nación y diferencia. Procesos de identificación y formaciones de otredad en contextos poscoloniales*, ed. Mario Rufer, 123–50. México: Itaca.

Boccara, Guillaume, and Patricia Ayala. 2011. 'La nacionalización del indígena en tiempos de multiculturalismo neoliberal.' *Forum for inter-American Research* 4(2) (November).

Briones, Claudia. 2004. 'Construcciones de aboriginalidad en Argentina.' *Societé suisse des américanistes-gesellschaft Bulletin* 68: 73–90.

Briones, Claudia. 2008. 'Formaciones de alteridad: contextos globales, procesos nacionales y provinciales.' In *Cartografías argentinas. Políticas indigenistas y formaciones provinciales de alteridad*, ed. Claudia Briones, 36–9. Buenos Aires: Antropofagía.

Chamber of Deputies of the Province of San Luis. 2009. Report of parliamentary proceedings No 14, August 19. San Luis.

Chamber of Deputies of the Province of San Luis. 2010. Report of parliamentary proceedings No17, September 16. San Luis.

Colombres, Adolfo. 2006. 'Diversidad cultural y proceso civilizatorio.' In *Diversidad cultural e interculturalidad*, eds. Aldo Amegeiras, and Elisa Jure, 317–28. Buenos Aires: Prometeo Libros.

Cuche, Denys. 2002. *La noción de cultura en las ciencias sociales*. Buenos Aires: Nueva Visión.

Farias, Juliana, and Adriana Vianna. 2011. 'A guerra das mães: dor e política em situações de violencia institucional.' *Cadernos Pagu*, 37: 79–116.

Grimson, Alejandro. 2013. 'Introducción.' In *Hegemonía cultural y políticas de la diferencia*, eds. Alejandro Grimson, and Karina Bidaseca, 9–20. Buenos Aires: CLACSO.

Hale, Charles. 2004. 'El protagonismo indígena, las políticas estatales y el nuevo racismo en la época del 'indio permitido.' Presentation for the conference, 'Construyendo la paz: Guatemala desde un enfoque comparado.' Misión de Verificación de las Naciones Unidas en Guatemala (MINUGUA), October 27–29.

Lazzari, Axel. 2007. Identidad y fantasma: situando las nuevas prácticas de libertad del movimiento indígena en La Pampa. *Quinto Sol*, 11: 91–122.

Mandrini, Raul. 2008. *La argentina Aborigen, de los primeros pobladores a 1910*. Buenos Aires: Siglo XXI.

Núñez, Urbano, and Vacca Duval. 2011. *Historia de San Luis*. 2 vols. San Luis: el tabaquillo. Orig. pub. 1967.

Parada, Mauricio, and Adriana Vianna. 2002. 'Infância e nação em desfile: o desfile da juventude e a Hora da Independência, 1936/1937.' In *Gestar e gerir. Estudos para una antropología da administração pública no Brasil*, ed. Antonio Carlos Souza Lima, 85–110. Rio de Janeiro: Relume-Dumará.

Pastor, Reynaldo. 1942. *La guerra contra el indio en la jurisdicción de San Luis*. Buenos Aires: Kraft.

Rufer, Mario. 2010. 'Memoria sin garantías: usos del pasado y política del presente.' In *Anuario de investigación 2009*. UAM-X. México: 107–40. http://148.206.107.15/biblioteca_digital/capitulos/333–4728sph.pdf

Segato, Rita. 2002. 'Identidades políticas y alteridades históricas. Una crítica a las certezas del pluralismo global.' *Nueva Sociedad*, 178: 104–25.

Segato, Rita. 2010. 'Los cauces profundos de la raza latinoamericana: una relectura del mestizaje.' *Crítica y Emancipación*, Año 2, 3: 14–43.

Shore, Cris. 2010. 'La antropología y el estudio de la política pública: reflexiones sobre la 'formulación' de las políticas.' *Antípoda*, 10: 21–49.

Souza Lima, Antonio Carlos. 1995. *Um Grande Cerco de Paz. Poder tutelar, indianidade e formação do Estado no Brasil*. Petrópolis: Vozes.

Souza Lima, Antonio Carlos. 2002. 'Introdução. Sobre gestar e gerir a desigualdade: pontos de investigação e diálogo.' In *Gestar e gerir. Estudos para una antropología da administração pública no Brasil*, ed. Antonio Carlos Souza Lima, 11–21. Rio de Janeiro: Relume-Dumará.

Taussig, Michael. 1992. 'La magia del Estado: María Lionza y Simón Bolivar en la Venezuela contemporánea.' In *De palabra y obra en el Nuevo Mundo*, eds. Manuel Gutierrez et. al, 480–517. México: Siglo XXI.

Taussig, Michael. 1995. 'Violencia y resistencia en las Américas: el legado de la conquista.' In *Un gigante en convulsiones. El mundo humano como sistema nervioso de emergencia permanente*, ed. Michael Taussig, 56–75. Barcelona: Gedisa.

8 Unearthing *patrimonio*
Treasure and collectivity in San Miguel Coatlinchán[1]

Sandra Rozental

In San Miguel Coatlinchán, a town located in the Texcoco Municipality, 35 miles east of Mexico City, stories of buried pots of gold and hidden treasure circulate broadly. The town's wealthier individuals are rumored to have serendipitously found stashes of silver coins buried inside the walls of old houses, unearthed lavish treasures hidden in caves by the town's past residents, or even by nineteenth century bandits who used its rather inaccessible topography as a hiding place for stolen bounty. In these stories, although treasure is prominent in the town's landscape and built environment as a form of hidden value outside of capitalism and traditional forms of labor, it is neither easily nor freely accessible. Supernatural forces, often related to specific historical moments of violence and plunder, guard treasure and work to keep it in place. At the same time, Coatlinchán's residents use the register of treasure to both describe and actively seek the hidden value that is embedded in their town and in its territory, a value that they translate into the town's collective inheritance or *patrimonio*.[2]

In Coatlinchán, patrimonio is made up of collective forms of property that, like treasure, are always under threat of being expropriated by others. Patrimonio is, however, also a kinship term that indexes the ways in which these forms of property constitute the material substances that sustain the community as a corporate being. In this context, patrimonio becomes both what produces and guarantees community over time, recalling Henry Sumner Maine's discussion of the relationship between property and the corporate personhood of kin groups in ancient law (1861). In fact, in Coatlinchán, patrimonio is also associated with ancient social and political formations—the *calpulli*, a kin group associated with a specific territory, and the *altepetl*, a city-state made up of various calpullis—as well as with more recent forms of corporate personhood and cooperation that were central to the *fiesta-cargo* system of Spanish colonial towns, now considered the basis for traditional Mexican village sociality under the rubric of *usos y costumbres*. What these past social and political formations have in common is that they functioned as amalgams of persons (both living and dead), matter (land, but also objects), and supernatural forces (whether pre-Hispanic deities or Catholic saints) that had to be nurtured to ensure the corporate body's endurance. By invoking these formations, Coatlinchán's residents are producing, reviving, and sustaining patrimonio as an ancestral form of value that can be accessed to counter contemporary forms of dispossession.

As anthropologists have noted since the 1940s and 1950s, treasure tales have been a common trope to explain sudden wealth in Mexico, in what George Foster called 'static economies' (1964) and Eric Wolf framed as tightly knit 'closed corporate communities' (1957). Although these scholars' assumptions about the 'static' and 'closed' nature of peasant societies have been largely contested, more recent work in other parts of Latin America has set such stories of hidden forms of value—mostly gold and silver (Collins 2015; Taussig 1994–2004), but also fat (Abercrombie 1998; Canessa 2000; Weismantel 2001)—in landscape and even in bodies, as the result of colonial encounters riddled with new kinds of inequalities that only intensified with the development of capitalist enterprises, escalating profits, and poorly paid local labor.

Coatlinchán's treasure tales in this sense are not unique to Mexico, nor to the region. And yet, here, they linger and merge with a very specific and deeply entrenched history of violence and continued dispossession that marks the town and its landscape as sites where particular kinds of value—in the form of land, natural resources, and ancient artifacts—can and have always been taken by force.[3] Such a convergence leads to slippages between local versions of treasure tales that imagine the town's territory as laden with hidden value, and *Tlacuaches*'[4]— as town residents are known in the area—own sense of the gradual yet forceful loss of an ancestral corporate body to which they belong. In Coatlinchán, then, treasure tales frame patrimonio as a form of collective wealth constantly being threatened by outside actors—whether individuals, private corporations, or even the Mexican state. At the same time, configuring patrimonio as treasure implies that no matter how many instances of dispossession Coatlinchán endures, the town and its landscape are somehow still full of buried and hidden forms of value that can, thus, be sought and eventually unearthed.

In this chapter, I focus on the associations between patrimonio and hidden treasure in Coatlinchán to shed light on the contested quality of patrimonio in Mexico, notably in a town known as the source of two iconic objects that are now part of Mexico's national heritage or *patrimonio nacional*: objects and substances legally claimed, owned, cared for, and administered by the Mexican state as the nation's inalienable property (Cottom 2008). Indeed, Mexico has a robust system of laws and state practices that produce patrimonio as a key site for state formation (Breglia 2006), as well as an idiom that sustains collective identities, including the nation, over time (Ferry 2005).[5] As Elizabeth Ferry has pointed out, the Mexican state enacts and reproduces itself through the preservation and administration of substances and artifacts claimed as national patrimonio such as oil, mineral ores, and ancient monuments and artifacts, while at the same time engendering parallel and sometimes competing collectivities that in turn rely on idioms of patrimonio to legitimate their place in the nation (Ferry 2002, 2005, 2006).[6]

Coatlinchán is such a collectivity, a town where idioms of patrimonio are crucial to producing and sustaining a sense of collective identity vis-à-vis the nation. Since the nineteenth century, scholars of pre-Hispanic Mexico, museum curators, and antiquity aficionados have known Coatlinchán as fertile ground for their collecting endeavors, buying pottery shards and figurines from locals, and even conducting professional archaeological digs in the town itself (Rozental 2014b). Yet it was only in the mid-twentieth century that Coatlinchán acquired national fame at precisely the moment that patrimonio nacional was put into practice. In 1964, through a spectacular and highly publicized engineering feat, a 167-ton pre-Hispanic stone carving representing an ancient rain deity was expropriated from Coatlinchán by the Mexican state, despite much local resistance (Rozental 2016). The state justified the removal through patrimonio laws that stipulated that archaeological finds are the property of the nation and need to be preserved and exhibited alongside other material sources of national identity in the rightful site for Mexico's treasures, the National Anthropology Museum (Rozental 2014a). The monolith was thus removed from the ravine where it had lain half-buried for centuries, and transported to the entrance of the newly built National Anthropology Museum where it stands to this day as one of Mexico's most iconic ancient monuments.

The second object from Coatlinchán that is also patrimonio is less well known, mostly because it is carefully kept in a vault on the second floor of the museum and rarely exhibited. The Coatlinchán Map is a sixteenth-century document that was probably removed from Coatlinchán sometime during the colonial period, and was eventually donated to the museum in the late nineteenth century.[7] It has since been part of the museum's most prized manuscript collections.[8]

Objects such as this map and the pre-Hispanic stone statue that once lay in Coatlinchán's territory are claimed as patrimonio nacional and discursively designated as 'national treasures' by the Mexican state. At the same time, in Coatlinchán, town residents are trying to reconstitute these objects as the town's communal property and as sites of ancestral corporate personhood. For Tlacuaches, like ancient artifacts and hidden treasure, patrimonio is located in landscape, or even buried underground, connecting the town's contemporary residents to the town's territory and to its past inhabitants.

Rendering the ways in which Tlacuaches frame patrimonio as treasure, both through narrative and in practice, and how registers of treasure come into dialog with state discourses and practices of patrimonio nacional, provides key insights for understanding how patrimonio is experienced and mobilized at a local level. At the same time, thinking of patrimonio in terms of treasure allows us to understand the contemporary stakes of Coatlinchán's deeply entrenched but also persistently threatened forms of collective property and corporate personhood. This sense of threat has heightened over the last decades, as Mexico has shifted from a mostly rural to a predominantly urban country, and from a protected economy and welfare state to a neoliberal model that favors privatization and individual entrepreneurship.

Patrimonio in the register of treasure

Coatlinchán is part of a region that, although once primarily rural, is increasingly being absorbed by what residents, as well as government officials, refer pejoratively to as the 'urban stain' (*mancha urbana*). For much of its history since colonial times, Coatlinchán had been organized as a relatively standard Mexican peasant *pueblo*.[9] Its residents lived off their lands, growing maize on their *milpas*, or working as *monteros* gathering wood and other resources from the community's forests. Their social and ritual lives were organized around the church and festivities in honor of specific saints. Since the 1910 Revolution and the agrarian reforms that ensued in the 1920s and 1930s, Coatlinchán's social, political, and economic life changed as the Mexican state gave the town a collective land grant or *ejido* that dismantled the large haciendas that thrived in the area from colonial times well into the late nineteenth century. The agrarian reforms were framed by the Mexican state as a form of restitution that returned ancestral lands to villages like Coatlinchán thought to have been altepetls deprived of their pre-Hispanic collective identity and communal property since the conquest in the early sixteenth century.

Today, Coatlinchán's ejido endures and collective bodies are still responsible for the administration of communal resources such as forests, sand mines, and the town's drinking water system. Yet Tlacuaches are increasingly ambivalent about belonging to and nurturing collectivity at a time when Mexico, like much of Latin America, is turning toward a political and economic system where the distinctions between private and public, individual and collective are not only uncertain but constantly shifting. In Coatlinchán, many town residents are seeking private title over their lands to sell them for profit. Scandals of corruption and illicit enrichment haunt town authorities in charge of the ejido and other collective bodies. At the same time, individuals and groups are working to revitalize the town's patrimonio, and in light of these threats, equate patrimonio with treasure because it is a hidden, even buried, historical source that fuels the collective and could ensure its future survival.

Marcelo, a native and resident of Coatlinchán sets up a stall every year for the annual *Tianquizko*,[10] an event that he helps organize around the summer solstice to promote and activate the town's pre-Hispanic roots through talks, workshops, food tastings, ritual dances, and offerings to ancient deities and the town's spirit guardians. Each year, with minor variations, Marcelo removes a sheet of thick glossy paper from an elegant dark green satin-covered box with great care and a certain air of reverence. He places the facsimile of the ancient map of Coatlinchán that he purchased in a bookstore in the late 1990s on an easel. This facsimile is part of a series of reproductions of ancient Mesoamerican codices and maps published by the National Institute of Anthropology and History (INAH) and the University of Puebla (BUAP) in the 1990s. Marcelo explains to all who approach his stall: 'the central glyph, the *calli* on top of a mountain with an emerging serpent, represents Coatlinchán.' This glyph (a house-like structure) is the largest pictogram on the map and is embedded in a spiral of pathways, smaller calli glyphs, and other pictorial elements that depict animals, *magueys*, and trees. 'This map,' Marcelo insists pointing to the facsimile,

> is real treasure (*es un verdadero tesoro*). It is like powdered gold (*oro molido*) for the people of Coatlinchán. We need to learn how to read it to understand

the hidden knowledge it contains. Only then will we be able to reclaim what is ours and preserve our patrimonio.

Marcelo's framing of the facsimile of the map as treasure, as well as a legible source of information to find and reclaim the town's ancestral patrimonio, illuminates how patrimonio is defined and activated at a local level in ways that challenge, or at least complicate, state discourses and practices of patrimonio nacional. Indeed, Mexican heritage laws are hinged on certain substances' and objects' uniqueness and authenticity making them inalienable national property. As Quetzil Castañeda has shown, such discourses of authenticity conceal the constructed nature of heritage sites that are often reconstructed based on the imagination and desire of a variety of actors such as archaeologists, museum curators, state officials, workers, and even tourists (1996, 2009). In Coatlinchán, what is revealed is perhaps not the constructed or 'inauthentic' nature of patrimonio, but rather the ways in which it is made up of other kinds of value that can be read, uncovered, and transmitted even through copies and replicas (Rozental 2014b). The singularity of the map is not the source of its value. Rather, the map is a treasure because it bears revelations that can be uncovered and mobilized in the present.

Marcelo and several other town residents have formed groups to study and preserve Coatlinchán's patrimonio, a configuration that they understand to encompass both material elements catalogued as national patrimonio by the Mexican state, but also the town's historic sixteenth-century church that towers over the main plaza, and pre-Hispanic material remains such as *tlateles* (stone mounds), artifacts, and pottery shards that lie buried in many of the town's plots. However, as Marcelo's discursive inclusion of a replica of an ancient map as patrimonio attests, other elements, some material and others more ethereal, are also included. In this context, Marcelo's description of the replica of the map as treasure could be understood as a metaphor, an evocative way to emphasize the priceless value that recovering the map, even in its facsimile form, has for the larger project of local patrimonio preservation and revitalization that he and others in Coatlinchán are so deeply invested in. And yet, in a place marked by such profoundly rooted histories of dispossession, Marcelo's framing of patrimonio in the register of treasure seems to be more than a mere evocation.

Looking for treasure in Coatlinchán

The analogy linking the recovery of what the map reveals with treasure and, specifically, with powdered gold (a substance that has been purposefully destroyed and needs to be reconstituted as such), echoes other stories and rumors that circulate regarding hidden treasure in this town. These stories mark Coatlinchán's landscape as treasure-laden, containing wealth stored and hidden by a variety of actors, each, at different historical moments, seeking to keep the town's wealth—its *patrimonio* —in place, despite outside actors' efforts to extract value from the community.

Tales of hidden treasure and avid treasure hunters lured to Coatlinchán's territory have haunted the town and its landscape at least since the nineteenth century. This was recorded by Mexican writer and chronicler Manuel Payno in his epic novel *Los bandidos de Río Frío* (1891) where Coatlinchán, its church, and caves feature as one of many of the famous bandits' hiding places for bounty stolen from merchants traveling from the port of Veracruz to the capital city's markets. In Payno's story, the bandits also visit Coatlinchán to steal gold and silver belonging to the town's mayor that was hidden by the local priest in the rafters of his bedroom (1996 [1891]). Indeed, Coatlinchán is geographically close to Río Frío, and on the Camino Real, a road that connected Mexico's most important port to the capital city since colonial times. In the novel, rather than a site where value is inherently located, Coatlinchán becomes a place where illicitly acquired value can be hidden from official networks, removed from circulation, and hoarded.

Around the same time as Payno was writing about Coatlinchán as a hiding place for treasure, Leopoldo Batres, one of the first specialists on ancient Mexico who went to Coatlinchán and studied the then-newly discovered monolith that was later transported to Mexico City in 1964, also recorded stories of hidden treasure, this time associated with the monolithic carving. Batres believed that the anthropomorphic figure was broken because colonial priests had cast down the statue as a false idol in the sixteenth century and extracted gold nails from it (1903, 12). This understanding of the statue's ultimate shape as the result of a combination of colonial iconoclasm and the attempt to extract pre-Hispanic gold by colonial authorities, places hidden treasure—and therefore hidden forms of value—in the language of conquest and colonial appropriation.

Even today, slipping between reality and fiction (much like Payno's epic reconstruction of the Río Frío bandits that had gained national fame during his lifetime), town residents tell stories of the treasures hidden in the town's surroundings by the bandits. In fact, many Tlacuaches today associate the value of the pre-Hispanic monolith, and its eventual extraction from Coatlinchán as patrimonio nacional, as the result of the bandits' hoarding practices. Echoing Batres, who believed the statue was broken because of colonial priests' thirst for gold, Flora, a resident of Coatlinchán in her nineties, attributed the monolith's broken features to outsiders' coveting the bandits' treasure in Coatlinchán. Over a cup of hot chocolate on her patio, she explained: 'during the Revolution, people had come looking for the bandits' treasures and thought they were hidden in the stone, so they blew its arm off with gunpowder.' Other versions of this story circulate in Coatlinchán; people often mention that the real value that the Mexican state was looking for in taking the monolith was in fact hidden: not the pre-Hispanic statue itself nor its potential use as a museum object, but rather the gold or silver coins thought to have been concealed inside or under the stone by the bandits, or by town residents hoping to elude others' expropriation of their wealth.

Jesús was in his early twenties when I met him in 2008. He was then an undergraduate studying social psychology at a public university in Mexico City. On one of our many excursions, he showed me a site near one of the rivers that crosses Coatlinchán's territory, a few miles from the ravine where the monolith lay before 1964. There, the entrance to a large cave could be accessed after climbing

Unearthing patrimonio 143

a series of big rocks. Jesús knew of the cave because he had tagged along with his father and some of his friends who, knowing the bandits favored caves, rock formations, and other natural landmarks, went on expeditions to places all over Coatlinchán's territory on weekends hoping to find hidden treasure. According to Jesús, they even designed homemade metal detectors for these outings. His father and his friends had dug a hole at the cave's entrance, but after many hours of digging, his father had gotten tired and went to rest. When he returned, his friends were acting suspicious and he became convinced they had found treasure and didn't want to share it. The next day, he kept on digging in case some of treasure was still there. He didn't find any gold or silver, but he did find a pre-Hispanic offering of stone effigies and ceramic vessels. For Jesús, this was more valuable than money: 'My father still has one of the ceramic figures and always tells me it is the most valuable thing he owns because it is part of our patrimonio. It belongs to us and makes us who we are.' In addition to these stories that frame Coatlinchán and its territory as laden with hidden forms of value—whether ancient gold or pre-Hispanic objects—the town and its residents constantly figure as participants in treasure tales. These are a genre of narrative that orally map hidden sources of value in specific sites in the town's territory: large rocks, caves, fresh water springs as well as old houses and pre-Hispanic ruins.

These are not just any treasures, but are rather, what remains of Coatlinchán's past as a pre-Hispanic settlement, a hacienda community, and a site for bandits to evade the authorities. Lupe, an elderly woman who was born in the 1920s, explained to her granddaughter one evening that, when she was a child, the richer families of Coatlinchán were those who had worked inside the old hacienda households as nannies and butlers, rather than as peons working in their fields. These families would every so often spread their gold on their patios and expose it to the intense sunlight of Coatlinchán mornings. When she was younger, she had asked her mother about this seemingly strange practice and was told that exposing gold to sunlight made it multiply, a theory of the accumulation of value that, like treasure tales, contrasts with capitalist notions of labor power and surplus value (Taussig 1994).

This gold, the wealth hoarded by a handful of families, also figures in more recent tales of sudden riches. According to many town elders, in the 1920s, revolutionary fighters came seeking refuge in Coatlinchán and turned the sixteenth-century church and its cloister into military barracks, raping women, burning the local archive, and pillaging households. Coatlinchán's elites, the ones that Lupe remembered working in the old hacienda households and exposing their gold to sunlight, fearing the revolutionaries' pillaging, allegedly buried their wealth inside their houses, in the thick adobe walls, or under the heavy stone floors. Old houses in the town's contemporary built environment are, therefore, thought to be filled with hidden treasure and are often dismantled in search of gold and silver by their old inhabitants' descendants.

As one of the older adobe houses on the town's main square or *plazuela* was being dismantled by its owner to build an Internet café, Concha, a woman in her forties, told me the house belonged to one of her cousins: 'he says he wants to make money off the rent instead of keeping the old house that is falling apart. After all, he lives in Mexico City. But surely, he wouldn't mind finding a pot of coins in the old walls!' Town residents like Concha attribute both locals' and other investors' purchase or renovation of old houses and dilapidated constructions not to the properties themselves, but to their interest in the hidden treasures they might contain.

In Coatlinchán, treasure bears witness to town residents' efforts to resist conquest and dispossession, and store value even beyond their own lifetimes. Indeed, treasure is not merely hidden out of sight; it is dutifully kept in place by supernatural forces that lurk in Coatlinchán. These supernatural forces are often thought to be the ghosts of town residents that buried their wealth in their homes, but more often reference very specific moments of violence and plunder experienced in Coatlinchán, first during the conquest, then during nineteenth-century capitalist expansion, and more recently in the aftermath of the Mexican Revolution.

Pablo, a man in his eighties who spends much of his time watching the *frontón* players in one of Coatlinchán's most public places, told me:

> It isn't just gold from the times of the Revolution. The tlateles here are also filled with treasure that the Aztecs hid so the Spaniards wouldn't get it. They were all killed but their gold is still here. That is why if you go to old houses and to tlateles, they spook you (*te espantan*).

Such stories recall Gastón Gordillo's account of the spatialization of social memories of violence through 'places that frighten' in the Argentinian Chaco. In Gordillo's words, these are places that 'bring to light the historical nature of space and the tensions and ruptures that have constituted it' (2009, 344). For Gordillo, sites marked by debris left in the wake of colonial expansion and capitalist infrastructures are not experienced by the residents of the Chaco as the ruins from past epochs, but as spaces with affective charges of violence and dislocation accumulated over centuries (2014).[11] In Coatlinchán, tlateles and old houses are such spaces, haunted not by the ghosts of pre-Hispanic or more recent ancestors, but by the violence of conquest and the sanguinary battles of a revolution that constituted the town as it is today.

The fact that nowadays stories of found treasure mostly refer to hidden pots of *centenarios*, the Mexican bullion coins first minted in 1921 to commemorate the 100th anniversary of Mexico's independence from Spain, rather than gold or silver, is in this sense revealing. Treasure being made equivalent to pots of centenarios dates and commemorates the revolution and the very local ways in which violence marked and transformed landscapes and towns in Mexico. What Aztec gold, bounty stolen by bandits from formal circuits of exchange, and the accumulated silver coins of Coatlinchán's wealthier families during the 1920s and 1930s have in common is that they are all treasures hidden from outside forces seeking to redistribute this wealth to other collectivities: the Spanish crown, the Mexican government, or other foreign actors seeking to profit from the collective.

In Coatlinchán, stashes of wealth are not just the legitimate property of the town's contemporary inhabitants; they are actively kept in place by supernatural forces that emerge from specific moments of violent transformation. It is only through the willingness of such beings imagined as ancestors or devils, that Coatlinchán's hidden riches can be accessed. For example, Micaela, a woman who owns a local shop told me when I asked her about the former owners of her house:

> It belonged to the richest man in town when I was little. It's a big secret but everyone here knows it. They realized it during his wake. Everyone knew he was a very cruel man. He wasn't from here, although he had lived here for a while. He was murdered and when they lifted the coffin to take him away, it didn't weigh anything and they realized the body had disappeared. That's how everyone knew he had made a pact with the devil in exchange for gold, and that's why he was so rich. The family tried to fill the box with stones, but everyone already knew. And after that, his family members started to suffer violent deaths: gunshots, car accidents, things like that.

This story, and others like it, cast Coatlinchán's treasures not just as the town's collective property, but as supernaturally guarded kinds of value that cannot be removed without risk or danger of reprimand. Thus, both the temporal specificity of treasure and its location mark and make Coatlinchán a place where wealth can be kept for future generations, a place that through patrimonio—the inherited communal legacy contained in the soil that takes on the form of gold and centenarios, but also pre-Hispanic artifacts and ruins—continually and even supernaturally resists becoming the spoils of conquest and violent appropriation.

Revitalizing collectivity as treasure in Coatlinchán

The register of treasure is not just present in stories about ancient gold hidden by pre-Hispanic ancestors or pots of centenarios buried in Coatlinchán since the revolution. Contemporary town residents invested in preserving Coatlinchán's patrimonio as the basis of the town's ancestral collective property and corporate personhood, activate treasure metaphors and treasure-hunting practices to counter new forms of dispossession.

Having helped found the Grupo Cultural in 2007, a group formed by various young professionals and local history aficionados, Marcelo and a few of the group's younger members went on to form the Calpulli Makoyolotzin in 2009. For those who founded the Calpulli, the new group was not the product of a division, but rather an offspring and affectionate relative of the Grupo Cultural. The Calpulli was in fact named after a *macollo*, a kinship term used in Mexico to refer to a sprouting shoot of a parent plant, and the term *yolotl* that means 'heart' in Nahuatl. The new group's members emphasize that the difference lies in each of the two groups' goals. The Grupo Cultural is invested in preserving the town's patrimonio broadly defined along the terms of the Mexican state's patrimonial institutions and policies: restoring the church and its murals, gathering community funds to mount exhibitions on local history, or sponsoring events related to local lore. For the Calpulli, in contrast, Coatlinchán's patrimonio is made up of much more than folklore and the material remains from distant pasts. For its members, restoring and preserving the town's patrimonio involves actually revitalizing, reactivating, and reinstituting past forms of collective sociality and ways of being in the world that they perceive as having been at the core of ancient Mesoamerican ontologies founded in collective forms of personhood and property. Perhaps the clearest marker of this can be found in the other component of the group's name. '*Calpulli*' is the Nahuatl term for a form of social organization that thrived in the Basin of Mexico during pre-Hispanic times. Historians have written about calpullis as kin-based groups responsible for managing collective resources, especially land, and for organizing social and ritual tasks related to the production and reproduction of community and territory.[12] The Calpulli Makoyolotzin, like others affiliated with the neo-Aztec movement *La Mexicanidad*,[13] borrows the term in its own revivalist efforts to reinstate an ancestral corporate body. The group's discursive bid and its practices resonate with the performative quality inherent in the reproduction and endurance of these collectivities in pre-Hispanic times that relied heavily on the ritual display of maps, as well as other forms of reenactment and staging practices related to the reproduction and sustenance of territory and territoriality.[14] The Calpulli chose its pre-Hispanic namesake in order to reference Coatlinchán's past as an important settlement and historic capital of the Acolhuacan, one of the most ancient and powerful political alliances, which united the pre-Hispanic towns of the Central Valleys of Mexico.[15] At the same time, the name performatively transforms the kinds of ritual work the group's members are engaging in into an age-old responsibility giving historical coherence and continuity to their efforts to rekindle this ancient social and political formation.

In addition, the members of the Calpulli Makoyolotzin frame their ritual and other tasks as a form of cooperation, or communal labor to guarantee the endurance of the collective over time. Each individual works to offer his or her 'essence' and physical labor to revive Coatlinchán's past as a cohesive, kin-based collectivity. On specific dates associated with the pre-Hispanic ritual calendar (like the summer solstice chosen for the Tianquizko mentioned earlier in this chapter), the members of the Calpulli go to certain locations in the community's lands identified as pre-Hispanic sites, which they identify using the facsimile of the map that Marcelo keeps. One of the sites most often visited by the group is the Santa Clara ravine also known as Tecomates, where the monolith that was removed in 1964 once lay. Having located and identified a site, the members of the Calpulli perform a 'cleansing' that is both literal—clearing overgrown weeds and trash—and ritual—burning *copal* incense, dancing, and making offerings to the site's guardians in the hopes they will once again provide for the town currently suffering from drought and its residents' abandoning their fields for other more viable sources of income.

The Calpulli's members use the term '*faena*' to describe their work as a form of communal labor, borrowing again from the region's past—this time a more recent past. Faenas were integral to the fiesta-cargo system studied by anthropologists working in the 1940s and 1950s in Mexican towns organized around their devotion to their patron saint. In such systems, each head of household was responsible for gifting his or her labor to the community for public works and community betterment.[16] Today, although faenas are still organized for community projects like cleaning the town's cemetery and drinking water network, and town authorities still demand certificates of participation in community labor projects in order to issue official documents, fewer and fewer of Coatlinchán's residents actually participate in them. Many residents purposefully avoid the organizing committees or simply prefer alternative modes of contributing to the town's welfare, such as cash donations.

When I asked about the Calpulli's work, Juan, another of the Calpulli's members in his mid-forties, explained the faena using the register of treasure:

> Coatlinchán looks just like any small town; we are poor, our fields are barren and the city is taking us over. Everything has been taken from us, but in fact, there are indescribable treasures lying just under our feet, latent, left there for us by our ancestors. We just have to learn to find them. That is what we are doing in the Calpulli, we are treasure hunters now.

For Juan and others who participate in the Calpulli, the discursive use of forms of communal social organization from both the pre-Hispanic and more recent pasts, as well as the actual work the Calpulli performs to cleanse ritual spaces and locate ancestral localities in the town's territory, are a means to simultaneously recognize, recover, and perpetuate the community's real patrimonio, its real treasure understood as the town's legacy as a prosperous and powerful collectivity that is currently under threat.

Illicit accumulation and corporate ambivalence

In Coatlinchán today, despite the efforts of town residents like those who joined the Calpulli, there is also growing ambivalence regarding the need to sustain the town's collective and corporate identity. New sources of sudden wealth have become the subject of gossip among residents who denounce the transformation of the town's patrimonio into private and individual property. Rumors of corruption and profitable illicit activities surround almost all those who are elected to administer the corporate entities that manage the town's collective property. 'That is the definition of being an *autoridad*' one man jokingly scuffed, 'to steal from the pueblo and become rich alone.' The relationship between sudden fortune and being a community authority is crystallized in the stories surrounding the pre-Hispanic monolith's removal from Coatlinchán in 1964, narrated by many as the result of illegitimate negotiations between a handful of town residents in office at the time and the Mexican state. Walking in town one day, Gaby, a young woman who worked at one of Coatlinchán's salons, pointed to a series of grandiose three-story houses that line one of the town's main avenues: 'you keep asking about the stone . . . you really want to know where the stone is, well, there you go. There, in those houses, in their pickup trucks and fancy cars. That is where it is!' Gaby was angry about the monolith's removal by the Mexican state, but she was even more upset by the transformation of the town's patrimonio that the ancient monolith stood in for, into the private property of a local elite who used their position as community authorities to illicitly exchange the statue for their private luxurious living. Nowadays, one still hears stories about newly acquired wealth resulting from unearthed treasures, but most often, Coatlinchán's newest elites are rumored to be involved in the illicit drugs trade, Mexico's more recent hyper-capitalist economy. Rumors of pots of gold and found treasures in old houses and ancient ruins are still present in the town, but they are no longer the only source of sudden wealth available to its residents. Whether through the drug trade or the sale of their plots of land, town residents have found new ways to prosper outside of the collective.

One of the most lucrative businesses in Coatlinchán today, aside from drug trafficking, is cattle farming. This relatively recent industry works as another mechanism for appropriating collective forms of property through bulls' bodies, purchased as calves, fattened, and subsequently sold to the meat industry. In other parts of Mexico, raising cattle is a capital-intensive industry with expensive inputs. In addition to paying for the calves themselves, cattle farmers have to sustain and nurture the animals' growth for many months before they are old and large enough for sale. However, in Coatlinchán, many Tlacuaches have turned cattle into an extremely profitable business by using communal resources as the main investment for sustaining fairly large herds, namely through community-owned water and fodder grown on ejido lands. Through such enterprises, a few families in Coatlinchán are profiting from water and land that are integral parts of the town's patrimonio and the basis for the corporate entity's survival over time.

Others have gained wealth by selling their newly privatized plots to investors, as well as to the local and federal governments that bought land for public infrastructure projects: a highway connecting Texcoco to Puebla—the Circuito Bicentenario —and a huge state-sponsored cultural center, the Centro Cultural Mexiquense Bicentenario. In May 2011, I received a phone call from Dulce, a young woman in Coatlinchán who works as a seamstress. She had been with me when I went to visit the dilapidated remains of the old Santa Monica ranch before it was sold by one of Coatlinchán's families to the state government for the Centro Cultural. This was one of the only expanses of land large enough for the project in the region, as well as one of the only plots that was still in private hands rather than incorporated into the ejido. Dulce called me with some urgency and out of breath:

> Guess what? Last night we overheard helicopters flying over the old ranch. The watchman saw how Peña Nieto [then governor of the State of Mexico] came to take everything. The workers are from here and they saw—well, actually they found a pot of *centenarios* when they demolished one of the old walls. But Peña's people came and immediately took the treasure away and closed everything off. Then, the helicopters left and when the workers came back the next morning there was nothing there.

When Peña Nieto won Mexico's presidential election a few months later, Dulce commented: 'Ha! See, that is where all our gold went, to his campaign!' In Dulce's narrative, no supernatural being appeared to keep value in place in Coatlinchán. The workers—also town residents—found the treasure through their labor, but Peña Nieto and his people—outsiders as well as cyphers for the Mexican state and its corrupt officials—extracted value from Coatlinchán that then contributed illicitly to his rise to power.

In this narrative, Coatlinchán's hidden wealth is no longer guarded by ancient spirits or by resistant ancestors seeking to redistribute it to a corporate entity made up of living and dead residents and of the territory that has sustained them over time: it is up for grabs. The helicopters in Dulce's rendering arrive from the sky, powered by an alien force and energy, and leave by the same means without leaving any trace, only the consequent appropriation of local value into political and economic power on a national scale. The sense in this story that Coatlinchán's wealth, its patrimonio, is no longer the collective property of its residents (living or dead) contrasts with the treasure tales and the Calpulli's project to rescue ancient forms of collective personhood and revitalize ancestral localities as a form of treasure hunting. The treasures that Coatlinchán's residents believe to be hidden in old houses and that Calpulli members are seeking in ruins and landscape are the sources of Coatlinchán's past collectivity, a form of social, political, and economic organization that is slowly fading above ground.

Notes

1 My fieldwork in Coatlinchán in 2008–2009 was funded through a Henry M. MacCracken Fellowship from New York University, a Tinker Summer Travel Grant, Research Grants from the Center of Latin American and Caribbean Studies at NYU, and a Wenner-Gren Foundation Dissertation Fieldwork Grant. An Andrew W. Mellon Foundation/American Council of Learned Societies Fellowship, an honorary fellowship at NYU's Humanities Initiative and a postdoctoral fellowship funded by Mexico's National Council of Science and Technology (Conacyt) provided time and space in which to write. This article came out of an extremely enriching conversation that took place during a set of panels on patrimony organized by Mario Rufer and Olaf Kaltmeier for the 2011 and 2014 meetings of the International Association of Inter-American Studies. I am very thankful to all the panel participants, as well as to my colleagues at the UAM-Cuajimalpa, and to Richard Kernaghan, Miruna Achim, Sabra Thorner, and Christopher Fraga for their comments on various drafts. Since 2010, I have continued to go back to Coatlinchán on short visits and day trips, and have sustained conversations with several of my informants through phone calls, email, and Facebook.
2 As I have written elsewhere, I favor the Spanish usage of patrimonio because it encompasses both the possible translations of the English terms 'heritage' and 'inheritance,' while at the same time indexing Mexico's deeply hierarchical and patriarchal state (Rozental 2014a).
3 Treasure tales are also common in other parts of the world with deeply entrenched histories of conquest and violent dispossession. For a fascinating account of treasure tales as a residue of such histories in Greece, see Stewart (2003, 2012). Anya Bernstein has also written about the emergence of treasure in Buryatia in southern Siberia as the result of both Buddhist object ideologies, and the region's histories of violence and rupture in the wake of the Russian Revolution and subsequent Soviet secularization campaigns (2011).

150 *Sandra Rozental*

4 Tlacuaches are opossums. It is also the nickname by which people in the Valley of Mexico refer to the residents of Coatlinchán. Most towns in the area have nicknames referencing local fauna or the trades of their residents.
5 For a historical rendering of patrimonio as a form of nation-state formation, see Tenorio (1996) and Bueno (2010).
6 In his recent work on community museums in various parts of Mexico, Mario Rufer focuses on the ways in which these idioms are translated into exhibition practices and discourses that, in turn, reveal the complex and, oftentimes, fraught relationship between local communities with very specific histories, and the abstract entity of the nation (Rufer 2014).
7 The map was exhibited for the first time in 2014 as part of an exhibition of Mexican manuscripts commemorating the museum's fiftieth anniversary. The National Institute of Anthropology and History (INAH) has published digital versions of many of its collections, including the Coatlinchán map: http://codices.inah.gob.mx/img/reel/9_MAPA_DE_COATLINCHAN/IMG1.jpg.
8 An image of the map was first published in the late nineteenth century by Alfredo Chavero in the first tome of *México a través de los siglos*. The map itself was purchased from Chavero by Dr. Rafael Lucio in 1880, and then by Francisco del Paso y Troncoso who donated it to the museum. A copy made by Antonio García Cubas was sent to the American Historic Madrid Exhibition of 1892 (Mohar Betancourt 1994).
9 In Spanish, the term pueblo refers both to a town as a physical, political, and administrative unit and to a more abstract entity that would roughly translate as 'the people.' In Coatlinchán, residents use the term to refer to their town as a community of people related to each other through kinship, co-godparenthood, and the communal administration of collective forms of property. For more on the term and its uses, see Eiss (2010).
10 'Tianquizko' is the local spelling of the Nahuatl term for market tianquiztli. In Coatlinchán, the tianquizko is framed as an attempt to revive a pre-Hispanic version of a market where things (and forms of knowledge) were bartered rather than exchanged through currency.
11 Gordillo's insights on treasure as the result of spatial violence and ruptures recall Charles Stewart's interest in treasures as 'secretions of history' deposited at moments of rupture. Stewart argued that treasures are 'paradoxically products of ruptures. Invasions, occupations and ethnic cleansings often produce treasures; they are punctuation marks in the past that give rise to the sequences and time frames of subsequent historicizations' (2003, 489).
12 The calpulli as a form of social, political, and religious organization has fascinated historians, anthropologists, political theorists, and legal scholars. The literature on the calpulli is, therefore, vast across the disciplines. I mention here only some of the most cited works, namely *Ancient Society* by Lewis H. Morgan (1877) and *On the Distribution and Tenure of Lands: And the Customs with Respect to Inheritance Among the Ancient Mexicans* by Adolph F. Bandelier (1878). The calpulli has been studied as a central category of Aztec society (Aguilar-Moreno 2007; Carrasco 1961; Caso 1961; Clendinnen 1995; López Austin 1974; Monzón 1949).
13 For more on the history of the movement of La Mexicanidad, see De la Peña (2012) and González Torres (2005).
14 In his detailed history of the altepetl as a political, social, and cultural formation in the Valley of Mexico, Federico Navarrete Linares describes the staging required for the production and reproduction of pre-Hispanic sociopolitical units such as calpullis through the ritual display of images and territorial representations. See Federico Navarrete (2010).
15 The members of the Calpulli have read and often cite recent editions of the histories of the Acolhuacan written in the sixteenth century by Fernando de Alva Ixtlilxóchitl and Domingo Francisco de San Antón Muñón Chimalpahin Cuauhtlehuanitzin.

16 For more on the faena in classic anthropological literature on Mexican peasant and indigenous communities, see Cowan (1954) and Sokolovsky (1978).

References

Abercrombie, Thomas. 1998. *Pathways of Memory and Power: Ethnography and History Among an Andean People*. Madison: University of Wisconsin.

Aguilar-Moreno, Manuel. 2007. *Handbook to Life in the Aztec World*. Oxford: Oxford University.

Bandelier, Adolph Francis Alphonse. 1878. *On the Distribution and Tenure of Lands: And the Customs with Respect to Inheritance Among the Ancient Mexicans*. Salem: Salem.

Bernstein, Anya. 2011. 'The post-Soviet Treasure Hunt: Time, Space, and Necropolitics in Siberian Buddhism.' *Comparative Studies in Society and History* 53.3: 623–53.

Breglia, Lisa C. 2006. *Monumental Ambivalence: The Politics of Heritage*. Austin: University of Texas.

Bueno, Christina. 2010. 'Forjando Patrimonio: The Making of Archaeological Patrimony in Porfirian Mexico.' *Hispanic American Historical Review* 90.2: 215–45.

Canessa, Andrew. 2000. 'Fear and Loathing on the Kharisiri Trail: Alterity and Identity in the Andes.' *Journal of the Royal Anthropological Institute* 6.4: 705–20.

Carrasco, Pedro. 1961. 'The Civil_Religious Hierarchy in Mesoamerican Communities Pre_Spanish Background and Colonial Development.' *American Anthropologist* 63.3: 483–97.

Caso, Alfonso. 1961. 'The Calpulli as a Clan Organization.' *American Anthropologist* 63.5: 1100–01.

Castañeda, Quetzil E. 1996. *In the Museum of Maya Cultures*. Minneapolis: University of Minnesota.

Castañeda, Quetzil E. 2009. 'Notes on the Work of Heritage in the Age of Archaeological Reproduction'. *Ethnographies and Archaeologies: Iterations of the Past*. Florida: University Press of Florida, 109–19.

Clendinnen, Inga. 1995. *Aztecs: An Interpretation*. Cambridge: Cambridge University.

Collins, John F. 2015. *Revolt of the Saints: Memory and Redemption in the Twilight of Brazilian Racial Democracy*. Durham: Duke University.

Cottom, Bolfy. 2008. *Nación, patrimonio cultural y legislación: los debates parlamentarios y la construcción del marco jurídico federal sobre monumentos en México, siglo XX*. Mexico City: Miguel Angel Porrua.

Cowan, George M. 1954. 'La importancia social y política de la faena mazateca.' *América Indígena* 14.1.

De la Peña, Francisco. 2012. 'Profecías de la mexicanidad: entre el milenarismo nacionalista y la new age.' *Cuicuilco* 19.55: 127–43.

Eiss, Paul. 2010. *In the Name of El Pueblo: Place, Community, and the Politics of History in Yucatán*. Durham: Duke University.

Ferry, Elizabeth Emma. 2002. 'Inalienable Commodities: The Production and Circulation of Silver and Patrimony in a Mexican Mining Cooperative.' *Cultural Anthropology* 17.3: 331–58.

Ferry, Elizabeth Emma. 2005. *Not Ours Alone: Patrimony, Value, and Collectivity in Contemporary Mexico*. New York: Columbia University.

Ferry, Elizabeth Emma. 2006. 'Memory as Wealth, History as Commerce: A Changing Economic Landscape in Mexico.' *Ethos* 34.2: 297–324.

Foster, George M. 1964. 'Treasure Tales, and the Image of the Static Economy in a Mexican Peasant Community.' *Journal of American Folklore* 77.303: 39–44.

González Torres, Yólotl. 2005. *Danza tu palabra: la danza de los concheros*. México City: Plaza y Valdés.
Gordillo, Gastón. 2002. 'The Breath of the Devils: Memories and Places of an Experience of Terror.' *American Ethnologist* 29.1: 33–57.
Gordillo, Gastón. 2009. 'Places that Frighten: Residues of Wealth and Violence on the Argentine Chaco Frontier.' *Anthropologica* 51.2: 343–51.
Gordillo, Gastón. 2014. *Rubble: The Afterlife of Destruction*. Durham: Duke University.
López Austin, Alfredo. 1974. 'Organización política en el altiplano central de México durante el posclásico.' *Historia Mexicana* 23.4: 515–50.
Maine, Henry Sumner. 1861. *Ancient Law: Its Connection with the Early History of Society and Its Relation to Modern Ideas*. New York: Dorest.
Mohar Betancourt, Luz Maria. 1994. *El Mapa de Coatlinchán: lineas y colores en el Acolhuacan*. México: INAH-Puebla: BUAP.
Monzón, Arturo. 1949. *El calpulli en la organización social de los tenochea*. México City: Universidad Nacional Autónoma de México.
Morgan, Lewis Henry. 1877. *Ancient Society: Or, Researches in the Lines of Human Progress from Savagery, Through Barbarism to Civilization*. New York: H. Holt.
Payno, Manuel. 1996 [1891]. *Los bandidos de Río Frío*. México D.F.: Miguel Ángel Porrúa.
Rozental, Sandra. 2014a. 'Stone Replicas: The Iteration and Itinerancy of Mexican Patrimonio.' *The Journal of Latin American and Caribbean Anthropology* 19.2: 331–356.
Rozental, Sandra. 2014b. 'Coatlinchán in Fragments: Where do they Belong?' *Ixiptla* 1: 34–53.
Rozental, Sandra. 2016. 'In the Wake of Mexican Patrimonio: Material Ecologies in San Miguel Coatlinchán.' *Anthropological Quarterly* 89 (1): 181–219.
Rufer, Mario. 2014. 'Paisaje, ruina y nación. Memoria local e historia nacional desde narrativas comunitarias en Coahuila.' *Cuicuilco* 21.61: 103–36.
Sokolovsky, Jay. 1978. 'Local Roots of Community Transformation in a Nahuatl Indian Village.' *Anthropological Quarterly* 51.3: 163–73.
Stewart, Charles. 2003. 'Dreams of Treasure Temporality, Historicization and the Unconscious.' *Anthropological Theory* 3.4: 481–500.
Stewart, Charles. 2012. *Dreaming and Historical Consciousness in Island Greece*. Cambridge: Harvard University.
Tenorio, Mauricio. 1996. *Mexico at the World's Fairs: Crafting a Modern Nation*. Berkeley: University of California.
Taussig, Michael. 1993. *Mimesis and Alterity: A Particular History of the Senses*. New York: Psychology.
Taussig, Michael. 2004. *My Cocaine Museum*. Chicago: University of Chicago.
Weismantel, Mary. 2001. *Cholas and Pishtacos: Stories of Race and Sex in the Andes*. Chicago: University of Chicago.
Wolf, Eric R. 1957. 'Closed Corporate Peasant Communities in Mesoamerica and Central Java.' *Southwestern Journal of Anthropology* 13.1: 1–18.

9 Processes of heritagization of indigenous cultural manifestations
Lines of debate, analytic axes, and methodological approaches[1]

Carolina Crespo

Bases of discussion or starting points: patrimonial poetics and politics in studies of heritage

Since the eighties, studies on cultural heritage became remarkably important within Latin American academia; meanwhile, its conceptualization and approach was being modified. 'Ideas, cultures, and histories cannot seriously be understood or studied without their force, or more precisely their configurations of power, also being studied' (Said 1977, 5), so researchers were drawn into inquiring not only the *poetics* found in processes of heritagization[2] (the ways of its functioning), but also the politics and forms of power they generate.

Indeed, at this point, several social scientists who were interested in these problematics shifted their focus from *essentialist* and *static* concepts of heritage and memory to their *dynamic* and *historically built* condition; from the study of an intrinsic quality of the object to the *process* and the *context* within which certain events and cultural practices get redefined and *selected* as constituent of a social group's identity, memory, and heritage; from their value as inheritance coming from the *past* to their construction in the *present*; and from their *authentic* or *true* condition to the *social relations* they express and how they *legitimize* such relations, that is, to the *uses and effects of power* they produce (e.g., Arantes 1984–1997; Bonfil Batalla 1989; Brow 2000; García Canclini 1989–1993; Hobsbawm and Ranger 1983; Rosas Mantecón 1998; Prats 1997; Rotman 1999).

Some of the aforementioned studies have especially emphasized the political–ideological dimension of cultural heritage, since it makes certain social groups visible in time and space and/or excludes others, it configures spaces and identities, it legitimizes or denies rights and resources, it establishes rules, values, and patterns for legitimate and illegitimate behavior, and it attempts to produce social consensus around them as it generates important conflicts (e.g., Arantes 1997; Bonfil Batalla 1989; Cruces 1998; García Canclini 1989; Prats 1997; Rosas Mantecón 1998). Within this frame, studies have been less focused on documenting the object and more interested on the history of its constitution, thus linking the object to a particular historical–cultural moment like the formation of nation-states (Prats 1977), the way it relates to political projects and hegemonic values, and how it excludes what does not adapt to these interests (Bonfil Batalla 1997; Florescano 1993). These studies are also focused on the discourse and the meanings associated to certain referents that have been constituted as such; the several interests and political usages that are set in motion (e.g., Florescano 1993; García Canclini 1989–1993; Prats 1997; Rosas Mantecón 1998); its constituting nature and its performative effects on social relations and practices; the inequality expressed in its selection, shaping, signification, and management (Cruces 1998); and/or the conflicts brought about by this situation among several agencies that are unequally positioned—not only nation-states, but also multilateral agencies, nongovernmental organizations (NGOs), different social groups, private sectors, and so on (e.g., Arantes 1984–1997; Cruces 1998; Rotman 1999). Others have undertaken the analysis of its more recent stages of activation and entry into the market as a form of economic resource (e.g., Aguilar Criado 2003; García Canclini 1993; Prats 1997), its insertion into 'policies of development with identity' arising from multilateral agencies that run through national state programs and actions (Benedetti 2007), and their connection to tourism.

For the last few years, the notion of heritage began to blend with discourses on the recognition of cultural diversity. Within the frame of what has been called 'neoliberal multiculturalism' (Hale 2004), which simultaneously implied the deepening of inequality and a claim on the recognition of cultural difference, heritage policies in Argentina—in accordance with changes generated in international programs—enhanced the activation of cultural references from social sectors that had previously been made invisible or included in a subordinated way to the repertoire of national heritage and so therefore read from an hegemonic key.

The incorporation of these other cultural references was brought about by the struggle of several ethno-political movements, gender movements, etc., as well as international regulations and programs by multilateral agencies and NGOs that have been interfering with state policies to a remarkable degree. But apart from being a political matter, heritage was linked to the rationale currently imprinted in a market where the promotion of a different and particular culture (e.g., Aguilar Criado 2005; García Canclini 1993) was constituted as a resource for economic development and a way out of 'poverty and marginality.'

In Argentina, anthropological studies on the heritagization processes of cultural manifestations and indigenous human remains have been focusing on state policies as well as those of international organizations and NGOs, aiming to elucidate their definitions, implementation methods, and effects. Otherwise, they focus on reviewing recent definitions and demands made by some indigenous peoples to the state and/or academics, around their signification, classification, belonging, and/or management. Most of them pay special attention to cases in which a contention on this matter has emerged, and they usually analyze the views or conceptions of heritage and memory that arise in each sector. On the one hand, they describe the perspective of indigenous peoples as groups, and on the other hand, that of state agencies—national and/or provincial—or other international organizations and NGOs, according to the case. Some even examine these processes by including how academic discourse and practice—both past and current—become articulated with them. Others also analyze relationships that come up within the group and with other agencies—state agencies, NGOs, academics, etc.—bounded by these policies and interrelated with asymmetric interethnic historical relationships.

That being said, the notion of 'indigenous diversity' and particularly the programs aimed at facing policies that focus on 'ethnic and cultural diversity' are far from offering a single common horizon of thought, definition, and action; in fact, they reveal a rather diverse range of conceptualizations and implications. As Hall (2010) suggests, the term multiculturalism is polysemic. Under the notion of recognizing and respecting the 'other,' different devices have been consolidated for the production of 'otherness' as a correlate to what we think of as 'us.' Meanwhile, indigenous peoples maintain a diversity of positions *vis-à-vis* these processes.

In this article, I am interested in discussing some possible axes or coordinates of analysis as well as methodological approaches for examining heritagization processes of indigenous cultural manifestations; that is, of memories,[3] multiple forms of knowledge, practices, and cultural goods belonging to social sectors that have been construed as 'subaltern' and 'others.'

My aim is to differentiate my work from those that, when looking at heritage, only see the instituted and the instituting in order to critically debate 'heritage' as a process and as a political practice, by considering less what heritage *is* from the perspective of a normative analysis and rather looking at what different social sectors *do* with heritage, as well as the relationships and the implications generated by this. This means that, in order to analyze these processes, we must see them not so much as a field for consensus but as a field of force that involves the setting of tensions within certain relationships, subjectivities, emotional attachments, ways of knowing and seeing the social world and the space, all of which is involved in the processes of creation and dispute for hegemony.

Therefore, two questions guide my work: first of all, how and to what extent is it possible to rebuild the voice and agency of indigenous peoples in this process without falling into dichotomist and bipolar understandings; and second, is it not necessary to review the analytic criteria with which we approach those hegemonic practices of heritagization regarding the significations, practices, and/or claims established around heritage by subjects that have been historically construed as others and subalterns, as it happens in Argentina with indigenous peoples?[4]

From an examination on how expressions and repertoires relating to indigenous 'past' and 'culture' are currently being considered as susceptible of heritage status and the hegemonic bases of discussion set by indigenous populations, this proposition's final aim is to rethink how to analyze the 'geographies of imagination and management' (Troulliot 2011) of 'ethnic diversity' within the processes of heritagization and construction of memory as well as the variable joints worked on by these sectors. In order to do this, I offer a selection of situations drawn from

156 *Carolina Crespo*

my own research and from the work of other colleagues dealing with this topic that, functioning as a state of affairs, will allow us to continue problematizing this field of studies and suggesting an approach that I consider appropriate to address the complexity of this process.[5] On the one hand, I am referring to certain coordinates of analysis that I consider fertile fields for the discussion on the heritage of indigenous sectors that have been construed as others and subalterns and which deserve a place for deeper exploration. On the other hand, and as a closure to this text, I address a perspective that, in my understanding, achieves a contemplation of the aforementioned analytic axes in their full complexity and dynamism.

Bases of anchorage or analytic axes

A On silencing and memories of silences

Heritage policies are revealing for that which they enable, recognize, and produce through their discourses, repetitions, and actions, but also for what they 'forget,' exclude, or render unthinkable, unspeakable, or marginal. Apart from configuring the rightfully acknowledged past and present, these policies produce—through their activations and omissions and even through their contradictions and paradoxes—certain authorized physical and social places as well as accepted subjectivities *versus* others that are denied.

Now, in spite of the fact that every process of heritagization implies the commemoration of certain cultural productions and memories within a hierarchy and the silencing of others, and that absences and silences 'of' and 'on' certain cultural manifestations have in fact been a constitutive part of heritage policies and programs faced both by state agencies and by international and nongovernmental ones, this is a field that has rarely been deeply explored.

Studies on these processes have virtually never focused on drawing the itineraries of silence of those subjects and/or cultural productions that have been left out or on the margins of history and heritage, or that have been left without a voice to speak about themselves and their relationships, or denied their own past. Neither have these studies attempted to place silence as the main focus of their endeavors. Rather, most of these works argue in favor of accounting for selective discourse and not so much on strategies, mechanisms, implications, and contexts in which silences are both created and transmitted not only from hegemonic sectors but among subaltern sectors as well. These aspects are particularly relevant, especially if we consider—as several academics already have (e.g., Sousa Santos 2009; Spivak 1998)—that silence and forgetting contribute to the very configuration of the processes that construe the subaltern and the other.[6]

In order to account for the centrality acquired by silence within these processes, especially when we refer to Argentinian indigenous peoples, allow me to illustrate this point with an example. In 2010, after about two decades of 'recognition of ethnic difference' at least within the legislative corpus in Argentina and after many more years of struggle for recognition by indigenous movements, the Historical Museum of El Hoyo—Andean Region of Parallel 42°, Chubut, Argentinian

Patagonia—opened its gates permanently with an exhibition in which native peoples and their heritage were absent.

Indigenous peoples had been silenced from local history in both the past and the present of this space, and the demands and territorial conflicts of several communities that had recently been publicly ascribed as Mapuche in that area had been omitted. These omissions could be tracked, although with differences between one and the other, according to the case, in mechanisms produced and diffused in the region of the 'Andean Region of Parallel 42°' where El Hoyo is located: in institutional practices and procedures; in documents from official historical archives; in many books about the history of the area sponsored by municipal agents; in political discourses of several local civil servants; in the common sense of many residents; in monuments, mural paintings, and sculptures exhibited in public spaces belonging to nearby localities; etc.[7]

The museum, as many of these mechanisms of power, can be read as 'itineraries or tracks of the unsaid' that reproduce—in other temporal contexts and with some variations, according to the case—a historical hegemonic silencing operating in the constitution and consolidation of the national historical narrative. Regimes of the quiet that have worked as part of the 'epistemic violence' exercised on and shaping—along with physical violence—of the experiences historically lived by these peoples.[8]

Silences—not only discourses—set up within processes of heritagization have a crucial political role. It is in the tension between what is said and what is kept quiet, but more importantly between how it is said and how it is not said, that objects and subjects are categorized, classified, and ordered according to certain *statuses* or roles such as 'national,' 'provincial,' 'foreign,' 'poor,' 'citizen,' 'deviant,' 'undesirable,' 'indigenous,' etc. Thus, specific kinds of social relationships are established as inclusive and/or exclusive, as are visions and divisions of the past and present world and, in the process, someone or something(s) are given existence, that is, they are rendered thinkable, sayable, and visible (Grassi 2003–2004) in certain ways, while others are overshadowed and/or stigmatized. Far from constituting voids, silences inscribed within processes of heritagization are sources and practices of production, imagination, and management of subjects, spaces, knowledge, and relationships.

Studies developed in the field of memory offer interesting inputs about this. Trouillot (1995) analyzes the silences in the production of official historical narratives and shows how silencing operates on the level of content by resorting to 'formulas of erasure'—avoiding to talk about something, as in the aforementioned example. But there is also the level of poetics—*how* things are said, by what Trouillot calls 'formulas of banalization.' Therefore, if the employed vocabulary or language and the actions implemented through policies create meanings and 'effects' (Shore and Wright 1997, 21), it becomes essential to examine, along with content, the style, the strategies, and the poetics used in practices of heritagization, which are boosted by the hegemonic sectors in order to impose silence. To give another brief example, during the last years, archaeological resources have been declared as national heritage and as belonging to the different provinces of Argentina. This constituted an important change for a country that has configured its identity around the figure of the *gaucho* and has stigmatized indigenous people. Nevertheless, the way in which this heritage status was declared shows important omissions, among which—and perhaps the most discussed by some indigenous peoples—has been the absence of any mention of them as 'inheritors' with rights to decide on that 'past' and its management.[9]

On this trend, the problematization of silence leads to another aspect that has been widely debated, not only among academics but even among indigenous people, such as the differential possibility of self-representation by sectors that have been construed as subaltern, establishing their own meanings and exercising control over their cultural productions.[10] Here I am referring to the importance of problematizing the instance of enunciation and shaping of authority and power within any heritage activation, that is, the importance of reflecting on who has the power of constituting and omitting something as the heritage of a group, the power of talking 'about' and 'for' which subjects and how they do it, and the power of communicating, spreading, and commercializing that heritage, and by whom it is considered meaningful (Cruces 1998).

Now, there is a double significance to the silences and the imposed asymmetries. Not only because these are structural processes that are expressed through official heritage policies built around cultural manifestations and memories of indigenous sectors construed as subalterns and others, but, simultaneously, because of the slides produced during their course, as they constitute their political–affective experiences and subjectivities. As Briones (1994) points out, within the frame of these processes of silencing, omission, and absence—not only of the elaborated and propagated discourse—where everything can be said and argued, these peoples construct themselves in variable ways and, whether it is done in a positive way or not, they make sense of the omitted discourse and, sometimes, they can recognize its political key.

Whether it is due to imposed silence or shame produced by stigmatization, traumatic experiences, expropriations, and lived discriminations, the public diffusion of some histories, cultural practices, and even forms of ethnic self-classification has not only been made difficult, in many cases they have also faced, as a correlate, the total or partial interruption of the communication of stories, knowledge, experiences, and practices by the elders with the family and private environment. In my own fieldwork, some members of the Mapuche communities are constantly commenting on the silence of elders over certain experiences, knowledge, and memories as a common practice both outside and inside of the household. While, sometimes, this is lived with sadness due to the limitations it involves, it is defined, at the same time, not just as an intergenerational void of knowledge, histories, and practices, but as structuring of relationships, feelings, and experiences—of which they are even a product—as constituting their subjectivities and, in changing contexts, as a drive toward mobilization and struggle (Crespo 2014).

If, as Pollak (2006) contends, there are certain social conditions that hinder the possibility to talk, to listen, and to think on some experiences and memories, others can turn them sayable and audible, or even a matter for contestation and for making claims within public space. Thus, in some circumstances, silences and, moreover, 'memories of silences' as I named them elsewhere (Crespo 2014), become—as lived and learned practice and beyond their contents—not only significant for their own subjectivities but also relevant as part of the reconstruction of a common trajectory, of 'structures of feeling' within collective social fabrics, since they exhibit the hegemonic conditioners they have suffered collectively. Besides, they can also be charged with a performativity that would have been unthinkable in other historical periods,[11] mobilizing emotions and cognitive processes in political terms and at odds with hegemony, since the latter only defines and grants heritage status to 'pure' indigenous manifestations that show continuity with the past.

In Argentina, members of indigenous peoples have reflected on and expressed the silences imposed through various means on the field of heritage. Since 'heritage' is a category both historically and culturally foreign to the indigenous worldview, a concept that belongs to a process of self-recognition within an order characterized by forms of domination, some started to reflect on it from political and revindicating instances (Crespo 2005; Slavski 2007). They resorted to 'heritage' to claim rights and they redefined it, first of all, not so much as a selection of significant and representative aspects of culture but as culture itself, that is, as a whole: *cultural heritage is everything* (Interview of the sub-coordinator of the 'Bilingual Education and Mapuche Cultural Heritage' agreement in the Andean zone, December 2005).

The totality attributed to 'heritage' by these indigenous people can be understood in different ways. Rotman (2010) suggests that in the case of some Mapuche communities from the province of Neuquén, this holistic and encompassing conception is crossed by a 'rhetoric of loss.' According to Rotman, this rhetoric is in itself a counter-hegemonic practice since it implies the recognition of many acts of violence, imposition, and material and symbolic loss suffered[12] as they emerge as products of 'what has been transformed into shortage or oblivion and that has lately been attempted to "recover"' (Rotman 2010, 24).

During my fieldwork with Mapuche communities of the northwest part of the Chubut province and the southwest of Río Negro, as well as in other studies developed with different Mapuche people in the province of Buenos Aires, I found another kind of reflection on the matter. Instead of configuring it within an interpretation frame centered around the notion of 'loss,' some Mapuches in this regions redefine and recategorize these 'oblivions' as 'knowledge that has been kept quiet, saved, and sleeping' among the members of the household (Crespo 2008; Sabatella 2011)—*They don't dare to say. They are not lost . . . it's like they are saved* (Interview with a member of the 'Rinconada de Nahuelpán,' March 2006)—and/or, sometimes, as 'secrets' or, according to Sabatella (2011), as 'valuable secrets.'[13]

Therefore, the concept of heritage and the processes of memory construction, in these cases, are not built upon the basis of 'shortage' but on a 'rhetoric of what has been silenced,' 'saved,' or of what 'survived in the quiet' and which is liable to be brought to light and redefined—according to the circumstances—and, even, in some more precise exchanges, as what is 'kept in secret.' The latter refers to the practice of *pewtüm*—a healing Mapuche practice through which sickness is visualized—whose silencing among the Mapuche people of Los Toldos, according to Sabatella (2011), became a 'valuable secret.' I am even referring to the way in which I have specifically heard how the archaeological heritage of the Andean Region is signified. Indeed, a Mapuche woman with whom I interacted in that region conceived archaeological heritage as a 'secret,' a mystery known and shared only by its ancient indigenous creators and by the elders of the Mapuche community, thus attributing both them and their cultural manifestations a hierarchical knowledge, power, and differential value (Crespo 2008).[14] This shifting of meaning from what is 'lost' to what is 'saved' and, on more specific occasions, to the 'practice of secrecy,'[15] invite us to rethink and discuss the specific relevance of the continuity of traditions, culture, and the past for hegemonic definitions as well as classical anthropological understandings of what indigenous peoples should 'be' and 'do.' It questions hegemonic views that appealed to the 'lack' of indigenous presence to discredit and stigmatize them,[16] and, mainly, it sheds light on the ways through which these subjects define and redefine, in different ways and in each context, values, experiences, knowledge, belongings, exercises of power, 'continuities and discontinuities' produced by imposed forms of violence as well as means of resistance elaborated *vis-à-vis* that violence.

Along with the study of discourse and concrete action, the dynamic of silences and absences as existing practices within heritage policies make up a privileged observation point to apprehend the power relationships involved in these processes, the systems of belonging-differentiation, and the forms of stratification that were established in both time and space. It also, and primarily, helps to understand asymmetric historical experiences, conditioners, and current standpoints as well as political-emotional answers produced by it, that is: possibilities of identification, construction of certain memories, forms of struggle, shared social fabrics, affects, experiences of mobility and circulation within the social space of subjects that have been construed as subaltern and others, as it happens with indigenous peoples. We just need to learn to perceive and interpret them in all their complexity, remembering that silences and omissions are never complete and that their significations and effects are nor permanent, homogenous, or equally strong, according to who conducts them and social context.

B *The place of ambivalence, heterogeneity, tensions, and contradictions*

As I pointed out in the beginning of this text, over the last years there has been room for expressions on 'indigenous diversity' in heritage policies. Nevertheless, how this diversity has been 'valued', spread, and commemorated reveals some subtleties and ambivalences in comparison with other manifestations from different sectors that have been granted heritage status. By this I mean that, in spite of the fact that the granting of heritage status is considered to be carried out by state agencies, multilateral agencies, or NGOs, it implies recognition, a symbolic, political, and economic 'valuing' where not everything that is configured as heritage has the same hierarchy or awakens the same interest. Some cultural manifestations from specific social groups that have been constituted as heritage receive less attention than others, as it happens with those linked to Argentinian indigenous peoples (Crespo 2008).

Besides, after a history of physical and symbolic violence, of stigmatization, expropriation, and visibility of the indigenous merely as part of a superseded past and/or one that has yet to be surpassed, 'ethnic difference' became thinkable, possible, and manageable within the field of cultural heritage in different ways for each level of the state—national, provincial, and municipal—and even inside the same institution and according to parameters that are sometimes congruent but other times contradict the policies formulated in other spheres—territorial, for productive development, etc.—(Belli and Slavutsky 2006; Citro and Torres Agüero 2012; Crespo 2008).

A revision of these heritage policies in different geographical-jurisdictional spaces and with regards to other policies directed at indigenous peoples allows us to show the diverse and complex way in which 'indigenous diversity' is created, defined, and attempted to govern, as well as current prevailing contradictions. Some national, provincial, and municipal state agencies' heritage policies on indigenous matters construe 'geographies of imagination and management' of the ethnic as something with boundaries and as opposed to the West,[17] so, as Hale (2004) proposes, the 'allowed indigenous' is differentiated from the 'inadmissible' or 'conflictive' one. Thus, within a single group, hegemonic sectors consider some manifestations and forms of knowledge as more legitimate or authentic than others and, therefore, as susceptible of being incorporated, preserved, divulged, and even commercialized as representative heritage of that ethnic group as long as they do not oppose ongoing hegemonic interests (Benedetti 2007; Citro and Torres Agüero 2012; Sabatella 2013).

These agencies institutionalize indigenous boundaries, memories, and cultural productions in a static and dogmatic way that leaves behind everything they have in common with the experiences of other social groups, when they have in fact been constantly changing.[18] But in other cases, municipal policies configure diversity from guidelines that differ from those of the provinces they are a part of and/or national ones. For example, some municipalities that have only recently and selectively acknowledged the existence of indigenous communities when it comes to cultural tourism policies, undermine ethnicity not so much for its specificity or over a radical difference, as in the aforementioned cases, than from their 'undifferentiated integration with regard to other ethnic-national groups,' thus making dissimilar histories equivalent and configuring them as 'foreigners or other inner residents,' as it has been historically done. Other municipal policies assert their integration as autochthonous peoples without distinguishing specific ethnic groups. In both cases, none revise the histories of instituted subjugation and invisibility (Benedetti and Crespo 2013).

The situated and dialogical analysis of actions undertaken at different levels of the state (Briones 2005)—not only international, national, and provincial, as it has traditionally been done, but also municipal—contradicts the idea of the existence of a univocal and homogeneous context of congruent public policies. Hence, the relevance of revising how 'multicultural regulations' in local spaces, where the conformation of alterity acquires its own styles in the construction of hegemony, are reformulated, re-appropriated, and re-signified (Rodríguez de Anca 2013). Similarly, it is important to observe the extent to which these heritage actions are crossed 'by contextual factors, personal wills, and relationships of clientele' as well as its effects (Citro and Torres Agüero 2012, 170).

We can also observe contradictions or contending standpoints within a single institution or organization. As Hall (2010) suggests, 'multiculturalism,' far from being only one strategy and a policy adopted to rule and manage cultural diversity, is based on multiple strategies and policies.[19] Within this multiplicity, sometimes implying contradictions, subjects must move and struggle to change their situation. Therefore, in the context of current 'multicultural rhetoric' where indigenist rights are legislated and limited spaces for 'indigenous participation' are opened, 'political dynamics operating on the basis of 'unfinished transitions' (Hale 2004), and combining the rationale of the recognition of diversity with the old rationale of subordinate incorporation of ethnic difference' can simultaneously prevail (Benedetti and Crespo 2013, 181).

Whichever the case may be, heritage policies, in their ways of saying, doing, and/or keeping quiet, produce knowledge and define subjects, spaces, values—affective, political, economic, and significantly symbolic—and relationships that have political implications and determine contesting political fields. Hence, their greater importance as practice than as 'representation' (Hall 1998); since these referents become prescriptive and regulators of social life, they establish a basis for conversation and a kind of morality, they condition and demand certain forms of performing difference, and they are internalized and/or confronted in various ways, thus configuring specific kinds of inter and intra-ethnic relationships.

Among the most frequent topics addressed by studies on the heritagization processes of indigenous cultural manifestations and human remains, there are the confrontations that occur between the different intervening agencies and, particularly in Argentina, recent processes of public claims over the archaeological heritage, especially of human remains, by some communities and indigenous peoples, according to each case (e.g., Arenas 2011; Curtoni and Chaparro 2011; Endere and Curtoni 2006; Di Fini 2001; Lázzari 2008; Oldani et al. 2011; Podgorny and Politis 1990; Rodríguez 2011). The transformation of archaeological resources into provincial and/or national heritage brought along discussions not only on the meanings assigned to these cultural productions and human remains, but also on the way in which indigenous peoples have been classified/categorized[20] and the possibility to self-manage them, which implies, as Slavski (2007) suggests, a dispute for the acknowledgement of their political rights: the right to self-definition, self-determination, and participation in matters that concern them.

The history of interethnic relationships in Argentina, the way in which their goods, productions, and human remains were collected by the end of the nineteenth and the first half of the twentieth century, explanations given to them until approximately the 1980s,[21] and the disputes around granting heritage status to practices, goods, and indigenous human remains give, in my opinion, a certain specificity or particular imprint to the processes of heritagization of cultural manifestations of other social sectors.

In the dispute to redefine their position, indigenous peoples gradually were appropriating, questioning, and/or re-signifying concepts set on the agenda by the dominant sectors of each context (Delrío 2005), and constructing in various ways their sense of belonging, their pasts, their presents, and their hopes for the future.

Over the last years, while some indigenous peoples resort to hegemonic vocabulary such as the concept of 'heritage,' redefining its meaning in order to frame their demands and stage a reflection on one's own and other's belongings and on the history of asymmetric interethnic relationships and deprivations experienced in different spheres of social life in Argentina (Crespo 2005), others demand the restitution of human remains as part of their 'forefathers/ancestors' (e.g., Di Fini 2001; Endere and Curtoni 2006; Lázzari 2008; Rodríguez 2011) or of some archaeological sites, re-accentuating them under the category of 'sacred spaces' over which they demand rights (Crespo and Rodríguez 2013).

Some academics look at indigenous claims around patrimonial manifestations as instrumental-political strategies. However, many who, like me, are involved in the study of indigenous problematics, discuss those views that reduce and explain identifications and claims over cultural manifestations as exclusive products of strategies or rationally and consciously calculated orchestrations with specific aims. We recover the importance of complex analysis. On the one hand, we differentiate the instrumentality attributed to the actions of hegemonic sectors around the patrimonial activation of those 'strategies' that—drawing on Bourdieu's formulations—result from force relations, 'the product of the practical sense [. . .] for a particular, historically determined game—a feel which is acquired in childhood, by taking part in social activities' (Bourdieu 1990, 62–63).[22] On the other hand, and aiming to detach from those instrumental views by showing its political implications in the field of ethnicity, some analyze the relationships established with that memory of longer duration from its political–affective quality (Escolar 2007; Rodríguez 2011a; Sabatella 2013); that is to say, it is conceived as a 'voluntary and affective affirmation based on feelings and perceptions, and not only on arguments and explanations' (Escolar 2007, 58) or as part of 'affective [experiences], alliances, and actions constrained by hegemonic social space' (Rodríguez 2011a, 2). Others, including myself, also observe in these claims a demand for justice and reparation of damages (Arenas 2011; Lázzari 2008), an attempt to revert an ongoing history of asymmetry, deprivations, and invisibility (Crespo 2005; Rotman 2010) that leads them to publicly connect with their ancestors as members of a specific people or as their 'descendants,' and to constitute themselves as a space for political–affective mobilization and attachment (Crespo 2005–2011; Rodríguez 2011b).

In many cases, even with different explanations and implications, identification with these memories and pasts is analyzed not only as a product of the present but of the complex articulation of historical and current experiences of dispute over hegemony. But as Appadurai (1981) points out, not all interpretations of the past made by sectors construed as subalterns and others are open to free acceptance. There are conditioners that limit what, how, why, and what for can something be said (Popular Memory Group 1982). To include the analysis of processes of heritagization and indigenous memories within processes of construction of hegemony means to also give account of other cases that have scarcely been addressed in Argentina and which allow us to keep adjusting theories and explanations in this field.

I refer, on the one hand, to those in which the absence of a public claim on heritage does not imply the lack of identification with a certain fragment of the past, with an experience, a tradition, or a cultural manifestation by a social group. As Gledhill (2000) pointed out, there is more than open claims and visible movements of resistance and opposition; there are also tactics and forms of resistance that operate more silently in everyday life. To give an example, some Mapuches do not publicly claim rights over archaeological heritage neither to state institutions nor to academics, but, in certain contexts, they refer to the distant past and its cultural manifestations as theirs. That is to say, within a frame of claims over territorial rights and as one of the ways to build autochthony *vis-à-vis* hegemonic historical views of them as foreign, as well as to explain other uses and definitions of territory, some Mapuches at Lago Pueblo started to spread—sometimes through the media and/or through personal interviews—the contention that Mapuche cultural manifestations related to an ancient past belonged to them and, simultaneously, they started to spread an interpretation of history before the 'Conquest of the Desert' that is opposed in many levels to the area s official historical narrative and to some aspects of academic discourse (Crespo 2011). Others, rather than making public demands, observe, in the context of interviews and more informal conversations, that the constitution of archaeological resources as part of the provincial and national heritage of Argentina is another form of expropriation and subjugation of their own history.

These situations illustrate why we need to take into account that identification with memories and pasts by sectors that have been construed as subalterns and others are not only a product of the present but of the complex articulation of historical and present experiences with hegemonic discourses and practices. We can also acknowledge the importance of observing not only that which is made visible and spread on public arenas, but also that which can take place in everyday life and private contexts through images and discursive genres considered as 'minor,' 'depoliticized,' etc. Often, the production of memories and silences around knowledge, experiences, and memories become vehicular not only through narratives chronologically organized in a linear manner, but also through legends, fantastic stories, cultural performances, and images. These expressive genres, which sometimes, according to the researcher's perspective are less used as sources, can, if they are examined situated and contextually, shed light on tensions, debates, senses of belonging, forms of resistance, and valuable aspects of social life, which are not always staged in other discursive genres or which are not always disseminated through words.[23] Before attempting to establish whether these stories are true or false, what 'matters is to unravel—as Gordillo points out—the force fields and collective experiences underlying its production' (Gordillo 2006, 28) and how they are inscribed and how we can access through them 'to the conflict between possible and impossible sayings' (Vich and Zavala 2004, 109).

But I'm also interested in adding the importance of starting to examine that the sense given to certain pasts, patrimonial productions, and/or traditions considered to be 'indigenous' can take upon more complex, heterogeneous, and ambivalent trajectories when it comes to identification, appropriation possibilities, and signification among the members of indigenous peoples. In other words, certain fragments of the past as well as experiences, practices, goods, spaces, and so on, can contain views, within the same self-identified group, that are ambivalent, simultaneously positive, and negative, expressing continuity and estrangement, all denoting ways of internalizing hegemonic discourses and practices alongside defiant visions *vis-à-vis* the established social order, whose political implications are, at the same time, divergent (Crespo 2008; Gordillo 2006).

Therefore, it is my understanding that the analysis of the heritagization processes of cultural manifestations and indigenous production of memories and silences cannot overlook these considerations. Besides, I think that these subjects' variable and contending positions can only be understood in their full complexity if they are historically located and connected with past and present structural processes experienced collectively by these social groups and with colonialist scientific discourses and practices (Gnecco 2005), as well as with subjective experiences, whose articulations differentially articulate significations and contentions on the matter of the past and of traditions within hegemonic relationships, and how these influence their political practices.

This would allow a contribution to the field in several ways. In the first place, it opens the possibility of accounting for and understanding the heterogeneities existing within a single group occupying the same position in the social structure by explaining how processes of subjection, subjectivity, and possibilities of indigenous agency operate differentially in the reconstruction of memory and heritage, framed by historical and current conditioners of them as social groups and, as Pizarro (2006) argues, the particular way in which past and present structural conflicts are mediatized. Second, it allows questioning the current common understanding of a calculated, strategic construction and self-interested usage of the past, heritage, and/or culture (whichever may be) by indigenous populations. Third, it allows to ponder, as Grossberg suggests, how certain cultural practices which, on one occasion, habilitated cultural *empowerment*, can lead to the opposite direction and, even, that some 'forms of empowerment which are effective as resistance over there, might be ineffective over here' (Grossberg 1992, 95).

Bases of approach: historical ethnography as an approach to processes of heritagization

The role played by processes of silencing, ambivalences, paradoxes, tensions, and heterogeneities are key to understanding the dynamics played out in the processes of heritagization. An ethnographic analysis crossed by a historical dimension allows an input into the necessary complexity of this kind of perspective, which emphasizes less the object and the rule, than the contending practices and relationships displayed before, during, and after the formulation of these policies and go beyond written norms. This is even more so if these policies and relationships are historicized within processes of construction and dispute over hegemony of longer duration.

Anthropology, centered on an ethnographic perspective, can 'underline the complexity and the lack of order within the processes of formulating policies, especially the ambiguous and often disputed ways in which policies are issued and received by the people' (Shore 2010, 29). Norms and policies that are based on determined ideological paradigms, on views and constructions of social order, and they are reformulated as the products of confrontations and negotiations. Far from a bipolar reality, we find ourselves facing a multidimensional world where complex dynamics of processes of domination and struggle are generated (Roseberry 2007). While, in certain cases, some subjects follow hegemonic scripts or they use them only partially and in specific circumstances, in others they abandon and defy norms, taking unexpected roads. The heterogeneous processes, practices, and effects of these policies, as Trouillot (2011) suggests, can be recognized by using an ethnographic strategy that studies not only within institutional contexts, but at its points of emergence, production conditions, and boundaries in different realms of everyday life and in the network of interpersonal relationships.

We advocate for a perspective that can de-naturalize behaviors, discourses, and silences, and which breaks with dichotomic and linear views and classifications that prevail in the field of heritage between: identity and market (Benedetti 2013), the material and the immaterial (Bialogorski and Fischman 2001; Lacarrieu and Pallini 2001), the political and the affective (Sabatella 2011), thus shifting the focus toward the study of how these aspects become contentious. We also advocate for an approach centered on the study of how local—municipal—heritage policies are articulated with and disarticulated from those of other instances of wider jurisdiction—provincial, national, and international. Finally, this approach should examine the emerging tensions within a single institutional context or agency in the processes of conformation of these policies, and should also give priority to the way it intertwines with other policies and demands at the local level.

Undoubtedly, the importance of conducting more local studies comes from the fact that the prevailing power dynamics in these spaces can complement, contradict, and overlap with the actions effected in other orders and state or non-state wider levels—NGOs, intergovernmental agencies, and so on—but, especially, as we noticed elsewhere (Benedetti and Crespo 2013), because it is in this relatively autonomous spaces that indigenous people constantly interact with local agencies of power and experience directly: the enabling and the boundaries imposed on their behaviors and the occupation of social and territorial spaces; relationships of inequality and subordination; expropriations and subjugations. Studying the dynamics of articulation between municipalities and other state or even non-state levels, while trying to shed light on how programs and wider policies intertwine with processes, relationships, social trajectories, and local power sectors, can contribute to sketch a less homogeneous and schematic panorama over epochal context frames. But, especially, it can contribute to a deeper and more complete understanding on how and why certain shifts and continuities of public policies implemented in different spaces occur, and on the thickness of the responses deployed by a part of the indigenous population.

Through different mechanisms and interpretations of ethnic diversity in each space, hegemonic sectors establish—within these processes of heritagization and of construction of memory—silencing, stereotypes, invisibilities, exercises of control, and asymmetries that have led indigenous people to undervalue themselves, to silencing and/or hiding their own cultural practices, experiences, knowledge, and pasts. Sometimes, as I mentioned above, certain contexts allow some silences and even 'silence' themselves as a practice to become an object of reflection, significance, and transmission, so they reach the public sphere by configuring themselves under a political–affective sense as constitutive of the group's subjectivity and a drive to struggle.

However, as I have also shown here, these interactions are not always in the form of open and visible opposition, nor do the confrontations occur only at the level of words. There are socio-historical conditioners which, combined with personal life trajectories, explain processes of interpenetration, ambivalence, heterogeneities, and/or questionings on silences, hidings, definitions, and contradictions of state and non-state agencies' programs and practices by indigenous peoples in each context. These processes are manifested through different expressive genres or forms of expression—different kinds of discursive genres, images, performances, and so on—which affect inter and intra-ethnic relationships in various ways.

An ethnography centered on a historical perspective allows a glimpse into the complexity of this phenomenon by de-naturalizing and contextualizing norms, discourses, practices, and programs, and distinguishing singularities within epochal frames, observing its historical nature and dynamism, burst into the study of the quotidian and the private as articulated with the public and the official, methodologically involving the study of how it emerges in different expressive genres, traditions, images, commemorations, ways of knowledge and exchange, and under which significations in each case, and shedding light on its usages and constituting power relations, tensions, ruptures, and crossovers.

If ethnography, with its thorough analysis, contributes to contemplate the extents, meanings, and political effects of the heritagization processes of indigenous peoples' cultural manifestations, showing how macro political coordinates intertwine with micro political phenomena and the dissimilar effects that progressively inscribe themselves in the local arena, then historicization of patrimonial practices contributes to calibrate its changes and continuities and to explain practices and relationships within longer processes. Nowadays, a great variety of actors coexist in the methodological design, with their own factions and inner divisions. A remaining matter for another article is to discuss the role of academics in this process, a significant task if our purpose is to 'constitute ourselves as a source of decolonizing knowledge whose contributions are not only directed at some sectors of society but at humanity as a whole' (Verdesio 2011, 8).

Translation: Lucía Cirianni

Notes

1 I wish to acknowledge the comments and the contributions to this work made by Sandra Rozental, Mario Rufer, and Frida Gorbach during the Third Biennial Conference of the International Association of Inter-American Studies that took place at Lima, Peru, on August 6–8, 2014. But I especially appreciate the generosity of Mario Rufer for the translation of this article and both editors of this volume for their invitation to participate in this book. And finally I thank Julieta Infantino for the revision of the translation.
2 I will use the term 'heritagization' instead of 'heritage.' That concept refers to the processes by which heritage is constructed.
3 Here, the term 'memories' is not to be understood as 'recollections' but as the multiple expressions of social and historical memory. (Translator's note)
4 Here, I am taking up a discussion from the current of studies on dominant and subaltern memory. For further information on this discussion as well as on the need for other theories to approach the processes of construction of the past among subordinate groups, see Briones (1994).
5 The following reflections are, in great measure, a product of my own experiences researching on memories and processes of heritagization in the area of the Andean Region of Parallel 42°—northwest of the Chubut province (El Hoyo, Epuyén, Lago Puelo, Cholila, and el Maitén) and southwest of the Río Negro province (El Bolsón)—in the Argentinian Patagonia. This work also draws upon experiences of extension-transference with the Indigenous Community of Quilmes in the Tucuman province —northwest Argentina—just as the exchange between indigenous leaders and public servants, and the reading of other studies on memory and heritage of indigenous cultural manifestations developed in Argentina and in other Latin American countries.
6 I understand the term 'subaltern', as Coronil (1994) proposes, less as a fixed position or the definition of a subject than as a process of subjection or a state of submission.
7 The formulas of silencing used and, specifically, the silenced aspects or dimensions in each of these mechanisms of power vary.
8 A deeper analysis of the mechanisms of silencing played out in this museum and their political implications can be found in Crespo and Tozzini (2014).
9 On the way archaeological resources were granted heritage status in certain provinces of Argentina, see Endere (2000), Crespo (2005), Rodríguez (2013), among others.
10 Many indigenous leaders actually define the silencing established by the state around heritage policies throughout time and even until today, as part of the outrages, subjugations, and expropriations lived in all spheres of social life—from things concerning their territory to symbolic matters (Crespo, 2008).
11 As Nahuelquir, Sabatella and Stella (2011) point out, meanings associated with silences vary within people's subjectivities throughout time and according to their social conditions.
12 Rotman points out that 'in processes of granting heritage status, the 'rhetoric of loss' (as defined by Gonçalves) related to the construction of a national culture and identity, is configured as a discourse from hegemonic sectors and it is structured as a hegemonic practice. This category, related to developments on ethnic identity of the Mapuche people, operates by enabling memories, legitimizing experiences and constituting

subjects—within processes that imply subjection and compliance as well as forms of reordering and resistance in subaltern conditions—thus allowing us to consider it as a counter-hegemonic practice' (Rotman 2010, 24).

13 In her thesis in Anthropology, Sabatella analyzes and introduces an interesting discussion about the displacement of 'silences' to 'valuable secrets.'
14 Although the limitations of this space do not allow me to analyze this here, I must mention that these secrets and mysteries are synchronized with some popular stories around archaeological heritage. For further information on this, see Crespo (2008–2011).
15 I consider 'secrecy' as a practice that allows to both create and maintain links of affective affinity, belonging, authority, and power, as well as to divide, isolate, and build otherness or even break social relationships by the more or less porous closure of information that is invested with a social 'value' (whether it is positive or negative) (Berliner 2005; Giraud 2006). Secrets are based on a game or a dynamic that implies closing and sharing information, hiding it. They can be linked to mysteries—as in the aforementioned example—that can incite fascination, and/or also with the register of something socially considered as a prohibition, a stigma, the inadmissible, or deviated. Since secrecy implies silence and sharing, it is often motivated by other factors around the practice of silencing and it entails other effects that are not necessarily equivalent, which makes it prone to other kind of connotations and meanings. About this, see Berliner (2005) and Giraud (2006).
16 For example, historical narratives from the Río Negro region produced after the territory was provincialized in 1955, have combined nationalization and foreignization of different ethnic groups within this land with racialization of the indigenous past, the emptying of these populations after the conquest, their later location in specific geographies within the province and into a class structure, and the loss or extinction of their culture in the present. As for the dominant anthropological discourse in Patagonia until the eighties, it defined the 'indigenous' from the notion of loss and backwardness, as a 'legacy of the past,' and it considered its own professional practice as the only one capable of 'rescuing' what was left of that difference from oblivion.
17 These boundaries of 'the indigenous' appear too in the actions of some NGOs and they are linked to a definition of ethnicity and the policies that are to be applied on these peoples determined by multilateral and international agencies.
18 As Gordillo (2006) contends, indigenous subjectivity is not so much something fixed and eternal, but the product of historical, cultural, and political experiences that are always changing and contradicting each other in regard not only to their ethnicity but to experiences that other social sectors have gone through.
19 For an analysis of 'multiculturalism' as an umbrella term, see Hall (2010).
20 The core of this questioning is the appropriation of the past by the national and provincial agencies of the state by classifying it as 'national and provincial heritage' and omitting the presence of indigenous peoples.
21 Over the last years, the collecting urge that impregnated science and the political violence implied in the way these collections were made, have been frequently criticized even within academia. Estanislao Zeballos, and attorney and an organic intellectual of the era of President Julio Argentino Roca, gathered a private collection of skeletons stolen from tombs in Patagonia which he later donated to the Museum of La Plata, in the province of Buenos Aires. Francisco Moreno himself, the first director of this museum and an explorer of the Patagonia region, declared to have exhumed remains from that area too. The private collection of the Police Commissioner of the province of Tucumán, Manuel Zavaleta, which ended up in the Ethnographic Museum of Buenos Aires, had been the product of plundering 'Calchaquí antiques.' Some of the human remains exhibited at the Museum of La Plata even belonged to indigenous people who, after the Conquest of the Desert, were transported to that institution as service personnel

and as scientific subjects of study, and who, after their deaths, were added to its patrimonial repertory and exhibited in one of its halls (Cf. Podgorny and Politis 1990; Di Fini 2001; among others).
22 It is worth mentioning that these 'strategies' are produced by force relations within the hearth of a group and they can be explained by rebuilding its history, its differential conditioners, the circumstances of their members, current revindications, and the trajectory followed by the constitution and signification, in this case, of that which is being disputed (Crespo, 2008). The variability of the strategies used to claim the recognition of rights and resources relates not only to the position of the involved agencies within the social structure, but also to the circumstances, social roles, trajectories, and specific social conditions of these sectors—even within the same positions. As I explain below, cultural practices or memories that can enable power and become effective forms of resistance at a certain point may not be seen in the same way by others who belong to the same group and social sector.
23 Archaeological resources and especially human remains are usually charged with performativity in stories. I have often heard indigenous people mention how the dead men participate and impact on the life of the living (Crespo 2008).

References

Aguilar Criado, Encarnación. 2003. 'Entre lo global y lo local. La revitalización de la producción artesanal en España.' *Artesanías de América*, no. 55: 73–98.
Aguilar Criado, Encarnación. 2005. 'Patrimonio y globalización: el recurso de la cultura en las Políticas de Desarrollo Europeas.' *Cuadernos de antropología social*, Vol. 21: 51–69.
Appadurai, Arjun. 1981. 'The past as a scarce resource.' *Man*, Vol. 16, no. 2: 201–19.
Arantes, Augusto. 1984. *Produzindo o passado: estratégias de construção do patrimônio cultural*. São Paulo: Editorial Brasiliense.
Arantes, Augusto. 1997. 'Patrimonio cultural e nação.' In *Trabalho, cultura e cidadania*, ed. Angela Carneiro Araujo, 275–90. São Paulo: Escritta.
Arenas, Patricia. 2011. 'Ahora Damiana es Krygi. Restitución de restos a la comunidad aché de Ypetimi. Paraguay.' *Corpus. Archivos virtuales de la alteridad americana*, Vol. 1, no. 1. http://ppct.caicyt.gov.ar/index.php/corpus.
Belli, Elena, and Ricardo Slavutsky, eds. 2006. *Patrimonio en el Noroeste Argentino. Otras historias*. Jujuy: Universidad de Buenos Aires.
Benedetti, Cecilia. 2007. 'Patrimonio Cultural y Pueblos Indígenas en Argentina: El Fomento a la Producción Artesanal en la Comunidad Chané de Campo Durán, Provincia de Salta.' *Revista de Antropología*, no. 19: 89–116.
Benedetti, Cecilia. 2013. 'La construcción de lo étnico y la producción artesanal en el Departamento de General San Martín, provincia de Salta.' In *Tramas de la Diversidad. Patrimonio y Pueblos Originarios*, ed. Carolina Crespo, 219–46. Buenos Aires: Antropofagia.
Benedetti, Cecilia, and Carolina Crespo. 2013. 'Construcciones de alteridad indígena en el campo patrimonial en Argentina. Algunas reflexiones a partir de estudios situados en Tartagal (Provincia de Salta) y Lago Puelo (Provincia de Chubut).' *Boletín de Antropología*, Vol. 28, no. 46: 161–84.
Berliner, David. 2005. 'An 'impossible' transmission: Youth religious memories in Guinea–Conakry.' *American Ethnologist*, Vol. 32, no. 4: 576–92.
Bialogorski, Mirta, and Fernando Fischman. 2001. 'Patrimonio intangible y folclore: viejas y nuevas conceptualizaciones.' *Revista de Investigaciones Folclóricas*, no. 16: 99–102.

Bonfil Batalla, Guillermo. 1989. 'Identidad nacional y patrimonio cultural: los conflictos ocultos y las convergencias posibles.' In *Antropología y Políticas culturales. Patrimonio e Identidad*, ed. Rita Ceballos, 43–52. Buenos Aires: Departamento de antropología y Folklore.
Bonfil Batalla, Guillermo. 1997. *Nuestro que Florescano.* Mexico City: FCE—CONACULTA, 28–56.
Bourdieu, Pierre. 1996. *Cosas Dichas.* Barcelopatrimonio cultural: un laberinto de significados.' *El patrimonio nacional de México*, ed. Enrina: Gedisa.
Briones, Claudia. 1994. '"Con la tradición de todas las generaciones pasadas gravitando sobre la mente de los vivos": Usos del pasado e invención de la tradición.' *Runa*, Vol. XXI: 99–129.
Briones, Claudia. 2005. 'Formaciones de alteridad: contextos globales, procesos nacionales y provinciales.' In *Cartografías argentinas. Políticas indigenistas y formaciones provinciales de alteridad*, ed. Claudia Briones, 11–44. Buenos Aires: Antropofagia.
Brow, James. 2000. 'Notas sobre comunidad, hegemonía y los usos del pasado.' In *Ficha de cátedra de Etnolingüística. El habla en interacción: La comunidad*, 21–32. Buenos Aires: OPFYL.
Citro, Silvia, and Soledad Torres Agüero. 2012. '"Es un ejemplo no solamente para los desu raza qom sino para toda la juventud formoseña". El patrimonio cultural inmaterial y la música indígena en la controvertida política formoseña.' *Runa*, Vol. XXXIII, no. 2: 157–74.
Crespo, Carolina. 2005. ' Qué pertenece a quién`: Procesos de patrimonialización y Pueblos Originarios en Patagonia.' *Cuadernos de Antropología Social*, no. 21: 133–49.
Crespo, Carolina. 2008. Políticas de la memoria, procesos de patrimonialización de los recursos arqueológicos y construcción identitaria entre los Mapuches de la Rinconada de Nahuelpán en Río Negro. Doctoral Thesis, Facultad de Filosofía y Letras, Universidad de Buenos Aires.
Crespo, Carolina. 2011. 'Patrimonio arqueológico, memoria y territorio. Procesos de autoctonización entre los mapuches de Lago Puelo, Chubut (Patagonia Argentina).' *Revista Frontera Norte*, Vol. 23, no. 45: 231–55.
Crespo, Carolina. 2012. 'Espacios de 'autenticidad', 'autoctonía' y 'expropiación': el lugar del 'patrimonio arqueológico' en narrativas mapuches en El Bolsón, Patagonia Argentina.' *Cuadernos Interculturales*, no. 18: 31–61.
Crespo, Carolina. 2014. 'Memorias de silencios en el marco de reclamos étnico-territoriales: Experiencias de despojo y violencia en la primer mitad de siglo XX en el Parque Nacional Lago Puelo (Patagonia, Argentina).' *Revista Cuicuilco* 21.
Crespo, Carolina, and Lorena Beatriz Rodríguez. 2013. '*"Como herederos legítimos de nuestros antepasados".* El proceso de pedido de restitución de la Ciudad Sagrada de Quilmes desde la mirada de la prensa local.' In *Tramas de la diversidad. Patrimonio y Pueblos Originarios*, ed. Carolina Crespo, 157–88. Buenos Aires: Antropofagia.
Crespo, Carolina, and María Alma Tozzini. 2014. 'Memorias silenciadas y patrimonios ausentes en el Museo Historico de El Hoyo, Comarca Andina del Paralelo 42°, Patagonia Argentina.' *Antípoda*, no. 19.
Coronil, Fernando. 1994. 'Listening to the subaltern: The poetics of neocolonial states.' *Poetics Today*, Vol. 15, no. 4: 643–58.
Cruces, Francisco. 1998. 'Problemas en torno a la restitución del patrimonio. Una visión desde la antropología.' *Alteridades*, year 8, no. 16: 75–84.
Curtoni, Rafael, and María Gabriela Chaparro. 2011. 'El Re-entierro del Cacique José Gregorio Yancamil. Patrimonio, Política y Memoria de Piedra en la Pampa Argentina.' *Revista chilena de Antropología* 19: 9–36.

Delrío, Walter. 2005. *Memorias de expropiación. Sometimiento e incorporación indígena en la Patagonia. 1872–1943.* Buenos Aires: Universidad Nacional de Quilmes.

De Sousa Santos, Boaventura. 2009. *Pensar el Estado y la sociedad: Desafíos actuales.* Buenos Aires: CLACSO—Waldhuter Editores.

Di Fini, María. 2001. 'Visibilidad/Invisibilidad en la relación Sociedad aborigen/Estado Nacional.' In *La Trama Cultural. Textos de antropología y arqueología*, 208–218. Buenos Aires: Caligraf.

Endere, María Luz. 2000. *Arqueología y legislación en Argentina. Cómo proteger el patrimonio arqueológico*, no. 1. Buenos Aires: Incuapa—UNCBA.

Endere, María Luz, and Rafael Curtoni. 2006. 'Entre lonkos y 'ólogos'. La participación de la comunidad indígena rankülche de Argentina en la investigación arqueológica.' *Arqueología Sudamericana*, Vol. 2, no. 1: 72–92.

Escolar, Diego. 2007. 'Arqueólogos y brujos. Ciencia, Cultura e imaginación histórica.' In *Los dones étnicos de la Nación. Identidad Huarpe y modos de producción de soberanía en Argentina*, 35–62. Buenos Aires: Prometeo.

Florescano, Enrique. 1993. *El patrimonio cultural de México.* México DF: Fondo de Cultura Económica.

Garcia Canclini, Néstor. 1989. *Culturas híbridas. Estrategias para entrar y salir de la modernidad.* Mexico City: Grijalbo.

Garcia Canclini, Néstor. 1993. 'Los usos sociales del patrimonio cultural.' In *El patrimonio cultural de México*, ed. Enrique Florescano, 41–61. Mexico City: Fondo de Cultura Económica.

Giraud, Claude. 2006. *Acerca del secreto. Contribución a una sociología de la autoridad y del compromiso.* Buenos Aires: Biblos.

Gledhill, John. 2000. *El poder y sus disfraces. Perspectivas antropológicas de la política.* Barcelona: Bellaterra.

Gnecco, Cristóbal. 2005. 'Ampliación del campo de batalla.' *Textos Antropológicos*, Vol. 15, no. 2: 183–95.

Gordillo, Gastón. 2006. 'Recordando a los antiguos.' In *En el Gran Chaco. Antropologías e historias*, 27–42. Buenos Aires: Prometeo.

Grassi, Estela. 2003. *Políticas y problemas sociales en la sociedad neoliberal. La otra década infame (I).* Buenos Aires: Espacio Editorial.

Grassi, Estela. 2004. *Política y cultura en la sociedad neoliberal. La otra década infame (II).* Buenos Aires: Espacio Editorial.

Grossberg, Lawrence. 1992. 'Power and Daily Life.' In *We gotta get out of this place. Popular conservatism and postmodern culture.* New York—London: Routledge.

Hale, Charles 2004. 'El protagonismo indígena, las políticas estatales y el nuevo racismo en la época del 'indio permitido.' Ponencia presentada en la conferencia *Construyendo la paz: Guatemala desde un enfoque comparado*, organizado por la Misión de Verificación de las Naciones Unidas en Guatemala (MINUGUA), 27–29 de octubre.

Hall, Stuart. 1998. 'Significado, representación, ideología: Althusser y los debates postestructuralistas.' In *Estudios culturales y comunicación. Análisis, producción y consumo cultural de las políticas de identidad y el posmodernismo*, ed. James Curran, David Morely, and Valerie Walkerdine, 27–61. Barcelona: Paidós.

Hall, Stuart. 2010. 'La cuestión multicultural.' In *Sin garantías: trayectorias y problemáticas en estudios culturales*, ed. Stuart Hall, 133–53. Popayán—Lima—Quito: Envión Editores—IEP- Instituto Pensar-Universidad Andina Simón Bolívar.

Hobsbawm, Eric, and Terence Ranger. 1983. *The invention of tradition.* Cambridge: Cambridge University.

Lacarrieu, Mónica, and Verónica Pallini. 2001. 'La gestión de 'patrimonio(s) intangible(s)' en el contexto de políticas de la cultura.' In *Primeras Jornadas de Patrimonio Intangible. Memorias, identidades e imaginarios sociales*. Buenos Aires: CPPHC.
Lazzari, Axel. 2008. 'La repatriación de los restos de Mariano Rosas: identificación fetichista en las políticas de reconocimiento de los ranqueles.' *Estudios en antropología social*, Vol. 1: 35–64.
Nahuelquir, Fabiana, María Emilia Sabatella, and Valentina Stella. 2011. 'Sentidos políticos de los olvidos: buscando perspectivas,' presentado en el *IV Seminario Internacional Políticas de la Memoria*. Mimeo.
Oldani, Karina, Miguel Añón Suarez, and Fernando Miguel Pepe. 2011. 'Las muertes invisibilizadas del Museo de La Plata.' *Corpus. Archivos virtuales de la alteridad americana*, Vol. 1, no. 1. http://ppct.caicyt.gov.ar/index.php/corpus/article/viewFile/319/101.
Pizarro, Cinthia. 2006. 'Somos indios civilizados. La (in)visibilización de la identidad aborigen en Catamarca.' *Anuario de Estudios en Antropología Social*, no. 3: 179–95.
Podgorny, Irina, and Gustavo Politis. 1990. '¿Qué sucedió en la historia? Los esqueletos araucanos del Museo de La Plata y la Conquista del Desierto.' *Arqueología Contemporánea*, no. 3.
Pollak, Michael. 2006. *Memoria, Olvido, Silencio. La producción social de identidades frente a situaciones límite*. La Plata: Ediciones Al Margen.
Popular Memory Group. 1982. 'Popular memory: Theory, politics, method.' In *Making Histories. Studies in history writing and politics*, ed. Richard Johnson, 205–52. London: Hutchinson.
Prats, Llorenç. 1997. *Antropología y Patrimonio*. Barcelona: Editorial Ariel.
Rodríguez de Anca, Alejandra. 2013. 'Políticas culturales y colonialidad. Acerca del régimen de visibilidad del Pueblo Mapuche en Neuquén.' In *Tramas de la Diversidad. Patrimonio y Pueblos Originarios*, ed. Carolina Crespo, 21–38. Buenos Aires: Antropofagia.
Rodríguez, Mariela Eva. 2011a. '"Casualidades" y "causalidades" de los procesos de patrimonialización en la provincia de Santa Cruz.' *Corpus. Archivos virtuales de la alteridad americana*, Vol. 1, no. 1. http://ppct.caicyt.gov.ar/index.php/corpus/article/view/325/107.
Rodríguez, Mariela Eva. 2011b. 'Reflexiones de los autores sobre el dossier.' *Corpus. Archivos virtuales de la alteridad americana*, Vol. 1, no. 1. http://ppct.caicyt.gov.ar/index.php/corpus/article/view/317.
Rosas Mantecón, Ana. 1998. 'Presentación.' *Alteridades*, Vol. 8, no. 16: 3–7.
Roseberry, William. 2007. 'Hegemonía y el lenguaje de la controversia.' In *Cuadernos de Futuro. Antropología del Estado. Dominación y prácticas contestatarias en América Latina*, ed. María L. Lagos, and Pamela Calla, no. 23: 117–39.
Rotman, Mónica. 1999. 'Diversidad y desigualdad: patrimonio y producciones culturales de los sectores subalternos.' Presentado en la *III Reunión de Antropología del Mercosur*, Posadas- Misiones. Mimeo.
Rotman, Mónica. 2010. 'El campo patrimonial: procesos de configuración y problematización de alteridades.' In *Memória em rede*, Vol. 1, no. 1: 22–42.
Sabatella, María Emilia. 2011. *Procesos de subjetivación política. Reflexiones a partir de un proyecto de medicina mapuche en Los Toldos*. IIDyPCa-UNRN-CONICET, Colección Tesis. Bariloche. http://iidypca.homestead.com/PublicacionesIIDyPCa/Sabatella/Sabatella.pdf.

Sabatella, María Emilia. 2013. 'De la tradicionalización a la politización: Analizando las políticas culturales y los procesos de alterización de una localidad bonaerense.' In *Tramas de la Diversidad. Patrimonio y Pueblos Originarios*, ed. Carolina Crespo, 39–66. Buenos Aires: Antropofagia.

Said, Edward W. 2002. 'Introducción.' In *Orientalismo*, 19–54. Barcelona: Debols!llo.

Shore, Cris. 2010. 'La antropología y el estudio de la política pública: reflexiones sobre la 'formulación' de las políticas.' *Antípoda: Revista de Antropología y Arqueología*, Vol. 10: 21–49.

Shore, Cris, and Susan Wright. 1997. *Anthropology of policy. Critical perspectives on governance and power.* Londres: Routledge.

Slavski, Leonor. 2007. 'Memoria y patrimonio indígena. Hacia una política de autogestión cultural mapuche en Río Negro.' In *Patrimonio, políticas culturales y participación ciudadana*, ed. Carolina Crespo, Alicia Martín, and Flora Losada, 233–47. Buenos Aires: Antropofagia.

Spivak, Gayatri Chakravorti. 1998. '¿Puede hablar el sujeto subalterno?' In *Orbis Tertius*, trans. José Amícola, Vol. 3, no. 6. http://sedici.unlp.edu.ar/bitstream/handle/10915/10384/Documento_completo.pdf?sequence=1.

Troulliot, Michel-Rolph. 1995. *Silencing the past. Power and the production of history.* Boston: Beacon.

Troulliot, Michel-Rolph. 2011. *Transformaciones globales: la antropología y el mundo moderno.* Cali: Universidad del Cauca—Universidad de los Andes.

Verdesio, Gustavo. 2011. 'Reflexiones de los autores sobre el dossier.' *Corpus. Archivos virtuales de la alteridad americana*, Vol. 1, no. 1. http://ppct.caicyt.gov.ar/index.php/corpus/article/view/317.

Vich, Víctor, and Viriginia Zavala. 2004. *Oralidad y Poder. Herramientas metodológicas.* Bogotá: Norma.

10 The ambivalence of tradition
Heritage, time, and violence in postcolonial contexts

Mario Rufer

Introduction[1]

> First, we will take away the time from you with our proverbial courteousness. Then we will take away the time from you with a criminal stupidity.
>
> (Herbert 2011, 30)

> [. . .] here all has become necessary, divorced from chance, categorized, set in order. And to feel sure of itself, the living Laudomia has to seek in the Laudomia of the dead the explanation of itself.
>
> (Calvino 1974, 140)

What is the use of tradition in our time? Furthermore, who does it serve? The multicultural discourse in its different versions has revealed the necessity of decentralizing the master narrative of national traditions toward the recognition of 'several cultures' in the same community imagined as a nation. What did that mean in the ways of narrating tradition, in the ways of displacing the univocal narrative toward another that raised awareness of that plurality? And, above all, which are the political dimensions of that displacement? In this text, I analyze the uses of tradition in devices of contemporary exhibition in Mexico. Basically, I try to make a counterpoint between the narrative of the ethnographic halls of the National Museum of Anthropology (NMA, established in 1964) and some community museums that emerged from the National Program of Communitarian Museums (NPCM), created halfway through the 1990s.[2]

In Mexico, the public discourses that formulated the exhibition complex had to deal, since the end of the revolution, with a problematic imaginary of double temporality: on the one hand, the singularity of the (political) apparition of the (mestizo) nation was the nucleus of what was expected to be exhibited as history (in terms of political development of the nation that ends since 1944 in the Museum of History of Chapultepec). On the other hand, the coexistence, *inside the people*, of decidedly non-modern indigenous cultures and studied by nascent anthropology, taken from the same moment of the revolution to think in a semiotic strategy that allowed the homologation of the notion of heritage patrimony, of modernity and of remnants (this last one understood in terms of what the nation should achieve with the exercise of political tutelage to those who still pertained to the most 'primitive' states of development).[3] The year 1968 was in many ways a turning point, and it clearly affected the Mexican museographic notion in terms of deciding what and how it exhibits the 'subjects of the nation' (Rosas Mantecón and Schmilchuk, 2010). Since the last part of the 1980s, the Directorate-General of Popular Cultures of CONACULTA (*Consejo Nacional para la Cultura y las Artes*, National Council for the Arts and Culture) started a clear vindication of the 'popular cultures' in the country, in terms of vindicating and exhibiting 'traditions, cultures, and customs.' That which was popular and indigenous mixed in a difficult solution that accompanied the dilemma of paternalist indigenism, which was expected to be outgrown.

The exhibitory strategy had three narratives at the end of the 1980s: the NMA in its 11 archaeological halls as the dead glories of the nation. In the upper floor, each departed has its corresponding remnant: the halls of ethnography replicate the 'present culture' of its archaeological past (which I will later refer to as *the relic*).[4] The monumentality of the ruins granted not only the possibility of dramatizing the indigenous past and 'the indigenous peoples of today.' Last, in 1982, the National Museum of Popular Cultures (NMPC) was created.[5] In the 1990s, the NMPC arrived to breathe new life to institutional narratives, proposing models of participative museology that—if we stick with one of the first statements of Latin American Community Museums produced in Chile in 1992— contemplates 'the dissemination of community forms of memory that show diverse forms of conceiving and transmitting the common past not registered in traditional history' (Balesdrian 1994, 43). Nonetheless, one of the pressing problems of the notion of extended heritage from governmental proposals to processes and social actors, has to do with the persistence of the notion of an 'educated/high' culture as part of 'heritage.'[6]

In this text, I pick two narrative fields for the analysis: on the one hand, a series of exhibitions of the NMA, specifically in its ethnography halls; on the other, some community exhibits where I include what draws my interest: the speech of the subjects in the selected communities, their appreciation of what they see, exhibit, and consider as heritage and tradition.[7] I specifically take two axes that I am interested in exploring here—the time and the violence—basically with two force arguments. The first is that the temporality of the nation is a political field in dispute. Ranajit Guha (1997, 154) proposed that in the representation of the colonial-national hegemonic discourse, the other always has the form of a past. The 'culture' of the other separates from the modern notion of history through a synchronous format of contemplation that has the form of backwardness. This vision would have annulled the possibility of understanding the heterogeneous temporality of postcolonial contexts, which always exceed the empty, homogeneous, and progressive time of the nation (and we add: of capital and historic disciplinary time). The vision of a unique time where *the other* is the past, is a narrative that habilitates the exercise of power: it is necessary to bring the other to the present, to guard him. What happens with that narrative the moment in which the nation has to move from the homogeneous discourse and recognize otherness, 'give them their place'? Which is that place in narrative, culture, tradition, time, history?

The second argument tries to understand the absence of narratives of historic violence that produce the difference in the multicultural nation. It could be understandable that it tries to exclude the continuity of violence in the halls of the NMA due to its narrative intention. But it is assumed that the new community museography, and even the guide from the NMPC had two proposed axes: conservation of local heritage and growth of the collective community memory (Camarena and Morales 2006). Amidst the structural violence that certain communities in Mexico are living through, for which there is a continuity in the plundering, exclusion, migrancy, and racialization since the colony, there is nonetheless a generalized silence over these points when speaking of 'community memory' in the discursive fabrication of memory–tradition–heritage. Why is it that if the actors talk of violence and it appears in the history that they tell through their objects, that so little of this is narrated in the community museums, even when the description cards present 'a collective memory of the community'? Why does the founding violence seem impossible to be connected with the present?

Time and tradition

The relatively recent policy of 'recognizing' the otherness as cultural policy extends with pedagogic force through national discourse. The effort to modify certain aspects of national tradition (no longer unique or homogenous but open and hospitable toward its internal 'others') is the trademark of the contemporary cultural devices in postcolonial contexts. Mexico is no exception (Díaz Polanco 2006; Ortega Villaseñor 2012). The notion of tradition fulfills an ambivalent role here: in modern discourse, it signified that which had to be overcome by secular, progressive, and empty temporality of the historic time, but it also had to maintain itself as the deep image of the *volk*, the ancestral substance that gives shape to the people. This tension between an illuminist and romantic will never solve itself in the poetics of the nation: it is, indeed, its trademark (Gorbach 2012). Both imply a different notion of temporality (the first empty and homogeneous, the second the mark of a synchronic continuum). Both involve a political dimension. Homi Bhabha (2002) suggested that the nation fabricates the dissemination of its meaning in terms of an ambiguity of time: it poses that the only possible destiny is the indefinite process of a future where things will never be as before, but that destiny requires identity and pedagogic force of the atavistic as the origin of what precedes it, fundaments it, and somehow returns at any moment. The point being that this ambiguity transformed into a powerful machinery in the hands of the state to differentiate: from the temporal unfolding, the colonial modernity continues to indicate the contemporary formations in our contexts to distinguish between subjects of the present (modern subjects) and subjects that should be conduced to the present (*fetched* from some type of past).

178 *Mario Rufer*

Nevertheless, in the 'multicultural era,' tradition would no longer (necessarily) occupy the space of the remnant past, but that of the scene of 'equivalent cultures.' To the new diverse nation, those cultures are there; they exist today.[8] What happens with that temporal tension in the multicultural era? Is historic depth conceded in the empty time of the nation that they also make up today? How is this shown in the exhibitionary complex (Bennet 1988)? The community museums were created exactly in the context of this new strategy of 'making plurality visible' in their own codes, and in Mexico, since 1994 and until 2009, 250 were created. That is why I am interested in understanding how ambivalence is worked in local contexts.

Time and tradition: the community

I will start with a scene of community exhibition. One of the central elements of these exhibitions is the notion of time, which somehow replicates the vision of national history—'traditional cultures.' One of the most visited community museums of Oaxaca is in Teotitlán del Valle[9]—a town with Zapotec roots, which has established a long history of textile creation and in particular colorful rugs. The community museum of 'Balaa Xtee Guech Gulal'[10] was founded in 1994, the same year that the NMPC was created (where some communities in Oaxaca played a central role). It is located in the downtown area of Teotitlán, in front of the town hall and some steps away from the central plaza where rugs and carpets are exhibited and sold. 'If you come here it is because you have finished shopping,' says Jorge, the museum's custodian, during my visit.[11]

The museum has a single divided hall with different divisions (very classic in style): archaeology, with pieces donated by the community for the museum's custody; handicrafts, a special space dedicated to the 'dance of the feather'; and lastly a composition with recreations in diorama and photographs called 'Traditions, uses and customs.' One of the first characteristics that caught my eye in the exhibition of 'traditions' was the peculiar use of temporality in the descriptions that referred to such subjects. The verb tenses are in indefinite past: 'It *was* done,' 'the bride *went* to help to the house of the family of the groom,' 'the groom *worked* in the fields,' 'the traditional food *consisted* of *mole de olla*.' At that moment I saw written in the cards, which gave indexicality to the photographs, a pervasive division of temporality that continues to work: separating societies of culture from societies of history through a typological narration of time. The photograph that I present in this section compares the 'traditional wedding' with the 'present day wedding.' The temporal limits are nonexistent. Traditions seem to stay over the background of no time of the culture, and the current wedding is stamped as an image that recollects the notion of modernity through a particular technology: the modern studio photography.[12] The photography of a 'present day wedding' announces a time not necessarily in solution of continuity with tradition, but juxtaposed. The studio photography, the religious rite, the groom's suit, the white bride.

Author: Are traditional weddings not held anymore?
Jorge: Do you mean the first ones? No, of course there are. There are, but few. Not here, inland. Far. Here the brides look like the present day photo, and they buy their dresses in Oaxaca.
A: And the banquet or the balls?
J: Well, a little bit mixed, there is a bit of everything, fandango, *cumbia* and what is called *reggaetón* . . . a bit of everything.

This is a feature that is repeated in a lot of formats of exhibition of community customs and rituals. Tradition appears encapsulated in a chronotope: it can be today, but far. The format of the museum seems to demand a narrative that cannot grasp the ambivalence of heterogeneous temporality, only in the chronicles do those significant traces of simultaneity appear.

When I was doing fieldwork in the museum of Teotitlán on July 2014, I heard the following conversation of two local middle-aged women:

A: Don't tell me we used to look like that . . .
B: Here it says 'nineteen hundred seventy five.' Oooh . . . that was so long ago!
A: If I wasn't seeing it, I wouldn't believe it.

The proper distance with the exhibited print is somehow a recurring element. They are and they are not what is shown there. There is an undertaken commitment of preservation that is not necessarily part of their everyday life. It is permissible to ask up to which point that cultural enunciation is not an administrable formula: they *come* to illustrate a plural present, to be a witness of what *still exists*, but they are not exhibited or narrated as future strength. In our times, the notion of future, Hartog (2007) would say, is still associated with a presentist regime whose subjects are prisoners of acceleration (not of tradition).

In the community museum of Tehuacán, Puebla, Doña Ángela (64 years old in 2013, one of the cooks of every year's *mole de caderas*) explains to me:

> The guy from the government, that guy from the culture bureau, came to tell us, that they were going to bring us modernity. 'She must be *chilanga*,'[13] I said jokingly just to bother him. *Uts*, and I came and the *guajes* from my grandmother were here. Modernity? This is all just old stuff like all of this [pointing at the town], and like me! And the *licenciado* tells me 'nooooo ña[14] Ángela, not old. Traditional. And you are its representative . . .' 'Oooooh well, if you put it that way,' I answered. But I didn't understand.[15]

This stub, to me, seems revealing of a temporal structure which displaces from ambiguity between new time and atavistic time as presented by Bhabha and aforementioned is: the atavistic temporality inhabits the multicultural present not only as a 'trace of the past' that no longer exists, but as something *testimonial*, *alive*, of that time in the present. Something that I would like to define here as a *relic*. In the most literal and Christian meaning: that which among all remnants of the magnificent past is worthy of veneration. Similar to the fragment that 'remains from a (past) body,' but definitely 'is' the presence in that body in the present.[16] And we know that everything that is venerable stops being historic, thought-of, disruptive.

It is impossible to continue proposing that the indigenous cultures or the pluricultural constitutions of the postcolonial states are unknown. The point lies in distinguishing, again, with which tools that incorporation is produced and in which way the current nation state is otherness-like, otherness-phobic, and otherness-producer at the same time' (Segato 2007, 138). I use the notion of incorporation as a hand-me-down effective image of the extension of territorial power as a result of warlike action, which morphs into the 'hospitable' image of the modern state that always allows another filiation among its ranks.[17] The narrative of the relic, I think, is one of those strategies of incorporation.

Doña Ángela speaks of an episode when in the community museum of Tehuacán she found identical pieces to those that existed in her house, an inheritance from her grandmother. She speaks a little bit of Spanish, she says, although it sounds perfect to me. The relocation of temporality through traditional 'culture' is the key here. Modernity, in that local stronghold, is not in the antipodes of tradition. It is the action of reordering the elements of context (some in dynamic action, others as distant to the subjects as the national heroes) and specifying them as *tradition*. In postcolonial contexts, it is fundamental that modernity incorporates the vision of (t)radition as a backup that *has its living guardians*. This discourse generates a double promise that finds in the field of culture, the most complete excuse as not to enter in contradictions with itself. The first promise has to do with rupture (Dube 2012, 14–19), the chiasm, the need to reform, renew. And if any metaphor persists from diffusionism as an epistemological pillar of colonialism, this is the idea that what is modern is 'brought' (to a peculiar chronotope that joins space and time: it is brought from the *capital*—it is '*chilanga*' says doña Ángela—and time because *it comes from some point* toward 'all that' which is old). The idea of modernity as a rupture is what is still present with minimal changes in the public discourse of the state, supported by notions of progress, development, economic reform, and activation (Comaroff and Comaroff 1993; Coronil 1997).

But there is a second peculiar promise of postcolonial modernity; it assumes the guarantee of the survival of tradition as a splendid altarpiece that distinguishes us. If in the most classic postrevolutionary nationalist discourse, the stone was the dead glory of the nation that was required to shine, the new multicultural text smugs in marking the 'subjects of culture and tradition' as a type of inheritance that must be *preserved* as live *testimony* of a double temporal mark: a form of the past that no longer belongs to those who have followed the acceleration of the present-day era, but which fulfills a crucial function. Its function is to guard the glory that legitimizes us. They are custodian-bodies of objects, languages, and forms of life; they also have the implicit duty of perpetuating them (with an exception: that the conditions of that perpetuation and its forms of manifestation be controlled by that which has been instituted, which in general has the form of state actions).

Time and tradition: the great museum

Of course, the most imposing cultural arm to deploy that narrative is the NMA. It was founded in 1964 in the monumental building designed by the symbolic architect of the 'second Mexican modernity,' Pedro Ramírez Vázquez.[18] On the first floor, the halls referring to 'Archaeology' are found; on the second floor, as I have already mentioned, to each archaeological culture, a matching correlative account is present in the 'Ethnography' section.[19]

In the halls of ethnography, a sufficiently dramatic distinction stands out between the 'ethnographic scene' and the 'ethnographic heritage' in terms of objects. In the introduction hall of the ethnographic precinct of the NMA called the 'indigenous peoples,' recently remodeled in 2013, two classic strategies of exhibition are combined: the diorama and the display behind glass cases.

In the recreated dioramas (stricto sensu, I will call them scenes for being, in many cases, three-dimensional planes with mannequins and objects), the order of the synchronic scene prevails, the romanticization of a 'captured' performance closer to the scene of a festival than of life: the neat outfits, the symmetrically displayed objects, the diaphanous look directed toward the other-spectator. The vision thought in that exhibition is that of the spectator of an unknown spectacle of beauty and harmony.[20] In the scene, everyday life is a spectacular show of the beauty of the other; the precious object showcased, an exhibition—valid here— of the cultural heritage *of the nation*.

One of the most outright examples of coloniality[21] that persists in the statement is cyphered in that usurpation: the surgical operation that extracts the object of the context to turn it into 'heritage of the nation,' it stops answering to the logics of use, creation, and circulation in the world of everyday practices to symbolize the patron of a culture. That conversion that goes from practice to display symbol is a metonymy of 'native culture' (Kirshenblatt-Gimblett, 2012). Exhibited through a series of distinctions, it is a syntagma of typological classifications; the cultural object suffers important displacements: from an object that makes sense in a local landscape, to an object that makes sense in a bigger unity (the national heritage). What is foreclosed[22] in those displacements is precisely the object-in-its history: the stamp of exclusion, the hierarchization, and the racialization of the conformation of a multicultural nation. Manuel, an indigenous Huichol who visited the NMA in 2008, states:

> when we entered the Museum of anthropology in Mexico it was nighttime and we saw the beauties our forefathers created. It was really strange. We had the same outfits, the same ones that were encased in the lit glass boxes and everything. But they were and were not the same, we were and were not ourselves.[23]

Manuel seemed to refer to that emptiness that the National Museums solves: the displayed piece painted and molded mannequin as an 'indigenous body,' in its purity of 'Huichol outfit,' speaks as an aseptic component of a nation in the politics of identities that conform to the diverse backdrop of 'national culture.'

In the words of Manuel we can read how, in the museological operation, various substantial processes are bypassed: a) that scene is produced from a place of usurped enunciation, replaced. It is not even that of the generalized speaker (the Huicholes), but a tacit one, implicit (the mestizo nation-state, molded over the base of criolle thought); b) that place of enunciation belongs to a regime of perception that orders, exposes, and classifies what is 'beautiful of the nation'; c) that regulation is translated into a syntax of the visible that throws off the sense of the processes that separate the object from its technique and the piece from its creators: 'they were and were not the same, we were and were not ourselves.'

If Walter Benjamin explained how an exhibition of machines and exhibitions of industrial novelties in the world at the end of the nineteenth century were a 'pilgrimage toward the fetish of capital' (cited by Bennet 1988, 96), in contexts like the Mexican one, the cultural object of the other becomes sacred (and therefore non-profanable) in pursuit of a 'pilgrimage towards the fetish of tradition.' In this case I emphatically use the Marxist notion of fetish, which tries to retain the ideological power of the apparatus: the object-tradition forecloses all violence, all common processes of designation and difference in which the racialized perception and the colonial source lays on over the 'subjects' of tradition. These subjects that visit the Museum of Anthropology 'by night' recognize the metonymy of the concealments of postcolonial order: 'the Huichol outfit' is a national heritage, but the suit of Manuel, perhaps washed out and with the stains of everyday use, is therefore the uncomfortable remnant of a distant passage (in space and time). The relic has, above all, its norms of presentation.

Violence and (non)memory: the impeded connections

One of the central elements of the discursive configuration of the Latin American multicultural nation from its institutional enunciation has been, in general terms, the plotting of violence that operates in the difference, hierarchy, and codification of cultural values (Briones 2005; Segato 2007). I specifically refer to the necessity of converting the problem of the *history of differences* produced by coloniality of power and the exercise of the postcolonial tutelary powers into a presentational celebration of the *cultures in difference*. The presentation of cultures as values of themselves does not historicize heterarchical configuration inside modernity. This is extended into the field of the exhibition complex: Tony Bennett called it 'zoological multiculturalism' (Bennett 2007), a glass display that equates them into the logic of the collection, an accumulation of presents without temporal depth. Where there is no displayed time, there is no space to explain violence.[24] What roles are tradition and heritage playing here?

I set out to write this section because when I visited different community museums in Mexico to understand how the community connection was being worked between heritage and memory, past and present (connection that the same NMPC was encouraging), I got a similar impression: they mostly were communities stricken by violence, racism, migration, and exclusion of long historic duration; practically none of the community museums (or community entourages, as they were known afterward) talk about this. There was no space for 'that' shown memory (which however burst in spurts in the colloquial scenes of the narratives of the actors that worked or visited the museums). What happens with the relationship between memory, heritage, and violence? If the initial act of local enrollment is the mimesis with the NMA, I first sought to understand what happened there with the violent foundational act, by excellence, of the national history, the conquest.

Violence and (non)memory: the great museum

In the last 50 years, the aforementioned ethnographical halls of the NMA practically represented the only 'citation' of the 'other' cultures in Mexico in terms of an exhibition complex. As interpreted by García Canclini, in the museum, there are no Black people, Jews, or Chinese as 'namable' components of the nation (García Canclini 2009, 175). Surely because the ordainment of the tutelary paradigm of the state—legally and judicially defining those who should be 'brought' into modernity through exercises of national 'guardianship'—was more comfortable and powerful than the definition of other heterarchies (non-anachronic, nor primitive or 'ours,' as a great part of indigenism called them 'our Indians'). This gave way to what García Canal refers to as 'visual machinery' of Mexicanness that configures the anatomy of the Mexican as hierarchical and racialized stamps clearly identifiable where 'our Indians' fulfill a crucial role of guardianship and rendition of the postrevolutionary country (stamps fed until the extenuation of muralism, movies, painting, etc.) (García Canal 2013, 70–74).

Upon the 40th anniversary of the NMA, Roger Bartra sustained that the Museum 'renounced to make an ethnography of modernity' by superimposing the archaeological spectacle with the 'zombies' that wander through the upper floor: the indigenous mannequin of the pluricultural showcase (Bartra 2004, 354). According to Bartra, the selected strategy was to send

> the cultural expressions of the surviving races to the attic of the Museum, to the upper floor rooms, to suggest a connection between the past and the present. What was achieved was clearly a terrible catastrophe which has blighted the indigenous societies since the Spanish Conquest, *but without explaining the process* (347, my emphasis).

In the NMA, the first two plaques mentioned by Bartra in the ethnographic halls, are titled 'Conquest and colonization' and 'Political, military, spiritual, economic, and cultural conquest.' In both, narrative features can be perceived. The first is a tacit temporal backdrop: the conquest is a moment (inaccurate in its limits) that culminated with the 'complex colonial order.' The second feature is absence: silence over violence (physical or symbolic), and even more, over the temporality of violence in the composition of the *Mexican tradition*. The card of the first plaque recounts 'The sixteenth century was the watershed of the cultural life of Meso-american people: ancient political, economic and social order crumbles when new populations arrive from across the Atlantic Ocean.' The glass display shows a medieval helmet, a cross, and a cassock without a descriptive card or explanation. The glass display that accompanies the last plaque registers objects of art, common use, and work of the sixteenth century: *molcajetes*, a painting of castes, vases, everything that shows hybridization of tradition 'in conjunction with ancient handicrafts and the cultural European influence' (NMA, 'Conquista política . . .') (See Figure 10.1).

I think it is important to highlight that the narrative of the conquest follows the cannon of the epic (not of history): it is the religious–military temporality that ends with pacification and the installation of the colonial order. It was a military moment (although the panel makes no reference of a cultural conquest which is explained with another temporality), with participating sketchy and exchangeable characters (the serviceman, the priest). 'The colony' works as a structural stamp of the indigenous people: it is the last precise historical reference. From then on, the indigenous peoples are objectivized in traditions, games, outfits, languages, against the timeless backdrop of 'ethnography,' with some inflexions about 'the present.' That is how ethnography of the glass-display culture is a counterpoint of the epic of the conquest: epic in the Bajtinian sense, which the substantial difference with the narrative way of history relies in that the epic prevents the possibility of reprocessing or reinterpreting because time is locked and, over all, it is closed to the personal experience (Bajtin 1989). The result is silence over the

Figure 10.1 Museo Nacional de Antropología
Photo by Maai Ortiz

repetition of violence, over the constant pillaging, over the long *historic* racialization of the indigenous people, over the 'marked' conformation of their culture as inferior, and above all, as part of the atavistic past (that past which is the background of the ethnographic no-time).

Another of the panels at the NMA, in the same hall, specifies under the title 'Physical Anthropology' (see Figure 10.2):

> The diversity of the Mexican population is found in the same cultural aspect as in the biological. At a first glance it is possible to perceive variations in physique of the inhabitants of the country, in which conformation American, European, African and in less measure, Asian components have intervened.
> (NMA, Ethnographic Hall, Panel 'Antropología Física,' permanent exhibition)

Other than crediting the already old separation between *bios* and culture, these panels (with various accompanying photographs) do not care for an element: those same images that show the perfect indigenous families proudly surrounded by their outfits, is not a sample of diversity upon *a first glance*. First because there is no first glance: every glance is informed by a code. It is that code which the halls of ethnography prefer not to problematize: those bodies carry in the history of Mexico (an all of Latin America) a sign of racialization: the historic footprint, perceptible, material, and corporeal of the conquest. Those bodies are read like that in the stable code of the 'production of a glance' over the others (García Canal 2013).[25]

This gathering of the past and the present makes evident that the order of modern, classical historicity, which fixates the historic past, is an artifice. But what is even clearer, due to contrast, is that in this postcolonial Mexican scene of gathering between dead glories and neat traditions—stamps over a timeless backdrop—lacks a notion of difference from a historic product of violence. I believe the following words of Said are important here:

> difference and otherness acquired in our time talismanic properties [. . .] It is evident that it is currently impossible to stay at the margin of what is magical, even metaphysical which they distill given the dazzling operations to which they were subjected by anthropologists, philosophers, theoreticians of literature and sociologists.
> (Said 1996, 37)

Violence and memory: the community

How does community museology answer, in its apparent 'duty to make its own memory?' In 2013, while I conducted interviews in the community museum (of recent creation and still budding) in San Pedro Actopan in the Milpa Alta municipality of the Federal District, Doña Juana mentioned to me:

Figure 10.2 Museo Nacional de Antropología
Photo by Maai Ortiz

It is our heritage, and again with the heritage thing. This guy seems a notary [referring to the promoter of the museum between laughs]. I tell you, I wanted us to talk about the photographs, did you see? He says they are our heritage also. Then? We have lost all this land around us to concessions which we don't know where they came from . . . we have the property titles, the decree from the King, we have it all, but go figure . . . that thing we don't have. They say no, they insist on our heritage . . . And there we are counting figurines and their little description.[26]

What is posed here is the split between the discussion of heritage and memory. When in South Africa (Rassool and Prosalendis 2001), in the Caribbean (Bastian 2003), or in certain spaces of Argentina (Lazzari 2008), the creation of museums or community entourages are promoted, there is a preoccupation of regenerating the collective link through the memories as a founding resource (not necessarily as *heritage*). There is a clear notion that the consumption that creates the occasion of signifying is an exercise of memory expressed in backings such as narrative, the creation of visual archives with one's own resources, the collective appraisal of objects, the collective narration and reconstruction of the landscapes as stalked by violence, displacement, and expropriation or urban–industrial depredation. Those memories are always plural, sometimes discordant. Of course, many times they have little to do with 'what really happened.' But that is not necessarily an issue of memory (and it is unclear if it is for history). The specificity of the question in the exercises of memory is not so much as what happened but 'how it became possible' (Schmucler 2000).

In Mexico, it is difficult to find that type of narrative structure that merges exercises of memory in so much negative cultural heritage—the name doesn't convince me but it is even used by UNESCO when referring to spaces of past violence (clandestine centers of detainment, ancient slave markets, etc.) that are preserved and commemorated due to their pedagogic value (Meskell 2002), and not due to the inhabitants perceiving it as unnecessary ('again with the heritage thing . . . I wanted us to *talk about the photographs . . . We have lost all this land around us* . . .'). The problem is the barrier that the processes of heritagization create to the most contingent and occasional processes of memory.

It is here where we could remember the famous short story *Funes el memorioso*, where Borges tackles a central dilemma that is related: his character Irineo Funes holds in his memory all the details, all the numbers, all the dates, and all the archives of the world. But he is *incapable of thinking*.[27] Juana of Actopan wants to talk, discuss, wants to think the photographs, the time, the drought, the expropriations. But the person in charge of the museum, the 'master,' inhibits her. She is satisfied with classifying and describing: 'counting figurines' and writing its description. On the eve of the National Encounter of Community Museums of 2012, Don Ramón explains to me: 'the problem resides in having found a lot of figurines. We have to classify them all, put them in the altars. They lose their beauty, *what each one has to show for itself.*'[28] Here, what is beautiful is exactly the opposite to the logic of the relic: singularity is beauty. The point is the necessity boosted by the institutions of the state (without forgetting the nuances of an affirmation like this) to somehow turn every discussion centered on the past and legacy into a *solemn* one. For the institutional voice, the heritage has to serve to take pride; the local 'possession' of that heritage serves to ennoble the community by instilling that memory, which is a *property of the nation*. Local memory guards a broader standard. As Juana does, counting figurines and describing them.

In mid-2012 in San Andrés Mixquic,[29] on the eve of the celebration of *Día de los Muertos* (The Day of the Dead), I had an interview with Don Alberto, one of the collaborators of the community museum of the town, perhaps the only one that stitched particular sedimentations of memory.

> You see . . . in this country we are occupied with obtaining what is buried because it is our history, we have to preserve everything, that is how they train us . . . But we bury in any garbage dump our dead youths, all of those people that die because of violence. Here, people are disappeared, you know? Everyone says, in Mixquic, are you serious? Well yes, there are some. Some family members came to see me, if we could put the photos up, it might just help. But imagine, my bosses . . . they would hang me. No, no. This is a museum, they say . . . Well yeah, it's true. A museum. *And what is a museum?*

The selected fragments show that the political work of memory over time is not only a work of reminiscence but of connection. When a fact is tried to be suppressed over the collective memory, the act itself is not necessarily repressed. What is tried to be suppressed is the connection of the event with the discontinuous times of the experience, erasing the footprint that connects heterogeneous temporalities. This is mostly a work of 'forgetting' in the national narrative, mentioned in advance by Ernest Renan (2010[1882]). Marc Augé points out with sharpness: 'remembering is less important than associating, freely associating as surrealist tended to do; associating, in other words, *dissociating the established relationships, solidly established, so others can flourish, that frequently are dangerous relationships*' (Augé 1998, 31, my italics). Classifying, naming, ordering, placed 'in altars' (please note the homologation between glass-display and altar) seems to be, for Juana, Ramón or Alberto—as much as for Irineo Funes—an obstacle to connect.

To put it clearly: it is false that in Mexico, in its patrimonialist or commemorative discourses, the conquest or its violence are not discussed. But, the narratives seem to have averted the connection of the conquest with the long-lasting violence that transformed it into a symptom of the national present; it is a matrix that formulates the position of social subjects in their hierarchies, differences, and ambivalences (Gorbach 2012; Rozat forthcoming). The classical syntax of the museum (and its attempt to not defile it) operates like a platform to dilute the association: the epic format of the military–religious conquest is neutralized in the ethnographic presentism that inaugurates the colony, where the history of subjugation is converted into the equivalent terms of a recognized culture.

In the community museum of Francisco I. Madero in Coahuila, Carlos, the 'guy from the government,'[30] told me about several episodes of recent violence with the milk and beer industries that drained the water, polluted, and managed to get permits to encircle communal land. To my question as to why this did not appear anywhere in the community museum, he answered surprised:

> You mean put something about the industries in the museum? That they take away our water and things like that? No, imagine that ... we would have more than enough of that material. But the problems it would raise ... Anyways, that does not go in a museum, does it? But it would be good to show: weren't we lacking in ruins? Things about the industries and all that stuff, that stays *between us* ...

The narratives of patrimonialization can act to suppress the connections that try to dissociate instituted relationships in the pedagogic complexes of statesmanship. The reflexive doubt on where to register the relationship between heritage and memory is constant in the actors: if the photos are their heritage, 'then?'; that does not enter in the exhibition, 'no?' Don Alberto puts it more clearly: why not put it together with the excavated pre-Hispanic pieces—buried by a specific form of conquest and colonization violence—the faces of the youths now buried by the necropolitical violence of the postcolonial state? Because that 'does not go' in a museum, says Carlos in Coahuila.

Even in its participative and communal aspect, the 'state–museum' imposes the syntax of the museum effect but from another place: the necessary separation is not what separates the exhibited piece or artifact from its context (Alpers 1991, 26; Kirshenblatt-Gimblett 2001, 51–54). Here a paradigmatic separation happens (not so much syntagmatic): it is the relationship of that community space with others way bigger (the National Museum, the pre-Hispanic monuments of the Central Valley), what should be kept sealed and supported: *there are ruins here too, there are remains here too* from a learned account that articulates the empty and unique time of the nation with its abbreviation, the community. That makes the notion of memory restrict itself to converge in a present where local tradition sutures any possible distance with the nation. The narrative of violence is conjured beforehand: not because it does not exist, but because it is dystopic; 'it does not' go there because it untidies the grammar of heritage. It is better spoken 'between us,' (where 'us' works as a deictic of the community), in an intimacy that is better left unmixed with the hospitality of the national chronotope.[31] This hospitality is, in any case, the first violence that institutes patrimonial narrative: in its gesture to conserve, preserve, showcase, patrimonial narrative runs the risk of annulling the experience and staying in a dictum of 'non-profanity.' In this sense, even if it is not necessarily formulating a counternarrative, community museums do open a gesture of warning: then, what is a museum?

Conclusion

The rhetorical question pondered by Don Alberto is what I wanted to partially answer in this text. Today a museum of tradition can answer four narrative forces: the epic, the monument, the relic, or the memory. In the first, a close narrative prevents reformulation, a temporary intervention, and a subjective experience (it is the narrative of the conquest of the NMA). The second erects the dead glories that reify themselves like 'forebearers' without explaining the processes that killed them (it is the archaeological narrative of the NMA). The third actually is a newer novelty as a discourse of diversity: it is a narrative that showcases a different culture as a *live witness* of the national plurality. By doing this, it praises the 'beauty' of that plurality. Regardless, the narrative of the relic leaves two things intact: on the one hand, the silence over the hierarchy and racialization of that object-culture that comes from another time, with a beauty that is maintained only in the framework of displays and asepsis. On the other hand, it also leaves the suture of power unharmed: the relic exists only when an authority legitimizes it and establishes *religio*, the link. That authority is still the state, which while beautifying acts and when naming, as in all of history, conquers and extends sovereignty.

The fourth, the narrative of memory is, at least in the Mexican case, a possibility, a horizon. The support of the community museum-entourage to establish subversive connections, political dimensions. I can't say that the new museology has impacted the alternative forms of building a local history through communal narratives. But evidently, communal spaces are crucial to alter the narrative of sameness, create doubt, build a dialogical supplement of the strong narrative of the nation-state (even in its multicultural trend). Indeed, they demand a presence when inscribing in master narrative, but there they question it: not too traditional, nor too nice. Historic and dialogical subjects, with a notable capacity to read the opacity with which the state-nation keeps proclaiming its wills of sovereignty and domination.

Notes

1 This paper is part of the project 'Subaltern memories of community museums: local narratives, cultural diversity, and tensions of the nations in South-South perspective,' financed by the National Council of Scientific and Technical Research of Mexico (CONACyT), No. 130745. I thank Mario De Leo, Maai Ortiz, and Carlos Alberto G. Navarrete for their search for material and photographic registry. I am grateful for the comments to the first version of this text by the participants of the Seminario Internacional Memoria/Patrimonio—Estado/Comunidad, which took place in Chapala, Mexico, in March 2014.

2 The NPCM was created in 1994 from an agreement between the Directorate-General of Popular Cultures and the National Institute of Anthropology and History. It decentralized into state bodies during 2000. The project under my command performed ethnographic monitoring in 17 community museums in Mexico in the state of Mexico, Federal District, Coahuila, Veracruz, Chiapas, Oaxaca, Yucatan, Zacatecas, Queretaro, and Tlaxcala. Presently there are more than 250 working community museums. Here we will dwell only in some examples.

3 For analysis of the official discourses and public culture to 'integrate the Indian' and forge the hegemonic discourse on mestizaje, refer to Alonso (2005). For a study on the genealogy of 'what is Mexican' as a product of cultural policies after the revolution, refer to Pérez Monfort (1999).
4 Anthropologist Paula López Caballero (2008) proposes that the theme of definition of historic identity in Mexico finds root in a problematic formulation over the 'authenticity' of the indigenous legacy in the present. In her reasoning, López distinguishes the past (as a reified figuration, exposed almost 'magically' as an original or authentic transposition) from legacy (as the mediations and latencies of that past in the present, ambiguous, contradictory and broadly textualized). The author explains up to which point the formula of national history was constituted into a tenacious search for origins that repressed the question of the colonial legacy and eulogized the unanswered question for the presence of the indigenous past. (pp. 330–1). From another place, historian Frida Gorbach (2012) investigates this problem as 'anthropologization' of history and questions up to which point that whatever is symptomatically absent in that historic latency is the conquest.
5 Due to space constraints we will not discuss the NMPC here. I will only highlight that it was an undertaking to break the indigenist discourse of the 'obstacle' of the Indian for national development. It was founded by López Portillo in 1982 and was under the charge of the great anthropologist Guillermo Bonfil Batalla during its first years, who gave it his own style. From the official discourse, the museum tried to boost the creativity of 'popular cultures' by erasing the indigenous adjectives due to three reasons: to accept the broad plurality of the Mexican nation; to un-stigmatize what had been the traditional view of the Indian since the revolution; and to empower the cultural creation of the popular sectors (seen only in terms of cultural consumers) (Bonfil Batalla 1983).
6 I agree with historian Buron Díaz (2012, 85) when he states: 'community museums aren't produced just by and for the community, they cannot only be faithful mirrors of the community it recognizes, they cannot because they adopt a language that denotes, first, its skillful appropriation of institutional codes that are traditionally alien to them, and therefore, a clear and decisive participation of the scientific community, with some historiographical notions that reflect the museum's community discourses, and which logically agree with a series of conceptual changes which are possible to track back.'
7 For a distinguished work on this point of reproduction of the notion of heritage tied to the creation of links of locality-collectivity, see Rozental (2014).
8 The most interesting judicial allusion in this respect exists in the Second Article of the Political Constitution of the United States of Mexico. In its reform of 2011, it explains that 'the Mexican Nation is unique and indivisible'; the next sentence explains that 'the Nation has a pluricultural composition originally supported by the indigenous people.' This ambiguity (unique and indivisible, yet pluricultural) highlights all the postcolonial enunciative strategy (CPEUM, Art. 2).
9 For some sources, Teotitlán ('land of gods' in Náhuatl) is considered the first settlement founded by the Zapotec (c. 1465). It is located in the state of Oaxaca, close to the capital city. In 2010, the National Institute of Geographic and Statistics stated that the population was of 4,357 inhabitants. Among the principal activities of this town is the commerce of 'grana cochinilla,' a parasite of the cactus, which dyes fabrics in a crimson color. In Teotitlán, inhabitants regularly speak Zapotec.
10 'Shadow of the Ancient Town' in Zapotec (according to the translation in a panel in the museum).
11 Interview of the author with Jorge, Teotitlán del Valle, July 14, 2014. Jorge was born in Teotitlán; he is aged 40, approximately. He works on the fields during the week but belongs to the community commission that rotates the members that work in the museum.

12 As to how modern studio photography stamped certain patterns in mestizo modernity (through a mimetic action with hyper-realistic European models), please refer to the studies by Deborah Poole on Peru (2005).
13 Popular expression meaning 'from Mexico City.'
14 Short for Doña.
15 Interview with the author, May 22, 2013.
16 The classic work by Ranger and Hobsbawm—reasonable against history and anthropology as tight disciplines—was pioneering not only in showing the invented character (while historically and strategically produced) of national traditions, but also in evincing the force of imperialism in the 'distribution' of national characters and the ways of tradition of the West and the Others (Ranger and Hobsbawm 2002).
17 Derrida mentioned that hospitality, as a term, shares the root with hospes (receptivity) and with hostis (hostility). Every community is paradoxically built in that sense: it defines an inclusion in the middle of a vigilant tension (Derrida 1997). In that tension, tradition occupies a central place. In the revised patrimonial narrative, we are before a state hospitality. In it, the other can be guest (another, indigenous, respected minority, etc.) in the measure in which it is biased in that reception by the major community of the nation. It is a hospitality that extends while retaining cultural authority and dangerously conceals the effective exercise of power, hierarchization, and the codification of cultural value.
18 The looting and pilferage mark from the beginning the relationship of nation-heritage-community. The famous Tlaloc Rock (deity of water and rain in the Mexican cosmogonical universe), which the NMA keeps since its beginnings, was withdrawn with violence from the community of Coatlinchán, where it lay. The neighbors of the community still declare that it has never rained as before. For an analysis on this subject, please refer to Rozental (2011).
19 Dora Sierra poses that the 'criteria that was used was that of 'continuity,' which means, first that whatever was going to be exhibited in the halls of archaeology was questioned, then what would be shown in the ethnographic section was decided, for the goal of having an ethnological sequence between the past and the present' (Sierra 1994, 83). This homologation goes back to the creation of the National Museum, whose department of Ethnography dates to 1887. 'Ethnology as an anthropological discipline was linked to archaeology inside the museum, in many cases subordinated to it, an in others to physical anthropology' (30).
20 Although we cannot delve into the subject here, it is interesting to criticize the use of wax mannequins in the museum: in which way taxidermy reaches the symbolism of the bodies (and annuls any possible likeness). For a criticism on the use of the mannequins and photos in the NMA refer to Dorotinsky, 2002.
21 To work on the concept of coloniality coined by Aníbal Quijano, I follow Rita Segato when she suggests that we have 'the necessity of perceiving the historic continuity between the conquest, the colonial regulation of the world, and the republican postcolonial formation that reaches until the present' (Segato 2007, 158). Of course, we are not talking of continuities in the terms in which the classic structuralism perceived it, or as certain serial historiography created them, with immutable beings that weigh as historical convictions over the social subjects that are living them. We speak, in change, of recognizing the silenced mimetic continuities which were created in its shadows, assumed, and practiced as 'new political orders,' metamorphosed in the apparent historic singularity of the national being present as autochthony, tradition, and heritage.
22 I take foreclosure as the mechanism described by Lacan by which a significant is excluded from the symbolic universe of the subject, therefore it is blocked from the signification of its historicity.

23 Interview by anthropologist Sonia Vázquez in the NMA, in September 2008. I thank Lic. Vázquez for her generosity in sharing her interviews for this work.
24 One of the first plaques in the ethnographic halls of the National Museum of Anthropology, under the name 'The indigenous peoples,' says: 'The social and cultural complex of present-day Mexico originated in the colonial era, when the Mesoamerican civilization—developed by local ethnic groups—got in contact with Western civilizations, through its Spaniard version, and with the African population and culture that had arrived by then. With these three fundamental ethical components, the Asians and those who arrived later, in each region a mixture of the present biology and culture operated' (NMA, Ethnography Hall, Plaque 'The indigenous peoples,' permanent exhibition). The discursive nodes are clear: complex, contact, civilization, culture, components. The conquest is mentioned under the euphemism 'to get in contact.' The African population 'arrived.' This is how slavery, racialization, and heterarchy that impregnates the division between groups does not seem to form a part of the present: merely their cultural components.
25 When I speak of race in so many 'signs,' I thoroughly follow the analysis of Rita Segato. A sign is a historic production of a signified code: in this case, indexical footprints of defeat, subordination, and subjugation. This point is not solved with the 'showing' of a glass-display of cultural diversity, because the image, if it is not worked from a gaze, can only bolster the historic reading of the sign (and not produce more than an effect of exoticism) (Segato 2007). On the problems of ethnographic museums, refer to Sturge (2014, Chapter 7).
26 Interview by the author, June 25, 2012. Doña Juana is one of the women that collaborates in the community museum of Actopan (museum that at the moment of my visit only had a gallery of photography in the district's office). She's a housewife and works in the fields. She was 63 years old in 2013. San Pedro Actopan is one of the 12 towns that constitute the municipality of Milpa Alta in the Federal District. There, several inhabitants still exhibit with nobility the concessions of land given by the Royal Edits of the seventeenth century (see López Caballero 2008). Milpa Alta is found in the southern limit of the Federal District; it is poorly developed compared to other municipalities of the Valley of México and it is one of its biggest natural reserves. Cooperative ownership acquired force here during the mid-twentieth century and it is a district with a high presence of indigenous population. San Pedro Actopan is known because it houses the National Fair of Mole (which takes place during October of each year).
27 'Funes not only remembered every leaf on every tree of every wood, but even every one of the times he had perceived or imagined it [. . .] He knew that at the hour of his death he would scarcely have finished classifying even all the memories of his childhood. I suspect, nevertheless, that he was not very capable of thought. To think is to forget a difference, to generalize, to abstract. In the overly replete world of Funes there was nothing but details, almost contiguous details' (Borges 1962, 115, my emphasis).
28 By 'figurines,' Ramón refers to archaeological pieces of the Remojadas culture, found where the highway to Veracruz was built at the end of the 1990s. Ramón, around 50 years old in 2012, born in Jamapa, was in charge of painting the mural at the community museum. Interview by the author.
29 San Andres Mixquic is a town of pre-Hispanic origin ('place of those who take care of water' in Náhuatl), located in the municipality of Tlahuac in the federal district. It is the tourist venue by excellence of the Day of the Dead celebration held on the 2nd of November of every year. It was named a 'Magical Borough of Mexico' (Pueblo Mágico) in 2011. It has a community museum found in the buildings of the municipality since 2006.

194 *Mario Rufer*

30 I use the expression 'guy from the government' because of the form as he was mentioned in several occasions by the neighbors while I was looking for him. Carlos was 24 years old in 2012; he had returned from Monterrey, where he was a professional dancer to occupy the 'Ministry of Culture' of Francisco I. Madero. That also included the community museum. Interview with the author, March 11, 2012.
31 I again refer to the hospitality as the aforementioned aporetic concept.

References

Alonso, Ana María. 2005. 'Territorializing the nation and 'integrating the indian': mestizaje in Mexican official discourses and public culture.' In *Sovereign bodies: citizens, migrants and states in the postcolonial world*, ed. Thomas Blom Hansen, and Fin Stepputat. Princeton: Princeton University.
Alpers, Svetlana. 1991. 'The museum as a way of seeing.' In *Exhibiting cultures. The poetics and politics of museum display*, ed. Ivan Karp, and Steven Lavine. Washington: Smithsonian Institution.
Augé, Marc. 1998. *Las formas del olvido*. Barcelona: Gedisa.
Balesdrian, Miriam. 1994. 'Los estatutos de una nueva museología social.' *Boletín de Museología*, XXI: 34–48.
Bartra, Roger. 2004. 'Sonata etnográfica en no bemol.' In *El Museo Nacional de Antropología. 40 Aniversario*. Mexico City: CONACULTA – Equilibrista.
Bastian, Jeannette. 2003. *Owning memory. How a Caribbean community lost its archives and found its history*. Connecticut: Libraries Unlimited.
Bennett, Tony. 1988. 'The exhibitionary complex.' *New Formations*, 4: 73–102.
Bennett, Tony. 2007. 'Exhibition, difference and the logic of culture.' In *Museum frictions. Public cultures/Global transformations*, ed. Ivan Karp et al. Durham: Duke University.
Bhabha, Homi. 2002. 'Disemi-nación. Tiempo, narrativa y los márgenes de la nación moderna.' In *El lugar de la cultura*. Buenos Aires: Manantial.
Briones, Claudia. 2005. 'Formaciones de alteridad, contextos globales, procesos nacionales y provinciales.' In *Políticas indigenistas y formaciones provinciales de alteridad*, ed. Claudia Briones. Buenos Aires: Antropofagia.
Burón Díaz, Manuel. 2012. 'Los museos comunitarios mexicanos en los procesos de renovación museológica.' *Revista de Indias*. LXXII, 254: 177–212.
Camarena, Cuauhtemoc, and Teresa Morales. 2006. 'Community museums and global connections: the Unity of Community Museums of Oaxaca.' In *Museum frictions. Public cultures/Global transformations*, ed. Ivan Karp et al. Durham: Duke University.
Comaroff, Jean, and John Comaroff. 1993. 'Introduction.' In *Modernity and its malcontents. Ritual and power in postcolonial Africa*, ed. Jean Comaroff, and John Comaroff. Chicago: University of Chicago.
Constitución Política de los Estados Unidos Mexicanos. Last version published in *Diario Oficial de la Federación*, May 27, 2015. www.diputados.gob.mx/LeyesBiblio/htm/1.htm [Last Access June 4, 2015].
Coronil, Fernando. 1997. *The magical state. Nature, Money, and Modernity in Venezuela*. Chicago: University of Chicago.
Derrida, Jacques. 1997. *El monolingüismo del otro*. Buenos Aires: Manantial.
Díaz Polanco, Hector. 2006. *Elogio de la diversidad. Globalizacion, multiculturalismo y etnofagia*. Mexico City: Siglo XXI.
Dorotinksky, Débora. 2002. 'Fotografía y maniquíes en el MNA.' *Luna Córnea* 23: 60–5.
Dube, Saurabh. 2012. *Modernidad e historia*. México City: El Colegio de México.

García Canal, María Inés. 2013. 'La producción de una Mirada: "La mexicanidad".' *Tramas*, 39: 67–83.

García Canclini, Néstor. 2009. *Culturas híbridas. Estrategias para entrar y salir de la modernidad*. México: Debolsillo [1989].

Gorbach, Frida. 2010. 'La 'historia nacional' mexicana: pasado, presente y futuro.' In *Nación y diferencia. Procesos de identificación y formaciones de otredad en contextos poscoloniales*, ed. Mario Rufer. México: Itaca – CONACyT.

Guha, Ranajit. 1997. *Dominance without hegemony. History and power in colonial India*. Cambridge: Harvard University.

Hobsbwam, Eric, and Terence Ranger, eds. 2002. *La invención de la tradición*. Barcelona: Crítica [1983].

Kirshenblatt-Gimblett, Barbara. 2001. 'Objetos de etnografía.' In *Estudios avanzados del performance*, ed. Diana Taylor, and Marcela Fuentes. México City: Fondo de Cultura Económica.

Kirsenblatt-Gimblett, Barbara. 2012. 'From Ethnology to Heritage: the role of the museum.' In *Museum studies. An anthology of contexts*, ed. Betina Messias Carbonell. Oxford: Wiley-Blackwell.

Lazzari, Axel. 2008. 'La repatriación de los restos de Mariano Rosas: identificación fetichista en las políticas de reconocimiento de los ranqueles.' *Estudios en antropologíasocial*, 1 (1): 35–64.

López Caballero, Paula. 2008. 'Which heritage for which heirs? The pre-Columbian past and the colonial legacy in the national history of Mexico.' *Social Anthropology*, 16 (3): 329–45.

Meskell, Lynn. 2002. 'Negative heritage and past mastering in Archaeology.' *Anthropological Quarterly*, 75 (3): 557–74.

Ortega Villaseñor, Humberto. 2012. 'México como nación pluricultural. Una propuesta de articulación sociojurídica en el siglo XXI.' *Boletín Mexicano de Derecho Comparado*, XLV (133): 215–51.

Pérez Monfort, Ricardo. 1999. 'Un nacionalismo sin nación aparente. (La fabricación de 'lo típico' mexicano, 1920–1950).' *Política y Cultura*, 12: 177–93.

Rassool, Ciraj, and Sandra Prosalendis, eds. 2001. *Recalling community in Cape Town: creating and curating the District Six Museum*. Cape Town: District Six Museum.

Renan, Ernest. 2010. '¿Qué es una nación?' In *La invención de la nación. Lecturas de la identidad de Herder a Homi Bhabha*, ed. Fernando Alvarez Bravo. Buenos Aires: Manantial [1882].

Rosas Mantecón, Ana, and Graciela Schmilchuk. 2010. 'Del mito de las raíces a la ilusión de la modernidad internacional en México.' In *El museo en escena. Política y cultura en América Latina*, ed. Américo Castilla, 145–66. Buenos Aires: Paidós.

Rozat, Guy. Forthcoming. 'Doxa y herejía en el relato de la Conquista de México.' In *El archivo, el campo. Interpretación, escritura y producción de evidencia*, ed. Frida Gorbach, and Mario Rufer. México City: UAM.

Rozental, Sandra. 2011. 'La creación de patrimonio en Coatlinchán. Ausencia de piedra, presencia de Tláloc.' In *La idea de nuestro patrimonio histórico y cultural*, ed. Pablo Escalante Gonzalbo. Mexico City: CONACULTA.

Said, Edward. 1996. 'Representar al colonizado.' In *Cultura y Tercer Mundo*, ed. Beatriz González Stephan. Caracas: Nueva Visión.

Schmucler, Héctor. 2000. 'Las exigencias de la memoria.' *Punto de Vista*. 68: 5–9.

Segato, Rita. 2007. 'Raza es signo.' In *La nación y sus otros*. Buenos Aires: Prometeo.

Index

administrating 7, 9, 48, 64
Adorno, Theodor W. 8
aestheticization 103
Afro-American 9, 10, 56
Alfaro, Eloy 10
America(s) (without Latin) 3–4, 14, 16–17, 19, 20, 32, 41, 44, 57–8, 65, 75–6, 79, 80–2, 85, 87, 133, 140, 146, 183, 185, 193
anthem, national 6, 37–9, 40–5
anthropologist 28–9, 110–16, 119, 138, 146, 150, 185, 191
Anthropology 5, 49, 90, 102–3, 109–13, 115, 118, 139, 166, 175, 181–2, 185
approximation 51
Archaeology 24, 90, 102, 110–11, 114, 118, 178, 181
Argentina 5, 21, 38, 47, 49, 55–6, 123, 127, 128, 130, 154–9, 162–4
authenticity 9, 14, 30, 41, 58, 63, 97, 116, 123, 128–9, 141
Aymara 27, 28
Aztec(s) 18, 24, 79, 111–12, 117, 144, 146

Benjamin, Walter 17, 49, 182
Bolívar, Simón 10, 30
Bolivia 10, 22, 26, 27–9
Bourdieu, Pierre 8, 15, 163
branding 9, 22, 32, 89, 93, 101–2, 105–6
Brasilia 19
Brazil 19, 29, 54
Brecht, Bertolt 17, 47
Buenos Aires 55–6, 59, 159

Canclini, Néstor García 7, 15, 153–4, 183
capitalism 7, 17–18, 137

Caribbean 5, 25, 48, 187
Certeau, Michel de 4, 74, 116
Chaco 129, 144
Chapultepec 110, 175
Chile 14, 24–6, 32, 176
China 25
city 28, 41, 47–8, 52, 55–6, 58–9, 65, 77, 89–91, 95–6, 112, 114, 123, 125–8, 137, 142, 144, 147
Coatlinchán 7, 137–9, 140–9
collection(s) 26, 63, 87, 88, 91, 95, 97–9, 103, 105, 112, 117–8, 139
collective memory 3, 37, 41, 52, 75, 177, 188
colonial(ity/ism) ii, 1–4, 6, 9, 13–15, 17, 19, 20–5, 27, 30–32, 58, 69, 71, 74–6, 80, 82–3, 87–8, 97–8, 103–5, 113, 117–19, 126, 131–2, 137–9, 140, 144, 165, 176–7, 180–4
colonizer i, 4, 13, 21, 24–5, 29, 71, 83
commodification 2, 8–10, 17–18, 22, 24
conquest ii, 2, 14, 18, 69, 75, 77–9, 81–3, 112, 118, 126, 129, 130, 140, 142, 144–5, 164, 183–5, 188–90
Córdoba 9, 47–9, 51–9, 61–4
Correa, Rafael 26, 32, 51
Cuba 38
cultural: 1–6, 8–9, 13–23, 25, 27–32, 37, 39, 48–50, 56–64, 69–77, 80, 83, 87–106, 109, 111–12, 14, 128, 130–1, 145, 148, 153–167, 177, 179, 181–4, 187; difference 128, 154; distinction 61; heritage 1, 4, 8–9, 17–22, 25, 27–29, 31, 48, 50, 56, 58–9, 61, 70–2, 75, 93, 98–106, 111–12, 153–166, 181, 187;

Index

identity 49, 53, 58, 60–1; management 9, 48, 60, 62, 64, 87–106; possession 96–100, 103, 105
Cultural Studies ii, 8–9, 49,
Cuzco (Peru) 94, 102

Derrida, Jacques 23, 69, 82
diversity 6–8, 45, 64, 69, 71–2, 80, 88, 109, 128, 154–5, 160–2, 167, 185, 190
Dresden 23

Ecuador 6, 10, 14, 22, 26, 32, 38
education 6, 38–9, 42–3, 45, 50–1, 54, 59–60, 69, 72–3, 75, 80, 110, 117, 159
El Alto 23, 27
Entangled Heritages 10
ethnography 47–8, 116, 118, 165, 167, 176, 181, 183–5
Europe 10, 13, 14–16,19, 21, 23, 25, 31, 45, 54, 57, 62, 64, 69, 79–80, 87–8, 91, 95, 97, 99, 102–3, 105
exhibition 5, 9, 13, 24, 26, 7, 87–103, 105–6, 112, 116–17, 120, 124, 146, 157, 175–6, 178–9, 181–3, 185, 189
exhibition (complex) 5, 117, 175, 182–3
exoticization 30

Fanon, Frantz 20
flag 6, 41–5
folklore 45, 51–2, 146
folklorization 30
forgetting 156, 188
Foucault, Michel 9, 16, 22, 49, 51, 64

gentrification 22, 23
German(y) 29, 87, 90–5, 100–1, 106
Gothenburg 26, 99
governmentality 9, 49, 64, 87, 89–90, 96, 98, 103–4, 106
Guatemala 28

hegemony 4, 39, 49, 74, 83, 117, 155, 159, 162, 164, 166
heritage: 1–10, 13, 37–45, 47–64, 69–80, 83, 87–90, 92–4, 98, 99,100–6, 110–112, 115–18, 126, 138, 141, 153–168, 175–7, 181–3, 187–98; cultural 1–2, 8–9, 17–22, 25, 27–9, 31, 48, 50, 56, 58, 61, 64, 69–70, 72, 75, 98–106, 111–12; depolitization of 102; field of 14–17, 23, 27, 29, 30, 159, 166; of humanity 19, 21, 48, 69; intangible 6, 16, 24, 25, 27, 102; management 89–90, 93, 98, 101, 104–6; policies 13, 18–22, 25, 27, 154, 156; tourism 18, 21, 28
heritagization 49, 60, 64, 153–68
high culture 49, 176
historian 23, 39, 60, 109–11, 146
historiography 2, 114
History ii, 3–4, 7–8, 10, 13–15, 17–21, 24–5, 28–32, 37–8, 42, 44, 48, 70, 72, 78–9, 82–90, 100–2, 105, 109–15, 117–19, 124–7, 130–3, 138–40, 145–6, 153, 156–7, 161–4, 175–8, 181–5, 187–90
Hobsbawm, Eric 42, 49, 153
Horkheimer, Max 8
Huichol 181–2
Human Heritage list 102

ICOMOS 15, 20–1
identity 3–6, 9, 14, 16, 18, 20–2, 24, 28–9, 31, 33, 43–4, 49, 53, 55, 58, 60–1, 64, 73, 75, 97, 101–2, 105–6, 109–11, 116, 119, 125, 128, 132, 138–40, 147, 153–4, 158, 166, 177
identity politics 4, 97, 106
Inca 9, 24, 87–107, 110
indigeneity/indigenism 3, 4, 9, 13, 14, 24, 30–1, 115, 176,
indigenous: 1, 3, 5–8, 10, 13–15, 18–22, 24–31, 41, 43, 45, 51–2, 58, 69–70, 72, 73–9, 81–3, 105, 109, 111–13, 118–19, 123, 128–9, 133, 153–167, 175–6, 180–1, 183–5; communities 1, 3, 5, 8, 25–6, 28, 75, 128, 133, 161; language(s) 6, 43, 45, 73, 74, 76, 81–3; people(s) 6–7, 15, 19, 24–31, 43, 45, 59, 72–5, 779, 123–5, 128–30, 132, 154–163, 165–7, 176, 181, 184, 185; population(s) 3, 14, 15, 18, 21, 29, 31, 73, 105, 132, 155, 165, 167
Institutional Revolutionary Party (PRI) 44, 45

intangible 2, 6, 15–16, 20, 24–5, 27, 37, 48, 69, 73, 102, 106
intangible cultural heritage 48, 69, 73
interethnic relationship 162–3

La Paz 23, 27
languages 6, 43, 45, 69–85, 94
Latin (language) 70–2, 80–2
Latin America 1–4, 6, 9–10, 13–15, 18–21, 23–4, 30–1, 38, 44, 49–50, 52, 88, 91–2, 138, 140, 153, 176, 182, 185
legacy 3, 7, 71, 76, 88, 94, 101, 105, 109, 126, 145, 147, 188
Lima 10, 21, 22–3, 50–1, 112, 124, 132

Machu Picchu 99, 100–2, 105
Mapuche 24, 25, 157–60, 164
Martín-Barbero, Jesús 15, 32, 118,
Maya 24, 28
memory i, 2–4, 8, 14–17, 24, 28, 32, 37, 41, 52, 60, 75, 78, 80, 118, 124, 127, 132–3, 153–5, 157, 159, 163, 164–5, 167, 176–7, 182–3, 185, 187–90
mestizo 6, 17, 27, 28, 31, 42, 45, 70, 72–3, 75, 79, 127, 175, 182
Mexican nation(alism) 6, 43, 44–5, 69–72, 74, 79–80, 111
Mexico City 114, 137, 142, 144
migration 6, 14, 21, 57, 81, 182
Moctezuma 77
monument 3, 5, 190,
multicultural(ism) i, 2, 4, 24, 30–1, 35, 49, 73, 94, 167, 177–9, 180–2, 190
museum 3, 5, 8–9, 17, 24–6, 49, 87–106, 109–11, 116–19, 138–9, 141–2, 156–7, 175–83, 185–90

Nahuatl 41, 71, 74–6, 145–6
National Anthropology Museum (of Mexico) 5, 109, 111–16, 139, 175, 181
nation-state 2–9, 16, 25, 50, 69, 100–10, 112, 115, 130, 154, 180, 182, 190
Natural History 100, 111, 117
neoliberal 2, 3, 8–10, 18–19, 32, 73, 87, 89–90, 96, 98, 102–6, 139, 154
neoliberal multiculturalism 2, 154
Neuquén 129, 159

New Orleans 22
New York 41
Nietzsche, Friedrich 29, 30, 32
nostalgia i, 3, 13–14, 17–19, 21, 77, 79

Oaxaca 73, 178–9
otherness 2–3, 5–7, 124, 128, 155, 177, 180, 185

Paraguay 38, 56
Paris 15
patrimonialization 45, 69, 82, 189
patrimonio/patrimony 37, 52 58, 70–1, 137–43, 145–9, 176
patriotism 39, 42
performation/performative 3, 5, 16, 22, 48–9, 51, 60–2, 64, 89, 93, 95–6, 99, 103, 106, 128, 146, 154, 159
performing/performance 6, 13, 42–3, 47–8, 51–2, 55, 58, 61, 63–4, 77, 90, 95–105, 127, 162, 164, 167, 181
places 2, 9, 16, 20, 27, 49, 61, 128, 140, 142–4, 156, 179
pluricultural state 6
policies of heritage 3, 7
popular music 5, 51, 55
postcolonial: condition 1, 14; society 4, 8–9, 14, 24
postcolonialism 1–4, 6–10, 13–14, 16, 18, 24, 27, 71, 75, 175–80, 182, 185, 189
post-neoliberal 2, 10
preservation 15, 20, 59, 94, 102, 117, 138, 141, 179
Puebla 40, 140, 148, 179

Quechua 94
Quito i, 16, 20, 22–23, 26

recognition 5, 7–8, 14, 24–5, 28, 30, 38–9, 48, 54, 58–62, 64, 70, 95–7, 104, 123–4, 127–33, 154–6, 159–60, 162, 175
representation 6, 13 16–17, 21, 54, 74, 79, 87, 96, 99, 103, 111, 116, 124–5, 129, 133, 158, 162, 176
retro 13, 17, 18, 21–2
revitalization 141
romanticism 14
Rosenheim 90–1, 94, 101, 106

ruins 19, 113, 117, 143–5, 148–9, 176, 189

San Luis (Argentina) 5, 38, 39, 123–30, 133
San Pedro de Atacama 26
silencing, silence(s) 1–2, 7, 18, 71, 75, 83, 105, 156–60, 164–7, 177, 183–4, 190
South Africa 187
Spanish 6, 18, 20–1, 40, 44, 56, 62, 69–83, 94, 117, 126–7, 130, 137, 144, 149, 180, 183
spectacle 42, 60, 181, 183
state formation 3, 8, 138
Stuttgart 87, 90–2, 94–6, 101, 106
Sucre 22

tangible or intangible goods 15
Taussig, Michael 15, 130–1, 133, 138, 143
temporality 3, 19, 29, 175–80, 183–4
Tenochtitlan 77
testimony 5, 39, 52, 78, 180
Tiwanaku 27–9, 31

tourism 9, 18, 21–2, 27–8, 50, 59, 90, 92, 93, 98–9, 101, 109, 131, 154, 161
tradition(al) 2, 5, 23, 26–7, 38, 42, 53–6, 58, 61–2, 74–5, 78–80, 88, 97, 106, 115, 117, 128, 132, 137, 160, 162, 164–5, 167, 175–87, 189–90
trauma(tic) 8, 15, 22, 71, 158

UNESCO 3, 6, 9, 13, 15–16, 19–21, 23, 27–9, 31, 48–9, 59–60, 62, 69, 73, 96, 102, 187
United States of America 23, 38, 116
Uruguay 38, 59
uses of the past i, 3–5, 10, 123–5

Vasconcelos, José 72
Venezuela 10, 38, 131
Veracruz 142, 190
violence 6–8, 21–2, 25, 32, 71, 78, 83, 118, 124, 126, 133, 137–8, 144, 149, 157, 159–61, 169, 175–7, 182–3, 185, 187–9

Yudice, George 8, 16, 48, 87, 93